THE ROYAL OPERA HOUSE IN THE TWENTIETH CENTURY

BLOOMSBURY READER

Discover books by Frances Donaldson published by
Bloomsbury Reader at
www.bloomsbury.com/FrancesDonaldson

A Twentieth-Century Life
Child of the Twenties
Evelyn Waugh
Freddy Lonsdale
The Marconi Scandal
The Royal Opera House in the Twentieth Century

THE ROYAL OPERA HOUSE IN THE TWENTIETH CENTURY

FRANCES DONALDSON

BLOOMSBURY READER
LONDON · NEW DELHI · NEW YORK · SYDNEY

This edition published in 2013 by Bloomsbury Reader

Bloomsbury Reader is a division of Bloomsbury Publishing Plc,

50 Bedford Square, London WC1B 3DP

First published in Great Britain 1988 by George Weidenfeld and Nicolson

ISBN: 978 1 4482 0583 7
eISBN: 978 1 4482 0552 3

Visit www.bloomsburyreader.com to find out more about our authors and their books
You will find extracts, author interviews, author events and you can sign up for
newsletters to be the first to hear about our latest releases and special offers

Contents

vi

Foreword

Sir Claus Moser asked me to write this book and Sir John Tooley made it possible, so I cannot pretend to impartiality. I have made every effort to give the facts accurately and, where there have been differences of opinion, to present both sides of the case.

I have most particularly to thank Mr Kensington Davison, the Organizing Secretary of the Friends of Covent Garden and Editor of the magazine *About the House,* and Miss Francesca Franchi, the Archivist of The Royal Opera House, for the immense trouble they have taken in helping me with this book. Many of the staff at Covent Garden have talked to me about the work of their departments and I have particularly to thank the ballet and opera press offices. Mr Pat Spooner and Mr Robin Dartington were kind enough to see me and explain the plans and problems of the second phase of the new building development. I must also thank the librarians of the Arts Council and the House of Lords.

Among those who have been willing to see me and discuss the book, I am particularly grateful to Dame Ninette de Valois,

Dame Merle Park, Sir Frederick Ashton, Mr Michael Somes and Mr John Denison.

My debt to the late Harold Rosenthal will be obvious to every reader. No history of the kind could be written without benefit of his two books.

Introduction

By two ordinances of the Long Parliament in 1647 all stage plays were forbidden and all players treated as rogues according to the law. Then at the Restoration, Charles II granted a patent to build a theatre to both Thomas Killigrew and Sir William Davenant – thus conferring on them a monopoly of the London stage. Killigrew built a theatre in a riding-yard at Drury Lane, almost on the exact site of the present theatre, but Davenant's patent was used at Lincoln's Inn Fields and various other places, until in 1731 John Rich, whose father had bought the patent from Davenant's heirs, built a theatre on the site of an old convent garden belonging to the Duke of Bedford. This theatre opened in 1732 with a performance of Congreve's *The Way of the World* and for more than a hundred years was used chiefly for drama, John Kemble (and after him his brother Charles) owning a part of the lease for many years and acting as general manager and stage director. All the famous actors of the period – the Kembles themselves, Garrick, Macready and Kean – appeared there at one time or another, as did Peg Woffington, Mrs Siddons and Fanny Kemble.

The Theatre Royal at Covent Garden was twice burned down

and rebuilt in 1808 and again in 1856. The architect of the first theatre was Edward Shepherd and that of the second Robert Smirke. All that is left of either today are the statues and friezes which were salvaged from the second one and which still adorn the front of the Royal Opera House.

Italian opera was first given at a theatre for which Queen Anne granted a third patent. Built by Sir John Vanbrugh, it was called the Queen's (later the King's) Theatre and was on the site of the present His Majesty's in the Haymarket. This theatre was vast and the qualities necessary for drama had been sacrificed to architecture. 'For what', Colley Cibber wrote, 'could their vast columns, their gilded cornices, their immoderate high roofs avail, when scarce one word in two could be distinctly heard in it?'[1] It failed therefore for the purpose for which it was built. Vanbrugh and Congreve, his partner, retired and, under a new lessee, the theatre was given over completely to Italian opera.

There are many parallels between the operatic scene at the beginning of the eighteenth century and that of today. In the first place the great popularity of opera in London in the early eighteenth century was almost entirely due to imported Italian singers, many of whom were *castrati*. Because of their success all libretti were written in Italian or translated into it. The universal use of this language created a demand for Italian singers comparable to that for today's international singers. From the first, therefore, performances were based on the star system.

The question of language was always a source of strong and differing opinions. At first the Italian stars sang in their own language, the English, in minor roles, sang in theirs. 'So the lover pleaded to his mistress in a tongue unknown to her, and the lady replied with equal fervour in rhythmical cadences of which he understood not a syllable.'[2] Since this situation seemed absurd, it was decided to sing entirely in Italian, a change which drew from Addison the famous comment: 'At length the audience grew tired of understanding half the opera and, therefore, to ease themselves entirely of the fatigue of thinking, have so ordered it at present that the whole opera is performed in an unknown tongue.'[3]

When Handel arrived in London in 1728, he became musical director at the Queen's Theatre, and Italian opera was composed by a German. In 1732, owing to the feuds between rival factions of society and the internal quarrels of the Royal Family, he was forced to withdraw from this theatre – by now called the King's – where the nobility, under the direction of the Prince of Wales, set up a new management. In these circumstances, Handel moved to Covent Garden where he gave three seasons of opera, composing for first performance there *Alcina, Atlanta, Arminio, Giustino* and *Berenice*. He lost his complete fortune, estimated at £10,000, on these seasons. There is some satisfaction in the fact that at the same time his rivals at the King's Theatre achieved a loss of £12,000. A benefit concert freed him from his debts and, although he wrote no more operas, he now began the series of oratorios for which he is more famous. During the next twenty years *Alexander's Feast, Samson, Judas Maccabaeus, Solomon, Theodora* and *Jephtha* all had their first performance at Covent Garden, while the *Messiah* had its first London performance there.

In the early nineteenth century opera continued to be given at the King's Theatre (burned down in 1789 and rebuilt), the works of composers such as Paisiello and Cimarosa now being followed by those of Mozart. *La clemenza di Tito* was sung by Mrs Billington at her benefit in 1806, and in 1812 Angelica Catalani who received £5,000 for a season in London introduced *Figaro*, singing Susanna. *Così fan tutte* and *Il flauto magico* followed in 1811, and in 1817 *Don Giovanni* was so successful that it played for twenty-three nights. Rossini and Donizetti came next and were followed in 1845 by Verdi's *Ernani*.

The quality of performance went up and down, largely following the degree of interest shown by the upper classes. Many complaints were made, not only about the performances at the King's Theatre, but also about the state of the theatre, the dinginess of the drop curtain, the general incompetence of the productions. Nevertheless, speaking of that theatre, Leigh Hunt wrote:

> This house is the only theatre, now, at which you are sure of hearing something both modern and masterly. There is occasionally some good at the English winter theatres, but the general run of the pieces is deplorable, and reminds one of nothing but the stage itself. . . . At the Opera, on the other hand, you are almost sure of hearing a work not only masterly, but of the first kind of masterliness in the art of music – some production from the first-rate composers . . . who, though of various ranks, are as great in their way as the great poets of England or painters of Italy.[4]

Yet, no matter how it was done, opera could never be made to pay. Handel, it was said, was too extravagant, the later managements not enough so, and all were beaten in the end by financial difficulties. Between 1807 and 1813 a man named Taylor managed the King's Theatre, and, always in debt, he lived for the greater part of the time within the King's Bench or its 'rules'. (His reign was notable also because for five years he employed

Lorenzo da Ponte as poet to the opera.) He was succeeded by a bookseller named Ebers who, overwhelmed by debt, said he never lost less than £3,000 in a season—and often considerably more. 'Thus, from its establishment in this country, we find that Italian opera, in spite of the fashionable patronage which had always been accorded it, was not only an unprofitable, but a ruinous speculation to all who undertook it.'[5]

Ballet came to London in the 1830s but did not last long, although its great popularity on the continent forced composers to introduce it into their works, so that the *corps de ballet* became a regular part of an opera company.

Opera was also given sometimes at Covent Garden, although to meet contemporary tastes it was usually in incomplete or rewritten versions – in *Don Giovanni,* renamed *The Libertine,* the tide part was taken by the actor Charles Kemble. The greatest event at this theatre was the engagement of Carl Maria von Weber as music director. In 1824, *Der Freischüstz,* one of the greatest successes in operatic history, was given six different productions in London alone. Following this Weber was commissioned to write an opera for Covent Garden and composed *Oberon.*

But opera came finally to that theatre through the jealousy, intrigues and intransigence of the singers at the King's Theatre, where the standards had seriously deteriorated. 'The *mise-en-scène* was simply contemptible', wrote one member of the audience of a production of *Così fan tutte,* 'and would have disgraced a minor provincial theatre in the last century.'[6] In 1846 it became known that Giuseppe Persiani, the husband of the famous singer, together with a compatriot named Galletti, had purchased the lease of Covent Garden and intended to open it as a second Italian opera house, and that Michael Costa, the conductor, and all but one of the leading singers would go with him.

The auditorium of Covent Garden Theatre was reconstructed by an architect named Benedetto Albano in 1846/7 and the years when performances were primarily of the dramatic art were over.* In 1847 the theatre was reopened as the Royal Italian Opera and a prospectus announced the purpose of 'rendering a more perfect performance of the lyric drama than has hitherto been attained in this country'. All the evidence suggests that singers who went with Michael Costa to Covent Garden were among the finest the world has ever known – the legendary Mario and Grisi, Tamburini, Rubini, Alboni – later joined by Lablache, later still by Pauline Viardot.

At Covent Garden Michael Costa had under him an orchestra of eighty players including sixty-one strings – an unheard of luxury for those days. He succeeded in making this one of the finest orchestras in the world, admired equally by composers and the public. Nevertheless Harold Rosenthal, in illustration of the operatic standards of the day, says:

> Yet this same Costa could sanction the production of *Ernani* in 1847 with Marietta Alboni singing the baritone role of Carlo, because Tamburini found it too high and Ronconi did not like it. He could agree to conduct *Don Giovanni* in 1858 with the title role re-written for the tenor Mario . . . even the overture is not spared: its masterly conclusion is destroyed in order that it may lead to the new key in which Leporello's first aria (the baritone Ronconi was singing the part) is transposed.[7]

---

* The Theatres Act of 1843 ended the monopoly of the Theatres Royal.

Alboni also sang the baritone part of Ernani in the opera of that name, because both Tamburini and Ronconi refused.

The first season under Michael Costa (1847) at Covent Garden opened with Rossini's *Semiramide* and included operas by Bellini and Donizetti, three by Mozart and *I due Foscari* and *Ernani* by the newcomer Verdi, while many others were introduced in the next two seasons, including Meyerbeer's *Le Prophete* and an excellent production of *Les Huguenots*.

By the end of the second season the artistic success of the new opera house was complete. Competition was offered at Her Majesty's Theatre by the arrival of Jenny Lind, one of the best-known singers in operatic history, but the productions at Covent Garden were in a class previously unknown both musically and scenically. Only one thing was wrong. The financial losses in the first season were so great (there was a deficit of £24,000) that Persiani and Galletti fled to Paris and surrendered the lease to a newcomer, Edward Delafield. By the summer of 1849 Delafield was bankrupt, having lost £60,000. The 1849 season was carried to an end by means of what Rosenthal calls 'a sort of co-operative effort', between the singers, who were by now unsure where their salaries were coming from.

Delafield's short reign is chiefly important because to assist him he engaged Frederick Gye as assistant manager, introducing to Covent Garden a name famous in the annals of the theatre. After Delafield was bankrupted Gye took over, backed by a committee of shareholders. In his first season he shared the direction of the theatre with the seven singers of the co-operative effort, but after that he reigned as sole director for twenty-five years, during which time Covent Garden was established as the only permanent opera house in London.

In his history of Covent Garden, Desmond Shawe-Taylor

remarks that Gye was a better business man than musician and says that 'it was perhaps fortunate for him that the first period of his management should have coincided with Verdi's great pair of successes, *Rigoletto* and *Il trovatore,* both of which he was astute enough to bring out only two years after their Italian premieres.'[8] Yet, if Gye was lucky that his management coincided with Verdi's great success, earlier managements had the advantage of the first productions of operas by Rossini, Donizetti, Bellini, and Mozart. It seems more likely that Gye's success was due partly to his ability to find sponsors willing to back this financially unattractive venture (the 1852 season lost £15,000 and Gye was able to continue only through the intervention of a guard's officer named Thistlethwate, who put up £12,000); partly to his ability to manage the turbulent, jealous and spoilt singers; and lastly to an element of brigandage in his nature which enabled him to outwit his competitors with unparalleled ruthlessness.

In the first years competition was silenced by sheer merit. Writing of the year 1852 and speaking of Her Majesty's Theatre, Chorley[†] wrote:

> The 'old house', then, was fairly beaten out of the field by the new one. And after all that had been whispered, and asserted, and published in print, the Italian Opera in Covent Garden had entirely superseded the house in the Haymarket with all its traditional fashion. . . . There was no questioning the fact that, long before 1853 set in, the tide, fashionable and unfashionable, had turned to Covent Garden to hear

---

[†] Henry Chorley, a famous music critic.

great musical performances, and that in 1853 'the dear old house' was closed.[9]

Opera seasons were summer seasons, averaging five months from the beginning of April until the end of August. In the winter the theatre was let for other entertainments. On 4 March 1856 a gentleman called Professor Anderson, known as 'The Wizard of the North', held a grand *bal masqué* at Covent Garden, which was described by a contemporary as 'a disgrace to everyone connected with it'. At five minutes to five in the morning, while what Shawe-Taylor calls 'this squalid function' was drawing to a close, the theatre was found to be on fire. Within half an hour the roof had fallen in and already there was no hope of saving anything. All the properties of sixty operas, the dramatic and musical library and four paintings by Hogarth were lost, and Gye's personal losses were estimated at £30,000.

The proprietors, who still included the Kemble family, called a meeting of one hundred and ten shareholders to discuss what should be done. We owe to Harold Rosenthal the following description of this meeting:

It was pointed out that the lease of the land from the Duke of Bedford still had thirty-eight years to run, at a rent of £2,085 a year. The proprietor's arrangement with Gye was for ten years from 1 October at a rent of £6,500 for the first three years and £7,000 for the remaining period. The last twenty or so years had been devoted to clearing a general debt of some £70,000 which by 1856 had been reduced to £9,000. The proprietors felt that because of the small annual profits (the 1855 season had ended in a profit of £1,500 for Gye, but he was in their debt for some

£1,700) it was beyond their power to do anything with the property. . . . In addition, the theatre was not insured, because the payment of the large sum necessary for the premium had proved impossible; Gye himself was insured for £8,000 but this sum would not go very far to meet even his personal losses.[10]

In spite of these appalling facts, Gye found that 'he had friends on all sides' and subscribers 'only too eager to help him manage'.[11] He negotiated a new lease with the Duke of Bedford to run for ninety years at £850 a year. It was to his phenomenal energy and the generosity of his eager friends that we owe the present theatre at Covent Garden.

The architect was Edward Barry, the son of the architect of the Houses of Parliament. Gye leased extra ground and, by running the theatre east to west instead of north to south as previously, fitted beside it the Floral Hall, where in the early days concerts were given.

Gye soon quarrelled with Michael Costa, whom he found too autocratic. After Costa left, there was a steady decline in artistic standards. Few novelties were given and until 1875 there was an almost total neglect of both Verdi and Wagner. That year was memorable for the first production of *Lohengrin*—nearly twenty-five years after its first performance and in Italian translation. The critic Hermann Klein said that it was the worst production of *Lohengrin* he had ever seen in an important theatre, and, after praising some of the leading singers, went on: 'But the remainder of the cast were beneath notice, while the chorus sang dreadfully out of tune, and the orchestra, under Vianesi, did its best to drown the singers throughout.'[12]

One of the most memorable events of Gye's period at Covent

Garden was the debut in 1861 of Adelina Patti, whose career lasted for almost thirty years, and who at times seemed to keep Covent Garden Theatre open almost single-handed – the only nights which drew fashionable society being Patti nights. But Patti was voracious in her demands for money and, since in New York the Metropolitan Opera House had by now opened to create competition with the old Academy of Music, she could hold Europe to ransom. She received as much as $5,000 for one performance in America (the dollar at five to the pound).[‡]

So, although to the end she could fill the house, Patti contributed to the decline of the Gye management. The copious burgeoning of talent of the earlier part of the century was in any case temporarily stilled, and journeying abroad, Henry Chorley spoke of 'the desolation which had swept over the world of Italian opera singing and composition'.[13] By 1877, when the management passed to Gye's son, the end was already in sight.

> Each year the subscription grew smaller; each year one noted a stiff deterioration in that atmosphere of stately pomp and stiff exclusiveness that had so long been the peculiar social appanage of the Covent Garden season. The history of the house in the early eighties furnished some melancholy chapters of decaying grandeur, of diminishing artistic effort and public support. The affairs of the limited liability company which had carried on the undertaking after the death of the old impresario went from bad to worse; and with the close of the season of 1884, the regime of the Gyes had passed for ever.[14]

[‡] See Appendix E, p. 351 for an approximation of this sum today.

Only short seasons were given at Covent Garden during the next four years – by J.H. Mapleson and by a Signor Lago who at one time and another had the distinction of introducing to London *Cavalleria rusticana* and two Russian operas, Glinka's *A Life for the Tsar* and Tchaikovsky's *Eugene Onegin*. Then in 1888 Augustus Harris leased the theatre and one of the most important eras of opera in London began.

1

1888–1910
Augustus Harris; the Grand
Opera Syndicate

At the north end of the front of Drury Lane Theatre there is
a memorial in red stone consisting of a pair of stone drink-
ing basins and above these, beneath a pediment and between
two pillars decorated with musical instruments, the bust of an
indisputably Victorian gentleman. This is Augustus Harris,
whose reign as manager of Drury Lane in the late nineteenth
century was the most prosperous since the days of David
Garrick, and who at the same time established a system of
management at the Opera House which, apart from the war
years of 1914–1918, persisted in one way or another until 1939.

He tried opera first at Drury Lane, in 1882 putting on a
season with a German company and another in joint management with Carl Rosa. Then in 1887 he staged a sensational
season with a company which included both de Reszke

brothers, Victor Maurel, Minni Hauk, Mattia Battistini and Lillian Nordica. The triumph of Jean de Reszke had been instantaneous and complete, and when Edouard arrived from Paris the two brothers appeared together in *Lohengrin*. Yet according to one account Harris lost £10,000 on this season, according to his own account £16,000.

In an interview with the *Strand* magazine, Harris said that he had intended to revive opera or bury it, and had found the burial ceremony 'rather a costly one'. He went on to describe what happened next.

> In the following year Lord Beresford wrote me a note asking me to call on him at the Admiralty. . . . When I got to Lord Charles's office he asked me whether I would do another season of opera. I shook my head and said there was nothing in it. . . . However, Lord Charles invited me to meet a few friends of his at Lady de Grey's to discuss the matter over a cup of tea. I went, and after we had had an exhaustive discussion, I said: 'If you will take half the boxes for the season I will take Covent Garden.' This was agreed to, and by the time I opened – there was not a box to be let.[1]

In this one conversation Harris secured two of the essentials for successful opera production at that time – financial backing in the form of a regular subscription and the patronage of the aristocracy. Lady de Grey (later the Marchioness of Ripon), a Victorian hostess of whom E.F. Benson said that 'Her beauty was of the quality that can only be described as dazzling; when she was there the rest appeared a shade shabby', was dissatisfied by the never-ending round of social engagements, disliked the country, was not a blue-stocking, but 'wanted a definite stunt to occupy her'.[2] According to Benson, she was not particularly musical, but found what she was looking for in the Opera House. Lady de Grey was in fact a powerful woman, powerful because of her position and also because of her character. She was also a friend of the Prince and Princess of Wales, as was Lady Charles Beresford.

A person of equal importance was Harry Higgins,[*] an able administrator, a member of London society and a noted wit. From the beginning, according to the critic, Hermann Klein, he acted between Lady de Grey and Augustus Harris conveying her suggestions to Harris, 'who knew better than to ignore them'. As time went on, Klein says:

> the *modus operandi* gradually altered. When Harris became overwhelmed with his various duties he was glad to rely upon Mr Higgins for advice, or even to go to Lady de Grey 'for instructions'. A new prima donna had to be engaged, a new opera to be commissioned, a Continental success to be mounted, a new box-subscriber to be passed and admitted. Ere any of these things could be done it was essential that Lady de Grey should be consulted. So by degrees her word became law. . . .[3]

Klein adds that he personally found Lady de Grey as amiable as the world supposed her to be, although he thought much might be said regarding the demerits of a system that depends so largely on individual fancy.

---

[*] Contrary to the statements of Klyne and other writers, Higgins was not Lady de Grey's brother-in-law.

A third essential for a successful operatic undertaking is a supply of creative artists. This condition was met for Harris with an abundance hardly known before or since. The golden age of singing stretched roughly from 1880 to 1910, and during that time the profusion of great singers was such that they cannot all be named. It is enough to say here that, when Patti retired, she was succeeded by Melba, who, almost equally beloved, reigned for thirty years. Jean de Reszke, who succeeded Mario, was himself succeeded by Caruso. Among the greatest singers, Desmond Shawe-Taylor counts Plangon (bass), Schumann-Heink (contralto), Battistini (baritone) and Lilli Lehmann, whose versatility was so great that she sang 165 roles ranging from the Queen of the Night to Carmen, Fricka and Ortrud. Of the singers of the late nineteenth century, Tamagno and Maurel were Verdi's own choice for the first performance of *Otello*, Tamagno being by all accounts the greatest Otello who ever lived, while Melba was unapproachable as Desdemona (as she was too as Mimi, Violetta and many other roles). Of the two Ravogli sisters, Giulia Ravogli, the most famous of all Carmens, so delighted Bernard Shaw that he said he doubted his opinion of her was worth the paper it was written on.

Then there were Jean Lassalle (a famous Hans Sachs), Marcella Sembrich (Lucia), the Wagnerian Emma Eames, Milka Ternina, of whom Puccini said no other Tosca could approach her and who triumphed in *Fidelio* and in Wagner, and a little later Emmy Destinn and Tetrazzini. Speaking of Melba, who like Grisi and Patti before her was reputed to be responsible for the fact that some of the best soprano voices were never heard at Covent Garden, Desmond Shawe-Taylor remarks that 'if this were true, the *diva* must have been off her guard in the autumn of 1907, when Tetrazzini's limpid flights of *colaratura* burst unheralded upon a half-empty house.'[4] Most of these singers were at Covent Garden during Harris's time, all sang either then or with the Grand Opera Syndicate which followed him.

To the riches thus showered upon Harris must be added the presence of Bernard Shaw, one of the greatest music critics of all time, who never ceased in his efforts to keep the impresario up to the mark. He purposely refrained from praise, he wrote, because 'The critic who is grateful is lost. Sir Augustus has given us *Otello* and revived *Fidelio*. Instead of thanking him I ask why he has not given us *Siegfried*. When he gives us *Siegfried* . . . I shall complain of the neglect *of Die Walküre*.'[5]

This continual harassment had its effect. In 1888 Harris gave the first entire *Ring* at Covent Garden. (The adventurous and musical Mapleson had given the first performances in London, with Richter conducting, at Her Majesty's Theatre in 1882, but these were badly received and London had to wait eight years to hear it again.) Harris's *Ring* was given on four successive Wednesday evenings but it began with *Siegfried*, because the tenor Max Alvary wanted to make his debut with his most famous role.

Harris restored Covent Garden to its place as one of the leading opera houses of the world and was responsible for some of the finest performances ever heard there. He introduced many new operas to London, including *Falstaff, Manon Lescaut,* and *Pagliacci,* and abandoned the practice of singing everything in Italian, giving performances of *Faust* and *Roméo et Juliette* in French, and of Wagner in German. He dropped the word Italian from the name of the theatre, which in future was known as the Royal Opera, and he introduced the habit, already known on the continent, of dimming the lights during the performances of German opera. In the interview with the *Strand* magazine, already quoted, he replied to a question about singers as follows:

I have had stars in all my pieces. I do not think the public want experiments in London. If you put a new singer on, he or she . . . must be good, and must sing without any sign of vibrato. In my first year I got the pick of young Italy . . . and they wobbled and toppled over like so many ninepins. It is no light ordeal for a singer to have to appear on the classic boards on which Patti, Tietjens, and Nilsson have sung. The memories of the past seem to haunt the place. . . .

When you go abroad and pay your five marks or five francs to see performances, you find that the artists are all more or less of the same calibre; you do not notice any striking difference between them. But when people pay a guinea or thirty shillings premium it is different; they expect the best, and I have endeavoured to give my public the very best talent that is to be obtained.

Sir Augustus also said that the big draws of the season were *Roméo et Juliette, Carmen, Lohengrin* and *Faust,* while *Cavalleria rusticana* and *Pagliacci* together made a good bill.[†6]

Harris died in 1896 but he left a viable organization behind him. He was succeeded by the Grand Opera Syndicate composed largely of the same people who had supported him: the Marchioness of Ripon (previously de Grey), Lord Esher and Lord Wittenham, with Harry Higgins (on whom Harris had particularly relied) as chairman. These were later joined by Baron Frédéric d'Erlanger.

The Grand Opera Syndicate appointed a managing director,

[†] Harris was knighted not for his services to music but as Sheriff of the City of London on the occasion of a visit from the German Emperor.

first Maurice Grau, who filled the same post at the Metropolitan Opera House in New York, and following him André Messager, the *directeur-général* of the Opéra-Comique in Paris. These appointments were possible because the opera season in London ran from April to July, while both the other opera houses had winter seasons. Neither appointment was entirely satisfactory and in 1906 Neil Forsythe, formerly private secretary to Harris, took over.

In 1902 Higgins had invited a young conductor and composer named Percy Pitt to luncheon. Pitt had earned some reputation as a composer and had written incidental music for Sir George Alexander's production of *Paolo and Francesca*. Here is what Pitt's biographer has to say about the meeting:

> In 1902 the managing director, widely known as 'Harry Higgins', who was, and always had been, anxious to lend a helping hand to British musicians, approached several composers to find out whether they had done, or would like to do, an opera suitable for Covent Garden. The fate of this suggestion was odd. The non-performance of works by British musicians was a standing grievance; yet no one seemed to leap at the opportunity.[7]

Higgins had been told, probably by Elgar, of Pitt's *Paolo and Francesca*, and he said that, providing a suitable libretto could be found, he would be prepared to commission him to write an opera for Covent Garden. This libretto was never found, perhaps, to quote once more from Pitt's biographer, because 'the very ardour of his desire made him [Pitt] too hard to please'.[8] instead, Higgins offered him the post of 'musical adviser', the duties of which were to act as musical coach, assistant stage conductor and general musical adviser. Then in 1906, when Messager left Covent Garden, Pitt was appointed musical director.

The Grand Opera Syndicate have much to their credit. They were responsible for bringing the great Austrian conductor, Hans Richter, back to London for the first time since before the Harris regime, and for an association with him which lasted for seven years. They continued to introduce French and German operas, they gave regular summer seasons and, in addition, let the theatre or acted in association with other companies (the San Carlo of Naples, the Carl Rosa and a company called the Moody-Manners), for autumn seasons. They kept Covent Garden financially viable for twenty-five years, even providing some £70,000 for improvements to the theatre. These included the installation of electric equipment, alterations to the stage and auditorium, enlargement of the opera pit and two additional entrances to the stalls. The small room under the Royal Box, known as the King's Smoking Room and said to be a copy of King Edward's Saloon on his yacht *Victoria and Albert*, was designed at this time for the use of the King, a regular attender at Covent Garden until his death.

In spite of all this the Syndicate have always been much criticized, both by the critics of their own day and by biographers and historians. There seem to be several reasons for this, of which the first is what one writer called their 'philistine' desire to put on operas, such as *La Bohème* and *Madama Butterfly*, which could be trusted to fill the house. The second, in which there is some justice, is the complaint that their seasons were not distinguished for innovative taste. However on this score they do not seem to differ so much from other managements who for one reason or another have had to attract a paying public. Thus, in the summer season of 1909 the operas given were as follows (number of performances in brackets): *Aida* (6), *Armide* (1), *II barbiere di Siviglia* (6), *La Bohème* (6), *Cavalleria rusticana* (3), *Don Giovanni* (2), *Faust* (5), *Les Huguenots* (2), *Louise* (5), *Lucia di Lammermoor* (3), *Madama Butterfly* (7), *Otello* (3), *I pagliacci* (3), *Pelléas et Mélisande* (3), *Rigoletto* (3), *Samson et Dalila* (9), *La sonnambula* (4), *Tess* (3), *Tosca* (4), *La traviata* (6), *Die Walküre* (2). This followed the winter opera season in English at which *Gotterddmmerung* and *Seigfried* had three performances, *Die Meistersinger* and *Die Walküre*, four.

A subsidiary and more justified complaint concerned the poor quality of the innovations the Syndicate did present. This is attributed to the influence of Melba who, like Patti before her, often wished to sing in operas unworthy of her talents. Out of more than forty new works presented, only a few have survived – *Tosca, Madama Butterfly, Louise, Pelléas et Mélisande, Parsifal.*[‡]

However, the most important cause of the unpopularity of the Grand Opera Syndicate concerned the question of language. Opera at Covent Garden continued to be given in Italian, or in its original language, and many people believed that it should, as in most other countries, be translated into the vernacular. This question was to remain the subject of strong differences of opinion until a satisfactory solution was achieved in the 1960s. In the meantime it was much discussed by music critics and remained a source of dissatisfaction to all who believed opera should be sung in English. The editor of *About the House* (the magazine of the Friends of Covent Garden) has given attention

---

[‡] The first London performance of *La Bohème, Elektra, Salome* and *Der Rosenkavalier* were given at Covent Garden, but the first was during a Carl Rosa season and the other three during seasons given by Thomas Beecham.

to the whole question of opera in translation and in a series of articles by experts has done something to clarify the issues.

The first reason for translating into English is obvious – for the better understanding of those members of the audience who do not know the language in which the opera was originally given. Curiously enough, although this end is clearly desirable, it was not the first cause of the strong feeling with which the argument was often conducted. This was inspired a little by patriotism, but chiefly by the belief that only by translation into our own tongue could influence be given to our singers, an English style be developed and British composers encouraged to write opera on native themes. The disadvantages, not so immediately obvious, are no less strong.

Among the most important of these is the artistic damage which any translation must do to sounds which have inspired music. The choice before even the most accomplished translators is often to alter the shape of the musical phrase or the finer nuances of the words. William Weaver illustrates both these points from the Italian translation of *Les Vêpres Siciliennes* (originally written in French):

> The very names of the hero and heroine meant trouble. Hélène, in becoming Elena, shifts its accent to the first syllable, and so instead of being addressed by her name, the heroine is usually apostrophised with 'O donna!', a more bombastic, less intimate and affectionate greeting. Henri becomes Arrigo, and the extra syllable often means that the value of the last note in French becomes halved in Italian, with an octave-drop. After an act or two (and there are five), I began to expect that octave-drop whenever anyone had to call the tenor by name.[9]

Both Andrew Porter, as translator, and Robert Lloyd, as singer, have used Verdi's *Don Carlos* (also written in French and translated into Italian) to illustrate the subtle changes to character translation may give, both choosing, among other examples, Philip's aria at the beginning of the fourth act. Porter says:

> Philip's aria as originally composed is a progression of thoughts: "She does not love me! No, her heart is closed to me. She has *never* loved me!" In Italian, this becomes, 'She never loved me! No, that heart is closed to me, love for me she does not have, for me does not have !'[10]

Commenting on this same passage, Robert Lloyd says of the French version:

> This is direct suffering, self-torturing. 'She doesn't love me, she never loved me' – the one thought leading from immediate pain to a more detached examination of the fact.

While of the Italian, he writes:

> Besides being less clear and succinct, by starting in the past, 'She never loved me', and moving to the present 'She does not love me' the sentiment seems at once more detached and contemplative rather than direct and suffering. If this seems too nice a point I can only assure readers that as I sit at that gloomy table the feeling I have is acutely different from one case to the other.[11]

These are the finer points in fine translation. In less sensitive hands the difficulties are often overcome by the use of

11

balderdash or words so inelegant they diminish the musical effect. Thus, again in *About the House,* William Mann quotes the following three examples from the E.J. Dent translation of *Don Giovanni:*

Zerlina: Feel what is beating here. There is my store.
Donne Anna: The traitor my honour who assaulted,
            My father who murdered.
Leporello: Master's in a pretty stew.[12]

Most of the other arguments against translation are of a purely practical kind. For all its theoretical benefits to the performers, it is of very little direct help to the audience if, as one of the earlier critics put it, 'the words might have been in Chinese, so little were they heard'.[13] And, although it is not popular to say this, it is a quite common experience to sit through the whole of an opera sung in English without under-standing any of the words.

In the first place, the moment more than one person sings, the words cannot be understood in any language. In the second, someone singing an immensely fast or otherwise difficult musical passage is not likely to pay very much attention to diction. Again, even in the case of operas with a great deal of spoken dialogue, one is often reminded that as long ago as Leigh Hunt's criticisms were written, and ever since, people have complained of the difficulty of hearing speech in the vast theatres suitable for opera.

For many years a lack of clarity has been put down either to the acoustics of the theatre or to the faulty diction of most singers. That there is something in this latter criticism cannot be denied, since some singers, Dennis Dowling, for instance, and

Derek Hammond-Stroud, have almost always been heard. Yet an article written by the late Dr Alfred Alexander, a voice expert (published again in *About the House)* puts some theory into what has seemed a purely practical matter.

He says that in ordinary conversation, on a topic with which we are familiar, we understand about ninety out of every hundred words and fill in the gaps by a subconscious process. When speech is accompanied by music, the rate of under-standing changes from about 50 to 80 per cent in melodic declamation to only about ten or fifteen out of every hundred words in true lyrical singing. He gives as reasons for this, first, the intervention of the orchestra, which acts as a concomitant noise in the same way as the background noise in a restaurant makes it difficult to understand a neighbour. Secondly, 'The singer's ingrained loyalty to the musical line makes him "play his instrument" to the best advantage of the sound he can produce',[14] which automatically precludes him from paying attention to enunciation when this interferes with the quality of the sound.

Both Rodney Milnes and Jane Glover have been made very cross by Dr Alexander's percentages, the former declaring that 'People who complain they can't hear the words in opera nowa-days simply aren't listening'.[15] To this one might reply that, since Dr Alexander has stressed that his ratio of words applies only to the *unprepared* listener, it is not really possible for prepared listen-ers to be dogmatic. Curiously enough, there is some evidence (from the average views of people replying to a questionnaire in *Opera* in 1957) that the *prepared* opera-goer – that is someone who has studied the libretto and score, sometimes the relevant language itself, or heard the opera very often – prefers to hear the opera in the original tongue, understands that there is a strong case for opera in vernacular translation, and has no rooted objection to bilingual performances if this is a practical way of bringing famous international singers to London.

The first time serious differences of opinion on the question of language occurred was in 1907. Dr Richter and Percy Pitt conceived the idea of giving an entire *Ring* in the English language at a winter season in the following January and February. They succeeded in casting this mainly with British singers – the exceptions being a Danish tenor, Peter Cornelius, who sang Siegfried, the German tenor Hans Bechstein, who sang Mime, and the Norwegian soprano Broghil Bryhn, who sang Brünnhilde.

On 5 December, immediately before the opening of this season, Dr Richter wrote to the press as follows:

An artistic success with the *Ring* would open a wide prospect: *the foundation of permanent English opera*. By that I mean performances in the English language. When, on my last visit to Bayreuth, I spoke to Frau Wagner of our English *Ring,* she greeted the plan with enthusiasm, and added that a profound influence on the public was only possible through the *national language*. But there must be no narrowness; the great masterpieces of the classical and romantic schools, the excellent existing works by English composers, must be conscientiously performed, and thereby native talent encouraged to produce new excellence. If this goal is reached, or at least the way prepared for it, I shall have achieved one of my highest aims and embodied my gratitude for the hospitality, which has been unstintedly and unceasingly bestowed on me in this country for thirty years.[16]

There was no narrowness. All through the autumn and winter of 1907 preliminary rehearsals were held daily, and extra trouble was taken with the stage rehearsals, since so many of the singers were concert artists without experience of acting. Curiosity was aroused by advance publicity, while 'at it given moment Hans Richter took over altogether and really moulded the whole ensemble into a marvellous state of homogeneity, both musical and otherwise'. After the first two performances the critic of *The Times* wondered whether the splendid standard set could possibly be kept up. *Siegfried* showed no falling off; and with *Götterdämmerung* Richter was said to have 'crowned his previous labours in England'.[17]

The English *Ring* was a great success. The season was repeated the following year and was again successful. Then Pitt and Richter asked to see Harry Higgins to put forward plans for a winter opera season. A letter from Higgins on the subject is interesting, not only for his refusal to undertake this season, but for many of the observations he makes:

> It is not a question of language at all: the fact is that, unless for some very special attraction, the London public will not come to the opera in sufficient numbers to make it pay . . . English people only come to the opera to hear something sensational or unusual. Autumn seasons are always a loss; and summer ones would be a loss too but for foreign auditors and the private subscriptions for boxes and stalls which depend to a great extent on fashion.

Higgins calculated that the cost of performances amounted to £550 a night and would probably be nearer £600, and then he went on:

15

Furthermore you must recollect that in this calculation there is practically no provision at all for new scenery, costumes, etc., etc., and if you were carrying on the season as an enterprise quite separate from the Syndicate who provide all these and charge them to their summer expenses, they would amount to a considerable sum. Wagner might be supported for a few performances; but for your other performances, such as *Orfeo, Samson, Fidelio,* etc., if your receipts average over £300 you will be lucky.

Under these circumstances I am not prepared to recommend my colleagues, who rely to a great extent on my judgment, to run their heads against a brick wall. I advise you strongly not to make an appeal for financial assistance without making it quite clear that in all human probability a loss will result. If the Doctor likes I am quite willing in 1911 to introduce English opera as a feature of the summer season in place of German. It will be an experiment, but one that we can afford to make. If anything will give an impetus to opera in English, that will, but to continue to lose money on English autumn and spring seasons, when there is not even a remote prospect of the enterprise paying its way, is worse than useless and will injure the cause you have at heart. My conviction is that there is very little demand in England for opera at all outside the season, and that, outside the small circle of those who have an axe of their own to grind, the idea that a craving exists for opera to be given in English is an absolute delusion. If we can do Wagner better in English than in German, by all means let us do it in English; I don't believe the summer public will care one way or the other. We shall see how they receive the *Valkyrie* in May.[18]

16

The performance of *Valkyrie* in English did not materialize as the American, Clarence Whitehill, who sang Wotan could not appear; consequendy it had to be sung in German.

Higgins's letter was never forgiven by Pitt or by Richter, who both saw it as a cruel blow to the spirit of artistic achievement. As Richter wrote to Pitt:

> Well! So there we have it. Higgins' letter is quite correct and sensible, he is right, but he is not far seeing, and he underestimates the public feeling for art; *our* works have made full houses and awakened the greatest enthusiasm, which promised abundantly for the future – So much work, talent, keenness and perseverance to be 'snuffed out'.[19]

So, although the Grand Opera Syndicate performed the astonishing feat of keeping Covent Garden open as an international opera house for more than twenty-five years (at first through backing Harris and afterwards in management), they are almost always presented as a self-indulgent society with a penchant for Puccini. One can understand that their contemporaries might take this view because their knowledge of operatic history did not extend beyond their own day. It is odd nevertheless that so many of the writers of posterity should feel the same impatience, because they have the experiences of Thomas Beecham to go upon.

2

1910–1926
Thomas Beecham

Thomas Beecham was the son of a rich man, Joseph Beecham, and in the spring of 1910 they together took the Royal Opera House for a season of twenty-two performances in order, according to the prospectus they issued, to find out the answer to the following question: 'Does there, or does there not, exist in England a public ready to take an intelligent interest in music-drama *per se* if it had the chance?' Later, Beecham wrote in his autobiography:

To anyone unacquainted with the character of the British public it would have seemed beyond question that what it was craving more than anything else in the world at this time was opera. Over a period of ten years there had been carried on in and out of the Press an unceasing campaign for the establishment of an English opera, or perhaps more accurately an opera in English; and according to dozens of writers on the subject, both professional and amateur, we should never be a really civilised nation until we had one.[1]

There is nothing here or in the prospectus to tell us whether Beecham himself felt strongly about the need to sing in English, but we know from his subsequent career that, with reservations, he thought it desirable. In *A Mingled Chime* (1944) he said there was no difficulty in gratifying the desire for performance of English works because there were 'dozens, even hundreds of pieces, unknown then as now', to choose from.[2]

The question of English voices was not so easy. Most had been trained for oratorios:

> Furthermore, English voices are unlike those of most other nations; really robust tenors and true dramatic sopranos hardly exist among us, and high baritones are as rare as a perfect summer. The best among them are of comparatively moderate volume, pure and excellent in tone but lacking in power and brilliance in comparison with those of Italy, Germany and France.[3]

To find out the answer to his question, Beecham tried the British public fairly high.

The Syndicate at Covent Garden owned not only the scenery and costumes but also the rights to perform many of the copyright operas in London. However, this did not worry Beecham, because he was determined to make some innovations. In his first season in 1910 he gave only three standard works, *Carmen*, *Tristan und Isolde* and *Hansel and Gretel*. To form a double bill with the last of these he used a stage version of

Debussy's cantata L' *Enfant prodigue*. In addition he gave *Ivanhoe* by Sir Arthur Sullivan, *The Wreckers* by Ethel Smyth, *A Village Romeo and Juliet* by Delius and Strauss's *Elektra*. *Carmen* and *Hansel and Gretel* were sung in English, the rest in their original language. At this first season Beecham had the distinction of bringing the young Bruno Walter to London.[*]

The success of *Elektra* was a foregone conclusion, because this opera, with its sensational and melodramatic story, had been much advertised by its success in Europe and America. All seats for the first performances were sold before the opening night. (At later performances the audiences grew smaller and smaller. It was not until 1957 when Gerda Lammers sang the role under Kempe that *Elektra* again was successful. See p. 200.)

In February 1910 the Beechams, father and son, announced that for thirteen weeks in the autumn they would give a second season at Covent Garden, and in March they announced that, in the meanwhile, they would give a seven weeks' summer season of *opéra comique* at His Majesty's Theatre. Alan Jefferson, Beecham's latest biographer, remarks that *opéra comique* means different things to different people. To Beecham it meant *Les Contes d'Hoffmann* (with John Coates), a performance of *Werther*, which survived only one performance and was not heard again in London for forty-two years, a French opera called *Muguette* with a score by Edward de Missa, a short Mozart season – a performance of *Il seraglio* with Maggie Teyte as Blonde, *Figaro* with Maggie Teyte as Cherubino, and *Così fan tutte*, produced for the first time in London since the days when Chorley condemned

---

[*]   Walter conducted performances of *Tristan* and *The Wreckers*.

it,[†] a one-act Strauss opera, *Feuersnot,* two British works, *Shamus O'Brien* by Stanford and *A Summer Night* by the music critic of the *Observer,* G.H. Clutsam, and finally *Die Fledermaus.*

In the autumn season at Covent Garden Beecham gave the first performance of Strauss's *Salome* (which, from the Lord Chamberlain's refusal to pass it without many changes to the original libretto, received even more advance publicity than *Elektra* and was again sold out before any performances) and productions of: *The Barber of Seville, Faust, Fidelio, Rigoletto, Tannhäuser, Tristan und Isolde, Tiefland* and *A Summer Night.*

On 23 October 1910 a writer to the *Sunday Times* complained that the results of these seasons had been very depressing:

> We have had opera under the conditions – cheapness of admission, our own tongue, for the most part, freshness of fare and artistic representation . . . which enthusiasts have assured us would enlist the support of all classes, and the public has held determinedly aloof. Save for the *Elektra* and Wagner performances the audiences of the season have been very thin, and even *Carmen* failed to draw a full house.

[†] The great music critic wrote of *Cosi fan tutte* as follows: 'The concerted music is marvellous in its beauty and ingenuity. In the second act there are some superb songs; there is a magnificent close to the opera. Yet what do they avail? The tiresome folly of the fable is even more fatal here than in the case of *Die Zauberflöte.* The utterly stupid trick put on the two girls by their two lovers, abetted by a nimble Abigail, cannot pass at this time of day; and thus, because of utter indifference on the composer's part, a mine of treasure is, as it were, drowned for ever and ever. There is no hope for *Cosi fan tutte* on the stage as the work stands.' (Chorley, *Thirty Years Musical Recollections,* p. 234.)

This does not look as if opera were one of the felt needs of our social life, and it is difficult to resist the conclusion that the English public is constitutionally unsympathetic to the music drama. . . . If anything opera seems more unreal to him when it is sung in the vernacular, because the association of his native tongue with histrionic and emotional abandon seems utterly unreal to him.

A correspondent of the *Daily Mail* (8 November 1910), having said that the artists were nearly all English, and that the productions met with unanimous praise not only from a musical point of view but also owing to the excellence of the singing and the presentation generally, asked 'Is Mr Beecham receiving the support he is entitled to?'

There were a few critical comments about language, since Beecham had not entirely solved the problems of presenting his ambitious repertoire in English. 'Don José sang in French to the Carmen', the *Evening News* complained, 'and in English to the rest of the cast and the chorus, all of whom sang in English. The Carmen sang in French to everyone.'[4] Moreover even when the entire cast sang in English, they could not always be understood. 'All the singers (except Miss Walker)', the critic of *The Times* wrote, speaking of a performance of *The Wreckers,* which is set in Cornwall, 'might also remember that the libretto is in English and not in Cornish, and ought, therefore, to be intelligible to the audience.'[5]

The *Chronicle,* summing up in January, said that seven months of opera during the year in addition to the usual three or four months from other sources was too much, but the writer added: 'Undoubtedly he [Beecham] has reason to complain for the public stayed away *en masse* from some very interesting performances.'[6]

According to a newspaper report Beecham himself was most explicit of all.

> Mr Beecham affirms in an interview that, although 'every-one had been grumbling and crying out at the lack of opportunity' when he provided the sort of entertainment for which so many people clamoured 'the public resolutely held aloof and declined to furnish support'.

The report continued that Beecham had then said:

> A year ago people cherished the fond delusion that it was only necessary for opera to be given on a large scale for everyone to take it up, especially opera in English. Now they have had it for a year and they have never come anywhere near the place. . . . There is no audience at all for opera. . . . To put on a new opera is to raise the most deadly danger signal; people at once avoid the district for weeks as though it were infected with plague. A new work absolutely sends a shudder through people.[7]

In an interview in New York Joseph Beecham said that the summer season of opera at His Majesty's had meant a loss of £40,000 and suggested that Grand Opera was inevitably bound up with society and Covent Garden was the only theatre where it could be made to pay. He went on to say: 'Some people spend their money on the turf; I prefer to devote mine to the popularising of Grand Opera and I do not begrudge the money.'[8] But Thomas Beecham said: 'Out of something like fifty works presented there had been unqualified approval of four only: the short and sensational blood-curdlers, *Salome* and

Elektra, and the tuneful lightweights *Les Contes d'Hoffmann* and *Die Fledermaus.*[9]

Before the 1911 season Beecham was approached by the directorate of the Grand Opera Syndicate at Covent Garden with the proposal that they should unite their forces to fight other competition and he joined the Board. The historically important result of this alliance was that the Diaghilev ballet company, which had already been engaged by the Beechams, gave their first performances at Covent Garden. There was a certain justice in this turn of events, because it was in fact the maligned Lady Ripon who, earlier famous for having brought Melba back to London after Harris had offended her, was now responsible for having persuaded Joseph Beecham to guarantee this first visit of the Diaghilev Ballet.

'The London season, which was now in full swing', Beecham wrote, Was running its usual placid course when, like a visitation from another plane, there burst upon it the Russian ballet.'[10] This was one of the major artistic events of the twentieth century. In the first three seasons the ballets performed included *Carnaval, Schéhérazade, Le Spectre de la rose, Cléopatre* (all with scenery by Bakst), *Pavilion d'Armide, Prince Igor, Swan Lake, Giselle* and *Firebird.* The artists included Nijinsky, Nijinska, Kshessinskaya, Pavlova, Fokina and Karsavina. In opera, the great event of these years was the first performance of *Der Rosenkavalier* in 1912.

In 1913 the Beechams left Covent Garden and leased Drury Lane in order to bring over not merely the Russian ballet but also Russian opera. With Feodor Chaliapin at a fee of £400 a night, this was a season the Syndicate at Covent Garden could not afford.

In 1914 the lights went down. Covent Garden Theatre was requisitioned by the Government and used as a furniture store during the whole course of the war. All German musicians had been sent home at the outbreak of war, but Beecham was able to engage singers from a defunct company which had been touring, called the Denhof, and some of those who had been part of his own season of *opéra comique* in 1910. On 2 October 1915 the Beecham Opera Company, with the Beecham Chorus and the Beecham Orchestra opened a season of opera at the Shaftesbury Theatre. The repertory included Gounod's *Romeo and Juliet, Carmen, La Bohème, Tosca, Faust, Madama Butterfly, Cavalleria rusticana, Pagliacci,* and *The Tales of Hoffmann.*

In wartime London there was no difficulty in filling the theatre for a season which lasted until the middle of December. Beecham conducted only twice himself and left the running of the company to his staff. On the musical side, his conductors included Percy Pitt, Hamish McCunn, later Julius Harrison, Landon Ronald, Harold Howell, and a very young man called Eugene Goossens, whom he appointed assistant conductor to himself with the duties of arranging scores, taking rehearsals, coaching singers and so on. Possibly more important to the success of the company than any of these was a man called Donald Baylis, a former employee of Sir Joseph Beecham,‡ and his right-hand man at Drury Lane who was a brilliant administrator. One of Beecham's biographers says of him that he was 'the *éminence*, the right-hand, the privileged intermediary'.[11] He was responsible for the efficient management of the company in London and on tour.

Following a successful season in London, the Beecham Opera Company appeared in Manchester with the Hallé orchestra and

---

‡ Joseph Beecham was created a baronet for his services to music in 1911.

northern choristers. During the war they visited Glasgow, Edinburgh, Birmingham and Manchester again, and gave seasons in London at the Aldwych from October 1915 to August 1916, and at Drury Lane from May to July and from September to November 1917. The repertory had been extended to include some Wagner, *Boris Godunov, Figaro* and *The Magic Flute.*

Beecham engaged a talented designer, Hugo Rumbold, and insisted on strenuous rehearsing and particular attention to diction. By every account the company reached a standard never before known in an English opera company and seldom surpassed since. Of the singers, Frank Mullings, whose name is hardly known today, was, according to Neville Cardus, by far the most poignant Parsifal of his experience. He writes:

> Mullings as 'Otello' in Verdi's opera, ran a good second, for magnificence of presence and intense characterisation, to Chaliapin's Boris. He was less demonstrative than Chaliapin. Mullings, a tall man and a big man, could incarnate Shakespeare's as well as Verdi's 'Otello', and also make us feel his softness of nature, caught in the snare of his own elemental passion. In the scene with Iago in Act II, his ferocity was terrible. . . . Mullings, for his all ravening lust for revenge, understood proportion, knew the force of silence. As he entered the bedchamber of Desdemona, his silence pervaded the theatre from stage to topmost gallery. Mignon Nevada, the Desdemona to Mullings' 'Otello', confessed that his quietness often chilled her with something of apprehension.§[12]

---

§　Mignon Nevada was the daughter of the great Emma.

Thomas Beecham himself says:

> The Desdemona of Mignon Nevada was the best I have
> seen on any stage. The gentle helplessness of the character
> and its simple pathos were rendered with perfect judgment
> and art, and the quality of the voice in the middle and
> upper registers suggested a tender melancholy admirably in
> keeping with the nature of this part.

Of Mullings, he writes:

> In the centre his voice had ease and uncommon beauty,
> and his singing of quiet passages had a poetry, spirituality
> and intelligence which I have never heard in any other
> native artist and in very few elsewhere.

But he says 'Both of these artists suffered from the same serious
weakness, an unsound vocal method.'[13] Other members of the
Beecham Company included Frederick Austin, Norman Allin,
Percy Herning, Rosina Buckman, Miriam Licette.

By 1918 Beecham was heavily in debt, even to moneylenders.
When war broke out in 1914 Sir Joseph Beecham had been
caught in a vast property deal which, expected to show quick
returns, was disastrously affected by the instant restrictions on
the transfer of capital. He had bought a large slice of the Duke
of Bedford's Covent Garden property, including the Royal
Opera House, an act which was to have some bearing on the
future of the theatre. The intention had obviously been to break
the property up and sell it quickly and advantageously, but an
accommodation, involving large interest payments, had to be
made for the duration of the war, and, when Sir Joseph died in

1916, he left a situation of extreme financial complication. Beecham (now Sir Thomas) nevertheless expected that, when peace came and enabled his father's estate to be settled, he would inherit a considerable income, and he continued to pour money into his opera company throughout the whole course of the war.

In 1919 he was invited to rejoin the Grand Opera Syndicate at Covent Garden and in the prospectus was described as 'artistic director', a post not previously known. The first international season after the war was made possible only by singers from the Beecham Opera Company, who were already engaged and could be cast in principal roles or take these over from visiting stars. The season ended with *La Bohème*: Melba singing Mimi, and Tom Burke (a Lancashire tenor) Rodolfo, Beecham conducting. International stars who returned included Destinn, Kirkby Lunn, Martinelli and Sammarco, and the operas performed included *Thaïs* (with Edvina), *Faust, Un hallo in maschera, Prince Igor* with a Beecham company cast and a production of de Lara's *Naïl* with Rosina Buckman, Frank Mullings and Percy Herning.

The 1919 season was, like so many things which immediately followed the artistic poverty of the war years, immensely successful, and the cheaper seats in the theatre were well filled. Even so, the days of a large and enormously wealthy upper class had gone for ever, and Beecham's personal friend and admirer, Lady Cunard, although a worthy successor to Lady Ripon in her devotion to opera, was unable to fill the subscription list as her predecessor had done. Too many of the stalls and grand tier seats remained empty.

Undeterred, Beecham followed with his own company for a winter season of two parts, November to Christmas and the end of February to mid April. During this period 104 performances of twenty-six operas were given by British singers including *Otello* and *Tristan* (with Mullings), *Le Coq d'or, Samson et Dalila* as well as some Puccini, and the *Mastersingers.*

Today it is difficult to speak with authority about the artistic standards of the Beecham Company. Following this season a critic in the *New Statesman* wrote: 'It is now certain that any company of foreign artists that can survive competition with the Beecham Company will have to be extraordinarily fine – far, far better than what Covent Garden habitually gave us before the war.' And he spoke of the all-round excellence of the company and the smoothness and polish of ensemble: 'Such is the result of five or six years constant work together under the stimulus of a conductor with artistic ideals who would stand none of the Melba, Tetrazzini, Caruso nonsense that made Covent Garden ridiculous. . . .'[14]

On the other hand Edward Dent in the *London Mercury* said this:

As long as Sir Thomas Beecham was fighting the battle of English opera with dogged persistence and unstinted expenditure of material in the face of apathy and indifference, and possibly the hostility of vested interests as well, there was a very general feeling that his courage and high idealism should not be hampered by a too searching criticism of his performances. It is inevitable now that it [the Beecham Opera Company] has taken possession of Covent Garden . . . it should be considered in a more impartial spirit.

And he went on to say:

29

In the case of new operas insufficient rehearsal can be pardoned, but it is not a sign of good management when the performance of stock classics is allowed to become slack and indifferent.[15]

A few years later, Ernest Newman wound up an article in which he said that London could not do without an international season, but that British opera should also be made secure both for London and the provinces, with the following words:

> The air is thick just now with schemes for putting British opera on its feet. Most of them are hopelessly idealistic, they would mean in practice little more than spending a vast amount of public money to get passable performances and worthless operas. It is hardly worth our while going to all this trouble and expense to make the operatic world safe for mediocracy.[16]

One may reasonably infer that the very high standards achieved at the beginning of the war had lapsed when Beecham left the running of his company to others.

For the 1920 summer season he again joined the Grand Opera Syndicate. Sixty-nine performances of seventeen operas were given and – most memorable of all – thirteen different ballets danced by the Diaghilev Company. Puccini came to London to conduct the first performances of the *Trittico* and a Spanish coloratura named Graziella Pareto gave what Beecham called 'easily the most attractive and satisfying performance of Violetta' of his recollection.[17]

Beecham had been asking for financial trouble for many years and at the end of the 1920 season it came. At midday on Friday,

30 July a notice was put up outside the Opera House stating that the evening performance of the Diaghilev Ballet had been cancelled. On the advice of his solicitors, Diaghilev had withdrawn his whole company and issued a writ against the Beecham Opera Company for non-payment. Beecham's landlords, the Grand Opera Syndicate, were understandably annoyed and refused to support him, 'not least because the season had made a staggering loss.'[18] In an attempt to keep the Beecham Opera Company together, it was sent out on tour, but after four weeks was forced to close. An order in bankruptcy was made against Beecham.

At this point in the story more than one writer has suggested that, if he had only stuck to his own company and avoided the colossal expense of the Ballets Russes, not only might all have been well with the 1920 season, but the future of a British opera company might have been assured. This view is put forward in spite of the fact that by the end of 1919, before the final season, Beecham's personal losses in opera had reached the figure of £104,000. However, his bankruptcy was only part of the much larger collapse of his father's estate. Beecham, who surprisingly had inherited some of his father's flair for financial management, left the operatic scene for four years to deal with these matters.

There was no summer season at Covent Garden in 1921, although the great English soprano, Eva Turner, appeared in autumn seasons given by Carl Rosa in 1920 and 1921.¶ In the meantime some of the leading members of the Beecham Opera

---

¶ Dame Eva Turner, regarded in her day as a great Aida and an incomparable Turandot.

31

had formed a new company, which they called the British National Opera Company (BNOC). Percy Pitt served as musical and artistic director and other directors of the company included three singers: Agnes Nicholls, Norman Allin and Frederick Austin.

In the next two years this company leased Covent Garden for four short seasons (a total of twenty-eight weeks out of ninety-five) and, apart from a four-week season by the Carl Rosa Company, gave the only performances of opera to be heard at the time. Without Beecham the BNOC, as it came to be called, suffered from a lack of professional management – not too little rehearsal but too much, and too heavy a schedule. Almost all accounts agree that the musical and artistic standards were not very high.

In 1924, the year of the British Empire Exhibition at Wembley, Harry Higgins, who said afterwards that the Syndicate were being constantly pressed to return to seasons of international opera, invited the Vienna State Opera to give a summer season, an invitation which, if accepted, would render the BNOC homeless. In the tremendous row which followed the protagonists of all sides had their say.

It began with the Musicians' Union who objected, not to the singers of the Vienna Company coming to Covent Garden, but to the orchestra that would accompany them, and threatened a strike. There is no doubt that many people were sympathetic to their stand, although this was largely because, as a writer to *The Times* put it, 'the artistic temperament takes naturally to the process of performing two themes in double-counterpoint'. In no time the action of the Musicians' Union, which was of a purely industrial kind, had become confused with a battle for the BNOC, which would not be able to appear at Covent Garden if the Vienna visit took place. Matters were brought to a head by a letter to *The Times* signed by the Principals of the Royal Academy of Music and of the Royal College of Music. Having made it plain that they would at any other time welcome an opportunity to hear the Vienna Company, they said they felt that it was inappropriate at a time 'which is to be dedicated to assembling all the best this Empire can produce'. Then, after praising the courage with which the British Company 'fights its plucky way', these gendemen said: 'However much we enjoy hearing the performance of other countries, we should see that a British organisation so worthy of support should not be robbed of the opportunity of doing battle at such a moment for opera in English at the home of English opera.'[19]

This letter, which would have been reasonable and persuasive if Covent Garden had been a subsidized state opera house, was too much for Mr Higgins, whose syndicate had been responsible for keeping it open to the opera public for so many years. A week after it appeared, he replied, making the following points:

No good object is served by calling things by wrong names and to describe a touring company that devotes its efforts almost entirely to performing translations of foreign operas as the British National Opera Company is an abuse of language. Why the latter [the BNOC] – he went on – should think they have any claim to perform indifferent translation at our theatre to the exclusion of those who prefer to produce operas in the original language, I cannot imagine.

The Carl Rosa, the Moody-Manners Company, and Sir Thomas Beecham have all in recent years engaged in precisely similar enterprises, but none of them claimed to be a British National Opera Company, for in their case also national opera has been the exception and not the rule.

The statement that Covent Garden Theatre is the home of English opera is about as absurd a misrepresentation as could possibly be made. The tide of Covent Garden Theatre was 'The Royal Italian Opera Company, Covent Garden' until 1892 when, in consequence of all operas being performed there in the language in which they were written, the word Italian was dropped.

Then, after saying that there had been no English summer season at Covent Garden until 1922 and 1923, when owing to 'fortuitous circumstances' the BNOC were granted short tenancies of seven weeks each, while outside the summer season there had been sixteen French, Italian or German seasons and fourteen English, the writer went on to say that the expenses incidental to ownership of Covent Garden were extremely heavy, 'and it is during the London season that my syndicate expects to earn sufficient to meet at least two-thirds of the amount required to meet them'.[20]

The practical arrangements for the summer season were solved by the Austrian ambassador to London advising his Government to abandon the visit, by Harry Higgins engaging many of the artists who would have come from Vienna and giving an eight-week season of international opera at Covent Garden, and by the BNOC taking His Majesty's Theatre, where they suffered from the competition at Covent Garden of Lotte Lehmann, Elizabeth Schumann, Frida Leider, Alfred Piccaver, Friedrich Schorr, Richard Mayr and other artists known to the public.

But, although this was the end of the row provoked by the

Musicians' Union, it was not the end of the immense feeling between those who believed in international seasons at Covent Garden and those who wished to have opera sung in English by a British company. Reading the newspapers of the day, one is surprised how early a deep emotional bias was felt against what is nowadays called 'the establishment'. Not yet known by this name, the people it denotes were spoken of with the utmost scorn. Musical journalists of the day apparently seriously believed that the very people who owned the largest houses in London spent much time and not a little money on Covent Garden in order to be able to dress up, wear jewellery and gossip. An article that appeared in *Punch* in 1928 is typical of the kind of thing that appeared week after week in the press:

> But fine clothes are no guarantee of artistic appreciation. The soul of music is not to be found in Peacocks. Covent Garden in the old days was magnificent but it was not music but mode that was worshipped in its auditorium.
>
> Today the people who care most for music and know most about it are not peers or plutocrats but belong to the middle class.[21]

At the risk of stating the obvious, it must be said that, although music has no class boundaries, appreciation of it among ordinary, untalented folk is most often found among those who have the greatest opportunities to hear it. Nevertheless, the second paragraph of the quotation from *Punch* expresses a belief, often put forward by journalists, that there was amongst the middle classes a body of seriously musical people longing for innovation and willing to support opera, providing it was sung in English. And this was all the odder, because not only was this fantasy disproved again and again, but little support for innovation was to be found in the columns of the critics themselves. Here is what Sir Thomas Beecham had to say about it:

> During the past eleven years I have introduced nearly one hundred novelties and revivals – which are virtually novelties – in the opera house. And I have done this to widen the area of public knowledge and to increase the pleasure of the intelligent musical amateur. I find it hard to believe now that all this labour has been in vain, but every time I return to London there is the same fight to persuade the public to come to the first performance of something they have not seen before. . . . I do not altogether understand the point of view of some English musical writers, who seem really to enjoy slaughtering works such as *Manon, Don Pasquale* and *Djamileh,* which the rest of the civilised world has for nearly a century agreed to regard as masterpieces.

Then, having said that music critics are always willing to praise musical comedy, Beecham went on:

> I have grown so completely accustomed to the accepted doctrine in England that bad or mediocre work must be allowed to go in peace, while the worthy or aspiring is something to be suspected and if possible 'downed' that I have ceased to worry myself about it.[22]

Nevertheless, before leaving the subject of opera in English, it must be stressed that the companies endeavouring to give work to British singers and to introduce opera to the middle classes all over England had some reason to resent the international seasons at Covent Garden. After the war was over there was in reality no public for opera sufficient to keep two companies going during the London season, when the BNOC had hoped to receive a large part of the revenue needed for survival. Towns such as Manchester and Birmingham also 'lapsed from grace' when a greater variety of entertainment was offered them and failed to fill the theatres for opera. It was, however, to the lack of support in London that the Chairman of the BNOC attributed losses of rather more than £10,000 a year during the first four years of the company's existence. Even at Covent Garden the summer seasons had to be reduced to no more than eight weeks at this time – approximately four weeks of German opera followed by four of Italian.

However, no matter what their views on language and singers in the 1920s, lovers of opera must have been glad of the international seasons at Covent Garden. For now there again occurred one of the golden ages of singers, although this time they came less from Italy than from the German-speaking nations. Bruno Walter, often regarded as the best conductor of his day, returned to Covent Garden in 1924 and remained until 1931 'as musical director in everything but name'.[23] Walter conducted mostly Wagner at Covent Garden, four Mozart operas – *Figaro, Don Giovanni, Il seraglio and Die Zauberflöte* – Beethoven's *Fidelio,* Richard Strauss's *Der Rosenkavalier* and *Elektra* and Johann Strauss's *Die Fledermaus.*

Desmond Shawe-Taylor was present to hear the singers of this glorious age. He tells us that, as compared with their formidable predecessors, the singers of that date were often deficient in sheer purity and tonal production and that their voices did not last as well; that Frida Leider never possessed the perfect technique of Lilli Lehmann, Milka Ternina or Lillian Nordica

('But her Brünnhilde and Isolde were none the less expressive, passionately human and marked in particular with a splendid *legato'*). He speaks of 'the warm voiced singer and excellent actress, Maria Olczewska', and of the huge Dane, Lauritz Melchior, whose voice remained fresh at the end of the last act of *Tristan* or *Götterdämmerung,* and he tells us that in the great bass-baritone parts, Friedrich Schorr and Rudolph Bockelmann 'divided our allegiance', while among the basses, Otto Helgers and Alexander Kipnis were outstanding. But it is on the performance of *Der Rosenkavalier* that Shawe-Taylor shows his descriptive powers at their best:

> It is . . . extremely difficult to believe that better performances of *Der Rosenkavalier* can ever have been given anywhere than those of the twenties and early thirties at Covent Garden. It was sung there time and again by the same ideal cast, until it began to seem as though Strauss himself must have had the very timbre and intonations of these voices in mind when composing the music, though none of them had in fact taken part in the Dresden *première.* The Marschallin was Lotte Lehmann's greatest part. . . . From this wonderful impersonation everyone has doubtless compiled his own nostalgic anthology; the famous aristocratic curl of the lip with which she commented on the departure of Baron Ochs . . . the intimate, varied, laughing ease of the series of conversations with Oktavian; the immense dignity and distinction of her appearance in the last act; the opening phrase of the trio; the final humorous–tragic 'Ja, ja' with which, on Faninal's arm, she left behind the young lovers – and her own youth.

As for those lovers – Elizabeth Schumann was the Sophie

of one's dreams; no one else came near her in those long soaring phrases with which she acknowledged the gift of the rose; 'exquisite' is an overworked word, but nothing else will do for that long, fine-drawn thread of sound, those ravishing *pianissimo* high notes at 'Wie himmlische, nicht irdische, wie Rossen vom hochheiligen Paradies'. None of the various Oktavians proved quite so inevitable a choice as that. . . . As for the Baron Ochs, there could never be any doubt during the lifetime of Richard Mayr. . . . One remembers him in the first act, sitting at his ease in the Marschallin's bedroom, pouring out a stream of scandalous gossip in that over-ripe Viennese dialect of which he was a master; he never seemed to glance at the conductor, or to trouble his head with such details as bar-lines and rests and cues; it might have been a bravura speech from some play by Sheridan – and yet every note was impeccably there. I shall never forget the first impact of this apparently careless display; it was a revelation of what acting in the opera house can be.[24]

Second only to the performance of *Der Rosenkavalier* was that of *Don Giovanni*, with Leider, Lehmann, Schumann and Stabile. Lauritz Melchior, not yet at his best, appeared in London in 1924, singing Siegmund, Toti dal Monte sang both Lucia and Rosina in 1925, Jeritza sang Tosca in the same season and Chaliapin sang Boris in 1922. Once more the list might be continued to include many others of the first rank. In the meantime, Eva Turner went to Milan to audition for Toscanini and to begin a notable international career.

Financially, in spite of these great artists, the season of 1924 had been as disastrous at Covent Garden as for the BNOC, and the Grand Opera Syndicate decided at last that they could afford no more. Then Mrs Samuel Courtauld came forward to help finance the seasons of 1925, 1926 and 1927. Apart from their conspicuous generosity, Mrs Courtauld and her husband are memorable for having introduced Colonel Blois as managing director of the new syndicate. Blois, who was one of the best directors Covent Garden has ever had, remained until his death in 1933, after the withdrawal of the Courtaulds, persuading the naturalized Hungarian banker, F.A. Szarvasy, to become Chairman of the Covent Garden Opera Syndicate Ltd.

Unlike Harry Higgins, Blois had a genuine sympathy with the aspirations of the English opera groups, and when, in 1929, the British National Opera Company was forced into liquidation, he took over a large part of the personnel and organized a tour. 'For the first time', he announced, 'international and English opera will be linked under one management, based on Covent Garden.'[25] Blois was very insistent that this was not merely the British National Opera Company under new management but a Covent Garden enterprise. In fact most of the singers were the same (they included the young lyrical tenor, Heddle Nash), but the standards had gone. Baylis, whom the Beechams had appointed to run their company, had died in 1920 and without him the administration of the company deteriorated along with the performances. The times were also unpropitious, and after two years, in 1929, the Covent Garden tour had to be abandoned.

The greatest importance of Blois, however, was that, for the first time in the history of opera, he made an attempt to analyse the financial returns of the seasons, and, having done so, to make it a policy to give the public at least some of the operas they were most willing to pay for. At the end of the 1925 season he issued a long statement in which he said first that, while there had been unauthorized reports that a profit had been earned, 'the fact is that a steady, substantial loss had been made from the very beginning to the final week.' After saying that the syndicate hoped later to publish a summary of the actual financial results and a comparison of the returns from the various works, which would enable those interested to gauge for themselves the possibilities of establishing international opera in London on a more or less permanent basis, the statement went on:

There seems to be no possibility of making such an undertaking self-supporting, but the present Syndicate will have accomplished one of their objects if they can show that the liabilities are not such as supporters of music need unduly fear, provided that a sufficient measure of public interest and support can be obtained. What has just been said may perhaps explain why the London Opera Syndicate has not been more enterprising in the choice of a repertory this year, and why they have included a certain number of old popular favourites instead of considering nothing but pure artistic interest . . . and the results seem to show that they were justified in their belief that – at any rate for a Season undertaken at such short notice – the inclusion of those popular items was necessary to ensure them against too great an average loss.[26]

Soon after this Blois did indeed publish most interesting details. He showed the operas of the season in three columns – the first being the order of popularity, gauged by the average bookings per performance, the second, the order of costliness, and the third the order of financial results beginning with the

most profitable. The results were sufficiendy unexpected, particularly in relation to the underlying belief expressed in the earlier
statement that the performance of popular operas would stem
the financial losses. Thus *Tosca*, which was the most popular, was
also the most financially profitable, but *Der Rosenkavalier* which
was the second most popular but very costly was ninth (out of
thirteen) in the order of profitability. *Butterfly*, very low in the
order of popularity but also low in the order of costliness, was
third in the order of profitability.

Certain other findings of his analysis are worth repeating. The
average loss on the last six operas (which included *Der Rosenkavalier)*
was nearly five times as great as the first five in the same column.
The average booking for German opera was 7.5 per cent better
than for Italian, but the average cost of German productions 20
per cent higher, the loss on this part of the repertoire for this
reason being twice as great as on the Italian. The soloists
accounted for 30 per cent of the total expenses, the orchestra for
21 per cent and the chorus and ballet 14 per cent – though a
subdivision showed that the orchestra for the German operas
cost 75 per cent more than for the Italian, the chorus 40 per cent
more, the soloists very little more.

Some deductions made from the figures were published. A
complete season of the works of Wagner and of *Der Rosenkavalier*
would show a loss if every available seat were sold for every
performance. A 10 per cent improvement in the receipts for the
season would halve the loss, but there was room for this improvement only in the more expensive seats. If 93 per cent of the boxes
and stalls were sold and the other bookings remained unaltered,
expenses would be covered, but if all the other seats were sold
and there was no improvement in boxes and stalls, the total
average booking would amount to 80 per cent of capacity instead

of the 94 per cent required. These figures proved what every manager from Harris to Blois had known – that, however distasteful to journalists were the manners of the wealthier classes, nothing but their presence could ensure the continuation of opera at Covent Garden.

The manners of all classes seem to have left a great deal to be desired. In an article complaining of some of the arrangements at Covent Garden, Ernest Newman said:

'But these are not the worst features of Covent Garden opera. The very worst of all is the audience: I make bold to say that we shall never have a real opera in London until there is a drastic improvement in this department.'

He went on to try to prove that the audience for German opera was not only different but that, 'although ludicrously limited in their receptivity', was rather better trained to musical standards than the audience for Italian, who 'have no standards at all'.[27] This is not borne out in Beachcomber's** account of a visit to the opera. 'Nobody', he wrote, 'seemed to notice last night that *Rosenkavalier* was the opera being played. The conversation was carried on at a pitch usually reserved for *Valkyrie*.[28]

Sir Thomas Beecham thought that the worst thing about Covent Garden was the music critics themselves. He went so far as to say that it was their attitude to any innovation which condemned the public to 'a tedious and sordid round' of

---

** For the benefit of later generations, Beachcomber, who wrote a regular column in the *Daily Express*, was regarded as among the great comic writers of all time.

Butterflies, Fausts and *Carmens* and, 'monstrous reflection, *Bohemian Girls*'.[29]

The great event of the 1926 season was Melba's farewell. Melba sang first at Covent Garden in 1888 and remained the supreme favourite for nearly thirty years. At first a high coloratura and a famous Rosina, Lucia, Gilda and Violetta, she later sang Marguerite, Mimi, Desdemona, Aida and Nedda. On 8 June 1926 at her farewell performance she sang the second act of *Romeo*, the opening scene of the last act of *Otello*, the third and fourth acts of *Bohème*. Desmond Shawe-Taylor wrote:

> Electrical recording had just been invented in time to preserve the occasion and to demonstrate for ever how much purity and steadiness of tone a singer can command in her sixty-eighth year, provided that her vocal method is absolutely perfect. An era of operatic history seems to have been ended by the departure of Melba and the death, in 1928, of Harry Higgins, that genial hoarse-voiced impresario who is the subject of so many anecdotes.[30]

3

1926–1939
Sadler's Wells and Glyndebourne

In the late twenties and early thirties the world of opera in England was dominated by Sir Thomas Beecham.* To understand this and also many of the later events at Covent Garden, something must be known about the man himself. An exceptional musician – many people thought a genius – he had a complete dominance over those who worked for him, and so much energy, generosity, charm and wit that most of these adored him. To his equals or to anyone he had to treat as such, he was not merely impossible to deal with, but ruthlessly

---

* He returned to his musical career in 1924 having sold most of the Covent Garden estate. In that year a public company called Covent Garden Properties was floated, owning an estate which included the Opera House. Beecham held a substantial share in this company and had an assured income.

untrustworthy, often implacably hostile. In an introduction to a memorial tribute, Humphrey Procter-Gregg said that to those who only knew Beecham by name he seemed a 'legend in a halo of delightful anecdotes', and went on:

> To those who knew him and those who also worked with him, he was a great deal more than that, probably the greatest conductor in the world and the most vivid musical experience in their lives. To the historian, Handel and Beecham must appear the most potent individual forces in the history of music in England: both operated on a lavish scale and both lost a lot of money.[1]

Berta Geissmer, who had been secretary to Furtwängler and worked for Beecham as General Secretary, said: 'In his effort to promote musical life, he has given to the British nation not only a fortune but also his heart's blood.'[2] Yet he had a sense of his own righteousness and unequalled brilliance which made him unreliable as an ally, dangerous as a foe: 'From Beecham's viewpoint, when he had a bee in his bonnet about something (as he usually had) there were only two camps. In one stood Beecham clad in shining armour. In the other grovelled the philistine. There was nobody in between.'[3]

In 1927 Beecham started a grandiose project which he called the Imperial League of Opera. He wished to 'found and maintain an organisation of the front rank that shall give seasons in six provincial cities'. To do this he reckoned would involve an annual expenditure of £50,000, which, with a safety margin of £10,000, would make an annual requirement of £60,000. Mistakenly, as the future would show, he asked for subscriptions towards this exact sum, saying that 'divided among 150,000 persons £60,000 works out at less than 10s per head or 2d a week'.

Unfortunately there were not 150,000 people willing to subscribe this amount, although there were some who subscribed a great deal more. Beecham actually raised £40,000, but, because this was short of the sum for which he had asked, in 1931 the trustees of the Imperial League thought it necessary to go to the Chancery Court for a settlement. Here an order was made that those subscribers who wanted their money back should have it returned to them.

In 1933 a circular was sent out suggesting that subscribers should agree to leave their money to be used for any purpose connected with opera, providing Sir Thomas Beecham was closely associated with it.[†] Subscribers agreed to the extent of between £17,000 and £18,000, but the appeal cannot be regarded as having been very successful, because the incidental expenses of verifying subscribers, and writing to them and so on (paid by Beecham and some others) was almost equal to the money received. But it did have the effect of leaving Beecham in possession of £17,000 to be used specifically towards the promotion of opera.

It was not for this comparatively small sum of money that the Covent Garden Opera Syndicate began in the early thirties to try to persuade Beecham to join them, but for himself. He had by now achieved the position of a Melba or Patti, who alone could be trusted to fill the house (although even then, as he

---

[†] The circular was part of an attempted amalgamation of the interests of all the various opera companies. This came to nothing and is therefore not of much importance historically.

proved with a production of Delius's *Koanga,* only when he conducted operas the public wanted to see). His response was difficult and uncertain. He expressed himself interested but he did not answer letters or accept invitations, nor could he be held to his word. Yet it was necessary to pursue him. 'I should like to get to him privately', Mrs Snowden, a member of the Syndicate, wrote to Colonel Blois. 'If there is a third person present, I can see he talks as though he were at a public meeting. I think if he will come and see me privately we can get down to it.'[4]

And, from a musical festival in Harrogate, she wrote:

> One thing I am convinced of: we ought to invite him to be our Artistic Director unconditionally i.e. whether his money is available or not. His qualities there are quite unmistakeable. People here who loathe his habits rave incontinently when he conducts. And they are right. He has been at the top of his form here and it has been glorious.[5]

Mrs Snowden was the wife of Philip Snowden, the Chancellor of the Exchequer in the Labour Government. Her presence on the syndicate was responsible for the first government subsidy to opera ever given in England, although this turned out to have very little value except as a precedent. It was tied to an agreement between the Royal Opera House and the BBC, giving the latter the right to broadcast opera from the theatre. A White Paper of 15 June 1931 stated that a retrospective payment of £5,000 would be made to the BBC for the autumn period of opera at Covent Garden ending 31 December 1930 and a further payment of £17,500 a year from January 1931 for a period of five years. The agreement provided that:

In the event of the determination of the principal agreement between the BBC and Covent Garden or the Corporation ceasing to pay to the Grand Opera Syndicate Ltd the annual sum of £25,000 for the presentation of grand opera at the Royal Opera House, Covent Garden and at suitable theatres in the provinces to secure the right to broadcast . . . then the said annual payment of £17,500 shall cease to be payable.[6]

From this it is clear that the BBC undertook to make the figure paid annually to Covent Garden up to £25,000. There was also an agreement that a further £5,000 would be contributed by the subscribers to the Opera Syndicate – £2,500 of which was paid by the gramophone companies. However, the BBC refused to commit themselves for the period of five years mentioned in the White Paper, and the principal agreement was finally concluded on the basis of two years. This enabled the National Government, which followed the Gold Standard crisis of 1931 and looked for cuts in public expenditure, to refuse to renew the subsidy for opera after the end of 1932.

The 1931 crisis also affected the attendance at Covent Garden and, while the summer season was financially depressing, the autumn season, given in English, was disastrous. By 1932, it seemed essential to amalgamate all operatic interests, and it was necessary to sue for Beecham's return to Covent Garden. Because of the difficulty of persuading him to answer cables or make any commitment, the desired result, although eventually achieved, was managed only with a left and right of maximum treachery and bad manners to others. First, although the German singers were asked to accept reduced fees for a four-week Wagner Festival in May, Bruno Walter, who had served Covent Garden so well, was left to learn from the newspapers that the chief conductor would be not himself but Beecham. In a letter to Blois, he wrote:

I feel that not only our collaboration of long years and our personal friendship but also the regard for a man of my standing in the artistic world should have been sufficient for you to inform me in the earliest possible moment what was going to happen, in order to prevent by any means that I had to learn the affair by the papers; and to co-operate with me how to publish the matter. For you, as a man of the theatre, could foresee like me in which distorted and malicious way the thing could be used by 'good friends'. This is now the case and only my good reputation will help against a serious damage. I do think that after all my work in Covent Garden I deserved a more considerate action from your side.[7]

Mrs Snowden was equally distressed. She had written to the manager of the London Symphony Orchestra, which normally played in the pit at Covent Garden, and to Malcolm Sargent, denying rumours that Beecham's new orchestra, the London Philharmonic, had been engaged for the 1932 season. In a letter to Szarvasy in which she spoke of 'the unfortunate position in which I am now placed through assuming that an important matter involving not only large expenditure but policy would only be decided at the Board Meeting', she said:

This is not the first, nor the second time that pledges to Sir Thomas Beecham, of which I was ignorant, have been made on behalf of the Syndicate. I have reluctantly come to the conclusion that the Board will work better without me,

50

and will ask you to accept my resignation as soon as the question of the subsidy is settled.

I am quite sure there was no desire nor intention to wound, but I find it less insulting to be insulted than ignored![8]

Historically more important than these matters was the death of Colonel Blois during the early part of 1933, which caused Szarvasy and his syndicate to terminate their lease of the opera house at the end of that summer season. Beecham, assisted by Lady Cunard, then formed a syndicate called The Royal Opera House, Covent Garden Ltd. This started with a nominal capital of £50,000 but the names of the members of the syndicate were sufficient assurance that the two requisites for success – money and social influence – were both present. These were Viscount Allendale, Lord Lloyd, Lady Cunard, Viscount Esher, Ronald Tree, MP, Lord Stonehaven, Benjamin Guinness and P.E. Hill. Some of the richest men in England were included here, while Philip Hill was the Chairman of Covent Garden Properties Ltd, which owned the theatre. Geoffrey Toye (the brother of Francis Toye) was appointed Managing Director and Sir Thomas Beecham Artistic Director.

In order to satisfy the requirements of the London County Council and the Lord Chamberlain, as well as for practical reasons, improvements which cost £70,000 were made to the theatre at this time. These included a new block of offices, dressing rooms, chorus and rehearsal rooms at the rear of the main building, as well as a new system of lighting.

The Beecham seasons of 1934–39 were not entirely without failures. Chiefly owing to Sir Thomas's exuberant liking for the musical strangers he met on his continental visits, various unsatisfactory castings and appointments were made – notably those of a conductor named Francesco Salfi – and the baritone, Cesare Formichi. There were also by now political difficulties in the engagement of German singers.

Members of the much scorned part of the audience who attended in the boxes and stalls nevertheless remember the period as a minor golden age. This was partly because it coincided with a resurgence of the glories of Italian opera. Rosa Ponselle had arrived as early as 1929, and in the following years London heard Conchita Supervia, Beniamino Gigli, Ezio Pinza, Mariano Stabile, Toti dal Monte and Lina Pagliughi.

Shawe-Taylor, who heard all these singers himself, tells us that Rosa Ponselle was a fascinatingly unconventional Violetta, while those delicious and still rarer comic operas *La cenerentola* and *L'italiana in Algeri* might have been specially written for Conchita Supervia:

> In both, beauty and immense stage charm accompanied an unusual faculty of investing the older florid music with its true dramatic significance . . . In Rossini's day the florid passages were doubdess more smoothly sung than by Mme Supervia, but the roles can never have been given with a more captivating *brio* or a more mischievous wit.
>
> Among her partners in these welcome Rossini revivals was the fine *basso cantante* Ezio Pinza; overwhelmingly ripe as the Rossinian equivalent of Baron Hardup he excelled no less in serious roles, the only pity being that the bass parts in Italian opera are so much less interesting and important than those written by German or Russian composers. Mozart's *Don Giovanni* really lay too high for his voice, but he made a fine thing of it all the same. That

accomplished *buffo* baritone Mariano Stabile created a great impression as Gianni Schicchi, and a greater still as Falstaff, a part in which he has no contemporary rivals.[9]

He complains that Toti dal Monte and Lina Pagliughi 'like so many of the better Italian singers' appeared all too infrequendy at Covent Garden, and describes Beniamino Gigli as 'a paradox among tenors':

> On the one hand a divine voice, certainly the greatest since Caruso (though of a lighter calibre), an admirable (not quite ideally flexible) technique, and an immense gusto, vivacity and charm; on the other hand sobs, gulps, exaggerated *portamenti*, street-corner vulgarities which could reduce the sensitive listener in a moment from ecstasy to despair.[10]

Shawe-Taylor goes on to say that Gigli represented at once the virtues and the vices of the star system and he says that these were even more noticeable in the Covent Garden appearances of 'the magnificent Russian bass' Chalia-pin.

> At Covent Garden, either he sang *Boris Godunov* in Russian while the rest of the company sang in Italian or near-Italian; or he would invest such French and Italian parts as Leporello, Basilio or Mephistopheles with a startling, but somewhat alien, sort of brilliance, and in doing so impose his will ruthlessly on the unfortunate conductor.‡[11]

---

‡ Chaliapin cannot be counted as part of the Beecham season. He appeared at Covent Garden in 1926, 1928 and 1929.

Among other singers were Lauritz Melchior, 'blessed with a truly heroic voice . . . [but] never a sensitive musician'[12] and several notable English singers, Eva Turner (Amelia in *The Masked Ball* and Brünnhilde in *Siegfried* in an Imperial League Autumn season in 1935, Aida and Turandot in the Grand Opera season in 1939, and Isolde in the autumn season of that year). Maggie Teyte (Gretel and Madama Butterfly in the 1937 winter seasons and Eurydice in the 1937 Grand Opera season).§ Other English singers included Heddle Nash, Dennis Noble and Edith Coates.

The year 1937 was also notable for the appearance of the Norwegian soprano, Kirsten Flagstad, who was considered the greatest Wagnerian soprano of her day. 'The steadiness of the tone', Ernest Newman wrote of her, 'is as remarkable as its purity; the ear is not afflicted by that constant "beat" we have grown accustomed to associate with Wagner singing.' And he added: 'So steady is the line, so good Mme Flagstad's ear, that even Mr Melchior's persistent deviation from pitch in the trying section of the second act . . . could not deflect her by a hair's breadth from the path of vocal virtue.'[13]

Not only the audiences but some of the singers remember the Beecham period as full of splendours. In her autobiography Lotte Lehmann, speaking of Covent Garden under Blois and Walter, says:

Dusty old stage decorations were the background to artistically incomparable performances . . . We had to climb up

---

§ Maggie Teyte was the most famous of all Mélisandes but, although Debussy's opera was in the repertory that year, she did not sing in it.

shaky old steps to rather doubtful dressing-rooms—but we all felt at home there and scarcely noticed the grotesque incongruity between our costumes, frequendy of regal magnificence, and our surroundings.

And she goes on:

> After Walter came Sir Thomas Beecham who brought Dr Erhardt with him as producer. Then came new ideas, modern productions, sparkling life, stage-reconstructions – Sir Thomas, witty, elegant, with a genius for comedy. Music danced in rainbow patterns through the stately house, an enthusiastic audience constantly filled balconies and boxes; now there was something to look at as well asusten to![14]

The engagement of Dr Erhardt as producer, of Gabriel Volkoff and Rex Whisder to redesign the *Ring* and *Fidelio*, ushered in what Harold Rosenthal has called the age of the producer—a change which he said was to have significant results at post-war Covent Garden, and which in fact presaged opera production as we know it today.

Among the conductors invited to London by Beecham were Vittorio Gui, Wilhelm Furtwángler, Fritz Reiner, Erich Kleiber, Felix Weingartner and Hans Knappertsbusch, the latter being so unpopular with the Nazis that in 1936 he was unable to get a permit to leave Germany, although he conducted *Salome* at Covent Garden in 1937. Malcolm Sargent conducted performances of *Louise* in 1936. Other French operas given at this time were *Pelléas et Mélisande and Les Contes d'Hoffmann*.

The partnership between Beecham and Geoffrey Toye did not last very long, and, as Harold Rosenthal has pointed out, since

Toye was paid £5,000 as compensation for loss of office, one must assume that he did not willingly resign his post. Gossip has it that Beecham and Lady Cunard were annoyed by Toye's engagement of the film star, Grace Moore, who, although inexperienced in opera, had a naturally fine soprano voice and the great merit of being able to fill the house. In any case, it seems unlikely that Beecham would have stood so strong a personality as Toye on equal terms for very long. No Managing Director was appointed to follow him but Beecham appointed first Percy Heming, and then in 1938 Walter Legge as assistant artistic director.

One of the great sensations of the Beecham period was the appearance in 1937 of a singer named Lisa Perli, announced to sing Mimi, who, when she appeared, turned out to be a well-known concert singer called Dora Labette, wearing a blonde wig. This imposture has often been put down to the difficulty of succeeding in England under an English name (although to the uninitiated Labette seems as improbable as Perli). In the audience at the time it was widely believed that the change of name had been made to give Beecham some peace during rehearsals from Lady Cunard, who was known to be jealous of Miss Labette. Certainly Lady Cunard, in a state of excited expectation to hear the new singer, took a party to Covent Garden and made no attempt to disguise her chagrin when, immediately Miss Labette appeared, she recognized the hoax.

Finally, it must be recorded that alone and unaided Beecham taught musical manners to the audience of Covent Garden. In 1934, while conducting the overture to a new production of *Fidelio*, he turned to the audience who, coming late into their seats, were still speaking and moving, and commanded them to stop talking. Later in the same performance he turned and told them to shut up. Speaking to the press the next day he explained his behaviour by saying 'that an audience should dream of applauding when you have begun the *Leonora* Overture No. 3 which is obviously a part of the whole business . . . is an incredible piece of barbarism.'[15] Following this, instructions were given that the audience could not enter their seats after the performance had begun.

However, the most important events in the history of opera at this time took place not at Covent Garden but at a small theatre in the north of London and at a country house in Sussex.

In August 1930 Miss Lilian Baylis walked on to the stage at the Old Vic and announced that opera would in future be run permanendy at that theatre and at Sadler's Wells, as long as she had the support of the public. Miss Baylis had been putting on regular performances of opera in English for some years and by 1920 was giving five performances a fortnight with an orchestra which, originally consisting of an eight-man band, had grown to twenty-two, augmented to twenty-eight for *Tristan*. After the failure of the Beecham Company in 1924, when Covent Garden was confined to very short international seasons and the visits of the Carl Rosa and the British National Opera Company, the Old Vic company, even if limited in scope, was the only one giving opera regularly in London. The productions were mainly of Verdi and Donizetti operas: *Carmen, Faust, Cavalleria rusticana* and so on; *Tannhauser* and *Lohengrin;* and in addition some English operas: *Maritana* by Vincent Wallace (1845), Sir Julius Benedict's *Lily of Killarney* (1862) and Michael Balfe's *The Bohemian Girl* (1843).¶

¶ The first and third of these composers were Irish, the second a German-born naturalized Englishman.

The history of Lilian Baylis at the Old Vic is well known. She was a woman of extraordinary strength of purpose, but she owed a great deal to the willingness of a high-minded generation of actors and actresses—John Gielgud, Edith Evans, Sybil Thorndike, Ralph Richardson, and later, Flora Robson, Peggy Ashcroft and others – to appear for very low salaries at her theatres. The best of the English singers had an incentive in addition to that of 'helping the Old Vic', because Miss Baylis's company gave them opportunities to sing leading roles. Artists such as Joan Cross, Edith Coates, Heddle Nash appeared regularly.

In 1925 Miss Baylis decided to buy and rebuild Sadler's Wells Theatre and to open it under the same terms as the Old Vic Foundation – 'to provide seats at prices within the means of labourers and artisans, financial gain to be debarred'. In order to raise funds for this project, she formed a committee (a surprising number of the distinguished members of which were the much scorned box-holders of Covent Garden) and launched an appeal. Garden parties and concerts (Melba sang at the Old Vic) together with direct requests for money, produced enough to buy the theatre, and, although Lilian Baylis was harassed by financial problems for the rest of her life, she opened Sadler's Wells in January 1931. Originally fortnightly performances of drama and opera were alternated at the two theatres, the companies moving over from one to the other, and Sadler's Wells opened with a performance of *Twelfth Night*, John Gielgud playing Malvolio and Ralph Richardson Toby Belch. A fortnight later the opera company made its debut with a performance of *Carmen* – conducted by Lawrence Collingwood, with Enid Cruikshank as Carmen, Arthur Cox as Don José and Sumner Austin as Esca-millo, the ballet being by Ninette de Valois.

The last of these names brings us to a miraculous event, most vital to the future of Covent Garden. This occurred not in opera but in the sister art of ballet.

If one had had to bet on the presence in London at the same time of Ninette de Valois, Frederick Ashton, Alicia Markova, Anton Dolin, Margot Fonteyn and Robert Helpmann – any one of whom was capable of raising ordinary standards of excellence to high art – the odds against it would have been immense. But, in one of those cyclical irruptions of talent, such as had produced the composers of the early nineteenth century and the golden age of singers in the late years of the same century, this convergence occurred. It ensured that, for more than thirty years, England would, outside Russia, be pre-eminent in the art of ballet.

Ninette de Valois had been a member of Diaghilev's company, later danced with a troupe of dancers led by Lopokova, Sokolova and Massine, and then joined the Ballets Russes led by Nijinska. In 1926 she opened a school in Kensington.

De Valois has confessed to remaining obstinately 'English' in the somewhat exotic atmosphere of Diaghilev's late period. Her Protestant spirit seems to have remained undimmed. She has absorbed many lessons from her two years with the Ballets Russes, but when she returned to Britain her impulse was to carry her in the opposite direction from that of Diaghilev. She came back to London determined to found not a roving avant-garde troupe like the Ballets Russes but a British version of the very organization against which Diaghilev had rebelled – a state company with a school and a theatre of its own.[16]

At about the same time as she opened her school, de Valois

59

wrote to Lilian Baylis asking to see her. Miss Baylis had already realized the need for a dance company to work with her drama and opera companies and, after visiting de Valois at her school, she began to use her at the Old Vic. 'Ninette de Valois is going to form a ballet company for us', she predicted, When we open at the Wells it will be on a whole-time basis.'[17] On 13 December 1928 de Valois presented the first ballet performance at the Old Vic, a curtain-raiser to *Hansel and Gretel* and, five months later, another curtain-raiser with music by Vaughan Williams.

Marie Rambert had also opened a ballet school in 1920. In 1926 she presented Frederick Ashton's first ballet, *A Tragedy of Fashion*, in a review at the Lyric Theatre, Hammersmith. Then, in 1930, an association called the Camargo Society was formed and played an important part in the promotion of ballet. Here is what Ninette de Valois had to say about it:

What was the role of the Camargo Society? I would say that it played the role of an important fairy godmother for English ballet, and it played this role for two or so years at the beginning of the thirties. . . . The Camargo Society (with Maynard Keynes as Treasurer) found time and money to organize the production of new ballets with which to enrich the English repertoire. The ballets were presented on a Sunday night and Monday afternoon in a West End Theatre, three or four times a year. The nucleus of the dancers was drawn from the already existing Mercury Theatre Ballet Club in Notting Hill (today, the Ballet Rambert) and the Vic–Wells Ballet (today, The Royal Ballet). . . . Many famous dancers appeared as guests. . . . These dancers were all willing to give their time and services, as the venture was far removed from the ordinary

theatre, nor could a Sunday evening and a Monday afternoon performance interfere in any way with their
professional commitments. I think one can say that honours
were equally divided between the Camargo Society, the
two young companies and the guest performers. The
companies could not have afforded to stage certain of the
ballets presented, yet these ballets could not have 'lived' if . . .
the Vic–Wells Ballet and the Mercury Theatre Ballet Club
had not been able to take over, between them, the more
successful ballets mounted by the Camargo Society and
preserve them in their repertoires.[18]

Both Ninette de Valois and Frederick Ashton danced in performances put on by the Camargo Society, as also did Anton Dolin.
Constant Lambert, later to be associated so closely with the
Sadler's Wells Company, conducted at one of the first Camargo
evenings.

At the first performance of opera at Sadler's Wells in January
1931 the Vic–Wells Opera Ballet (dancing in *Carmen)* consisted
only of girls, but in May 1931 when they gave a whole evening's
programme, Anton Dolin, Stanley Judson and Ivor Beddoes
danced with them. In 1932 Robert Help-mann joined the
company and in the same year Ashton for the first time created
a ballet, *Les Rendezvous*, for them, still part of the repertory of
ballet today. In 1934 de Valois gave a performance of *Giselle*,
mounted by Nicholas Sergeyev and danced by Markova, Dolin
and Helpmann. Four weeks later the company danced *The
Nutcracker*, this time with Markova and Stanley Judson.

When Markova left the company in 1935, her place was taken
by a very young girl named Margot Fonteyn. In the same year
Frederick Ashton joined the company as a performer and

resident choreographer. Constant Lambert had attached himself to the company 'almost as through a natural process'.[19] When, also in 1935, the company presented the first authentically English ballet to be created for this company, *The Rake's Progress*, choreography by de Valois with designs by Rex Whisder, the future was assured. In 1934 the governors of the Old Vic altered the charter of that theatre, enabling drama alone to be played there, and Sadler's Wells became the home of the opera and ballet companies.

The other historically outstanding event of the middle 1930s was the opening of the Mozart festival at Glyndebourne. Once more this was the result of the conjunction of several people of great and uniquely complementary talents at a fortunate moment. John Christie, the heir to 1,500 acres of land and a large Elizabethan house in Sussex, had married the singer Audrey Mildmay. He was already known for spectacular eccentricity and, among other things, revered by a whole generation of Etonians because, as a master there, he took 'Early School' in his pyjamas. In an essay written for the fiftieth anniversary Celebration of Glyndebourne, Isaiah Berlin says:

He had the single-mindedness of a secular visionary; he swept aside objections and apparently insuperable difficulties pointed out to him by cautious advisers. His boldness, indomitable will and total independence – above all this last attribute, more often found in England fifty years ago than it is today . . . were a major cultural asset to our country. Like every great Intendant in the history of opera, he displayed a degree of personal authority, indeed, of the indispensable element of *terribilatà*, which rivalled that of Diaghilev and Toscanini.[20]

These are splendidly descriptive words but it must occur to anyone who has followed this history so far that, without any loss of accuracy, they could have been applied to Sir Thomas Beecham. It must therefore be attributed to good fortune that, when John Christie wrote, as he several times did, begging Beecham first for help and advice and later to associate himself with the festival, the latter regarded his letters as the preposterous outpouring of a maniac and did not even bother to answer them. With hindsight it seems clear that the future of Glyndebourne depended absolutely on an immediate, unqualified and striking success. One can think of no way in which this could have been achieved by a combination of the talents of Christie and Beecham. One such character is necessary for magical theatrical performance; two of them are good only for volcanic eruptions.

At this time, Christie himself seemed not to know quite what he wanted to do. There had long been music in the Organ Room (at the present day open to the public during the festival months) given for the benefit not merely of house guests but of estate employees and tenants, and his original idea was merely to build a small theatre to extend this. The foundations for a house to seat about 300 people were actually dug at right-angles to the present building, when Christie's wife, Audrey Mildmay, suggested to him that, if he was going to spend so much money, he might as well do it properly.

The second circumstance, obviously fortunate to this enterprise, however evil its effects in other ways, was the reign of terror in Germany. This meant that many fine musicians were exiled and therefore available to take part in an amateur attempt to run opera in an English country house. Christie met Fritz Busch, who, bringing with him Carl Ebert, agreed to direct the first season of a Mozart festival (Christie had proposed Wagner) at Glyndebourne. These two and Rudolf Bing (later Director of the Edinburgh Festival and afterwards of the Metropolitan Opera House, New York), who came as assistant to Ebert, were given designers and technicians, technical and electrical equipment, all the paraphernalia of the modern ensemble as yet hardly known in England. Above all they were given almost unlimited rehearsal time.

Christie had early decided that there were two possibilities: to offer superb performances for people who could pay for them; or educational performances for the ordinary public, with the best possible stage setting and with English orchestras and little-known singers. He chose the first and, from the depths of his fantasy, recommended that evening dress should be worn by the audience—with the improbable result that, with the exception of the war years, ladies and gentlemen have appeared at Victoria Station at three o'clock in the afternoon throughout the summer months wearing dinner jackets and evening dresses from that day to this.

Isaiah Berlin attended one of the first performances of *Figaro* at Glyndebourne. Here is what he wrote about it fifty years later:

> In 1936 I . . . heard a performance of *Le nozze di Figaro* which, as I can confidently testify after almost fifty years, I still remember vividly: and remember as having been simply wonderful. Mariano Stabile was the best Figaro I have ever heard, in Salzburg and Milan as well as Glyndebourne. . . . The Countess, at Glyndebourne in that year and later was the Finnish singer, Aulikki Rautawaara . . . Busch was the equal of, and at times superior to, even Franz Schalk and Bruno Walter; and the Glyndebourne orchestra

under him rose to unexpected heights. Ebert must have
been the best director of classical opera in Europe. Both
were, as is not always the case with even the most gifted of
artists, men of inborn aesthetic sense and taste; and no
composer requires this as much as Mozart. The orchestra
was far less accomplished than the Vienna Philharmonic,
yet the freshness, the wit, the sheer verve, the inner pulse,
the forward movement, the marvellous enthusiasm, lifted it
above any performance of *Figaro* I had heard in Salzburg,
Munich or anywhere else.[21]

And the historian of Glyndebourne, Spike Hughes, wrote:

When, after the first night of the new *Magic Flute* in 1963,
George Christie asked how it had compared with the 1935
production, I found it difficult to answer; to discuss with
anybody who hadn't heard it exactly what it was about the
performance that made it an incomparable experience was
an impossible task. It had a quality most of us had never
encountered before and few of us, I believe, have ever
encountered since. Between them Fritz Busch, Carl Ebert
and Hamish Wilson created what one can only think of as
an exceptionally *complete* performance; the pitfalls were
avoided, the heights attained; what can so often sound silly
in this opera sounded enchanting, what can so often sound
dull was intensely moving.[22]

The only people not absolutely happy with Glyndebourne
were the critics, and they had their usual worries about whether
an upper-class audience is worthy of such quality. These worries
have continued to this day, the only curious thing being that,

right from the beginning, it was obvious that, if many of the audience at Glyndebourne came from the dreaded upper social strata, the middle classes were also there in force.

It does, however, cost a good deal of money to go to Glyndebourne, and if the question is asked: What has all this to do with Covent Garden? the first answer is that, while one end of the Covent Garden audience was being educated to opera at Sadler's Wells, Glyndebourne performed the same function for the other. The second service came from a flair for discovering young singers, many of whom went on to Covent Garden.

However, no services to Covent Garden were rendered intentionally or even willingly. Christie shared with Beecham one further characteristic – in his mind those who were not with him were against him. The historian of Glyndebourne said:

> From the first moment that Glyndebourne became an operatic reality John Christie had lost no opportunity to abuse and denigrate Covent Garden, more often than not as a matter of deep-rooted principle than as an expression of personal opinion on artistic matters. It was difficult to get Christie to go to Covent Garden at any time and Bing was to spend anxious years trying to persuade him to do the polite thing and put in at least a token appearance at the Royal Opera House from time to time.[23]

He also quotes this letter from Christie, written in 1938:

> I hope there may be a reasonable chance of managing Covent Garden as well as Glyndebourne, but I suppose it depends on whether Beecham makes a muddle and a loss again this year. This is in confidence, but I want Covent

Garden to be combined with us. . . . It would mean I suppose thirty performances at Covent Garden followed by thirty performances at Glyndebourne – about twelve weeks.[24]

None of these things was to matter much for several years. In 1939 the Royal Opera House was closed for a few months, and then let to Mecca Cafés, who used it as a dance hall throughout the war.

4

1939–1946
The Arts Council

The Council for Encouragement of Music and the Arts, known as CEMA, was founded in the early days of the war. Originally the idea of William Emrys Williams, then general secretary of the Institute of Education, it was enthusiastically taken up by the president of the Board of Trade, Lord De La Warr, who persuaded Tom Jones, chairman of the Pilgrim Trust, to put up money for it. In a broadcast given in 1945 Lord Keynes, its first chairman, said:

> It was the task of CEMA to carry music, drama and pictures to places which otherwise would be cut off from all contact with the masterpieces of happier days and times; to air-raid shelters, to war-time hostels, to factories, to mining villages. ENSA was charged with the entertainment of the Services; the British Council kept contact with all other countries

overseas; the duty of CEMA was to maintain the opportunities of artistic performance for the hard-pressed and often exiled civilians.[1]

Although started with private funds, CEMA was soon taken over by the Board of Education and supported entirely by a Treasury grant. Before the end of the war it was decided to put it on a permanent basis and its name was changed to the Arts Council of Great Britain, while the responsibility for the public grant was transferred direct to the Treasury. Keynes went on to say:

> I do not believe it is yet realised what an important thing has happened. State patronage of the arts has crept in. It has happened in a very English informal, unostentatious way – half-baked if you like . . . At last the public exchequer has recognised the support and encouragement of the civilising arts of Life as a part of their duty.[2]

He also said that it was hoped that Covent Garden would be reopened 'early next year' as the home of opera and ballet.

Coinciding with the formation of the new Arts Council a parallel movement had taken place at Covent Garden. The inspiration behind this was Philip Hill, the Chairman of Covent Garden Properties Ltd, who had been a member of the Board of Directors at Covent Garden during the Beecham period immediately before the war. Although the Mecca Cafés' lease of the Royal Opera House was due to expire in December 1944, they had an option to renew it unless the theatre was required for the presentation of opera and ballet. In order to prevent the exercise of the option, Hill approached the impresario Harold

Holt, and suggested to him that he should take a lease of the theatre and put it to its proper purpose. Holt did not take up this offer himself but he passed it on to Leslie Boosey and Ralph Hawkes, partners in the firm of music publishers.

Boosey & Hawkes responded very generously. They were prepared to spend a considerable amount of money in the interests of opera and felt that the theatre at Covent Garden should become the home of the lyric arts in England. They consulted the Arts Council (still CEMA), where they met 'such enthusiasm that they took a lease of the Opera House for five years from December 1944 with the option of being able to terminate the lease earlier at certain intervals.' Messrs Boosey & Hawkes felt certain that they could not themselves undertake the production of opera and ballet and (again with the encouragement of CEMA) they set up a committee to consider the use of the opera house and the type of organization suitable to take responsibility for it.

Since, as lessees of the theatre, Boosey & Hawkes did not propose to present opera and ballet, Mecca Cafés were able to question the legality of their right to the lease. An action dragged on into the early months of 1945, although Boosey & Hawkes were assured that it could not succeed and were not deterred from pressing on with their plans. The matter was settled amicably early in 1945, when Mecca Cafés were granted a licence to continue to use the theatre as a dance hall until September of that year.

The consultative committee set up to consider the future of the theatre consisted of Leslie Boosey and Ralph Hawkes, Sir Kenneth Clark, Samuel Courtauld, Edward Dent, Sir Stanley Marchant, Dr William Walton and Steuart Wilson. The Chairman was Lord Keynes, also Chairman of the new Arts

Council. This committee decided to develop a resident opera and a resident ballet company, and from time to time to invite opera and ballet companies from abroad. At a fairly early stage they agreed that the organization best fitted to pursue the objects they had in mind would be a charitable trust, which, being non-profit-distributing, would ensure relief from the payment of entertainment and other taxes, and would enable the organization to receive full benefits from gifts. This Trust was not formally set up until February 1946, when the members of the committee became Trustees.

The main points of the agreement reached between Boosey & Hawkes and the Covent Garden Opera Trust were as follows: Messrs Boosey & Hawkes undertook all the preliminary expenses of the Trust and made an agreement whereby they took full responsibility for rent, rates, insurance, the administrative staff of the theatre and of the Trust, together with the front of house staff and the nucleus stage staff. They licensed the Trust to use the Opera House for a rental based on a percentage of the gross takings, and they retained the bar rights and the sale of programmes. Messrs Boosey & Hawkes further agreed that if the receipts from these various sources more than covered their expenses, they would hand back any surplus by way of reduction of rent, whereas if they incurred any loss they would make no claim on the Trust.

Although in the first place the committee set up to act for Covent Garden was purely consultative, it quickly took one very important decision. In February 1944 David Webster received a letter from Anthony Gishford, a cousin of Ralph Hawkes, telling him of the plans for Covent Garden and asking whether he would care to be considered for the 'Key Post'. On 6 April 1944 Gishford arranged a luncheon for Webster to meet Hawkes.

Webster's biographer reports the meeting as follows:

> Webster was overflowing with ideas, and he and Ralph
> hit it off instantly together. After lunch Gishford went
> back to the War Office . . . leaving David and Ralph, still
> talking excitedly, to wander off together up Bond Street,
> along Oxford Street and into Upper Regent Street, where
> Boosey & Hawkes had their offices. That's the time it
> took for Ralph to be convinced that he had the man for
> the job.[3]

Webster was a large, burly, rather ugly man. Edward Dent
wrote this description of him at that time:

> He is rather fat and prosperous looking, not unlike John
> Christie, but whereas Christie has the 'powdery' pink and
> white surface of a Raeburn, and looks so Victorian that you
> almost think he's got mutton-chop whiskers, Webster is pink
> with a high polish, and ought to be Lord Mayor of some big
> provincial town.[4]

However in spite of these not very attractive looks, Webster
was impressive all his life. Kenneth Clark describes a meeting
with him in Liverpool during the war.

> We had been to Liverpool to hear a performance by the
> Liverpool Philharmonic of William Walton's *Belshazzar's
> Feast,* and had met the Chairman of the orchestra, David
> Webster. He loved opera, knew it well and was an experi-
> enced administrator. As we went home after dining with
> him we said 'That is a man who might run Covent Garden

if ever it became a National Opera.'[5]

He goes on to say that when he was asked by Boosey & Hawkes to suggest a possible administrator for their project he pronounced 'rather hesitantly' the name of David Webster. The double recommendation was enough. Webster must also have been approved by Keynes, because in July 1944 he spent two months investigating the Arts Council financial organization and advising on its future.

In August 1944 he signed a contract with the Covent Garden Trust, although he could not enter the Opera House until October 1945, when the Mecca Cafés released the theatre. Webster's appointment, which was originally to run to 31 December 1945, with an option for renewal for a further twelve months, was as surprising as the speed at which it was made. As general manager of Lewis's, a large department store in Liverpool, he had proved himself a first-class administrator. He was very much interested in the arts, particularly the performing arts, and had some experience with amateur companies both as actor and director. He was largely responsible for keeping open the Liverpool Philharmonic Hall during the war, and had been Chairman of the Liverpool Philharmonic Orchestra, of which Malcolm Sargent was chief conductor. Pursuing his theatrical hobbies, he had come to know many actors and musicians, but had no professional experience of any sort. He was just over forty when he went to Covent Garden.

With this appointment, the Covent Garden committee made it clear they had decided that a state-aided opera house should be administered by a Board consisting of distinguished members of the various artistic professions, as well as patrons of the arts, and by a strong General Administrator; without, however, that 'indispensable element of *terribilità*' characteristic of so many of the greatest intendants in the history of opera. This was a shock to those who, having given evidence of possessing this quality, were waiting to be called.

There is no evidence in the files of the Royal Opera House that an invitation to Beecham to collaborate in any capacity was ever considered. This circumstance is sufficiently extraordinary that one can only suppose that a decision on the question was taken so early and with such unanimity that it never reached print either in minutes of the meetings or in letters. Haltrecht (Webster's biographer) tells us that Lady Cunard had spoken with confidence of Beecham's future at Covent Garden and that Beecham had taken out options on a number of singers for the season of 1945. Walter Legge, who had been Beecham's assistant director before the war, speaks of being 'fondly confident that Beecham and I would be in control of opera at Covent Garden, as we had been in 1938 and 1939.'[6] And, speaking of Beecham on his return to England (he had spent the war years in Australia and America), Legge says:

By then he must have known that the control of Covent Garden Opera House had fallen into the hands of people who feared and disliked him as much as he rightly despised them. It seems that with this banishment from Covent Garden an iron entered his soul. It was not mentioned between us for many years, not until 1951 when for some unfathomable reason he accepted the near insult of Covent Garden's invitation to conduct eighteen performances of *The Bohemian Girl*—he who nearly forty years before that had introduced in

74

that very theatre, *Elektra*, *Salome*, and *Rosenkavalier*.[*7]

Beecham's biographer, Charles Reid, talked to him towards the end of his life about Covent Garden. He wrote:

> With a bitter eye, he reverted to a matter which fretted him more nearly: the Trust's great sin of omission. In 1945, when setting up house, the directors and their advisers had never (was it to be believed?) consulted or approached him. They never came near me!' In his day as an impresario he had given over a thousand performances of opera in English alone. To Covent Garden's benighted rulers this was evidently a matter of neither moment nor interest.[8]

According to his own evidence, Walter Legge was considered for the post at Covent Garden but turned down. In the thirties he had acted only part-time as Beecham's assistant and had been in the employ of HMV Gramophone Company. He was responsible in 1931 for a scheme by which subscriptions were received in advance to cover the cost and make a small profit on the recording of great unrecorded musical works. He began with an album of six records of Hugo Wolf songs, sung by Elena Gerhardt, with German and English texts and annotations by Ernest Newman, and he went on to the Beethoven Sonata Society, which included in fifteen volumes all the piano sonatas

---

[*] In fact there is evidence in the Royal Opera House archives that it was Beecham who wanted to do *The Bohemian Girl* and it was given a new production only because he asked for it. See p. 138.

in recordings by Arthur Schnabel. These Society albums had an enormous success and sold throughout the world. They gave Legge a commanding position in this field. Then in the war he took over the organization of serious music for ENSA about which he wrote: 'I kept three orchestras, the Liverpool Philharmonic, the City of Birmingham and the Hallé, busily occupied with these concerts as well as dividing up the work nearer London.'[9] Because of his position with the gramophone company, he was by now very influential with both conductors and singers. In 1953 he married Elisabeth Schwarzkopf.

In a memoir published posthumously by his wife, there is an account of a luncheon given by Ernest Makower, founder of the pre-war London Museum Concerts. Legge wrote:

> Leslie Boosey, at that time, I believe, chairman of Boosey and Hawkes, was with us and he had made arrangements to put Covent Garden on its feet again. Boosey told me that although I had all the necessary knowledge and experience to run Covent Garden my standards were notoriously higher than those they aimed at – how right he proved to be – and that I was too intransigent.[10]

The third person who confidently expected to take part in the running of Covent Garden was John Christie, and he was hardly less bitter and a great deal more persistent. Christie believed, or gradually came to believe, that in 1944 he had tried to buy the theatre at Covent Garden. Spike Hughes says this:

> Christie had also set out to buy the freehold of Covent Garden House. He had employed a leading firm of property dealers and was prepared to pay up to £100,000 for it;

he was told he could probably get it for a good deal less. 'But owing to the hostility which existed in certain quarters', he said, 'I did not go on with it.'[11]

Christie, who after the war used the term 'Glyndebourne' when he meant himself, gave a slightly different version of this in a letter to the *Observer*, written in 1950.

During the war Messrs Boosey and Hawkes and Glyndebourne made attempts at almost the same time, the one to rent Covent Garden, the other to buy the freehold for opera. Six weeks later Glyndebourne retired in favour of the attempt to rent the place, but on the basis of 'all right, let's do it like that.' As soon as the lease was fixed, Glyndebourne and its individuals were totally excluded from Covent Garden. In consequence Mr Bing left this country to take over the Metropolitan [Opera House, New York] and Professor Ebert also went to America. The rest of Glyndebourne's team stayed here, but the Arts Council froze all funds for opera at Covent Garden.

I believe that Covent Garden's annual operatic work should be divided into three seasons based on Festival and not merely routine standards, and that this country could lead the world in this work. But it must be handled by an executive of operatic experts.[12]

In 1957 David Webster asked Leslie Boosey what he knew of this matter. Boosey wrote back, saying that Christie had asked him to lunch at Brooks' Club, and had there said that he understood Boosey & Hawkes were negotiating for a lease of the theatre at Covent Garden and that he himself was negotiating to buy it. Boosey wrote that he was sceptical about this statement, and made up his mind to enquire further.

> I therefore went across the road to the office in King St and asked Mr Goddard[†] point blank whether Covent Garden was for sale as Mr Christie had said he was negotiating to buy. Mr Goddard said that there was absolutely no question of their selling Covent Garden to John Christie or anyone else. I therefore decided J.C. was 'shooting a line' as they say in the Navy.
>
> I am perfectly willing to believe J.C. had actually approached Goddard and Smith to see whether Covent Garden was for sale but as far as the lease was concerned B&H was first in the field and there was no question of our having supplanted him. J. C. has suggested on various occasions that he agreed to withdraw on the understanding that he should be on the new Board. This is a figment of his imagination. No such arrangement was ever discussed let alone made. All the same I did try to get J.C. on the Board but Keynes flatly refused and there was nothing more I could do about it.[13]

The exclusion of Christie from Covent Garden is usually attributed to Keynes who is said to have disliked him from the time they were at Eton together. Kenneth Clark puts it more strongly: 'Keynes had an ancient, implacable hatred for John Christie, which Christie returned with interest'.[14] In speaking of

---

[†] Of Goddard & Smith, a firm who were handling the property for Covent Garden Properties.

the necessity to find a director-general Clark says the obvious choice was Rudolf Bing, but that this was ruled out because of his connection with Glyndebourne. However, Keynes was not alone in thinking that Christie was temperamentally unsuited to collaborate in a state-aided project. At a meeting of the Arts Council on 25 July 1944, Lord Esher asked whether Christie had been invited to join the new committee of management at Covent Garden. Kenneth Clark (acting Chairman in Keynes's absence) replied that his name had been considered 'and, indeed, pressed by myself, but that the committee had decided against him. Then on 3 August the matter seems to have come up again because Mary Glasgow, Secretary of the Arts Council, reported to Keynes that there had been much discussion at a meeting of the Covent Garden Trust about the appointment of Christie: We rather pressed, to begin with, for his inclusion. It was decided not to invite him for the present. It is really a question of whether he will be more bother inside or out.'[15] One other mention of Christie's name about this time deserves attention. He had been made a member of the Arts Panel of the Arts Council and, commenting on this, Keynes wrote to Mary Glasgow: 'Glad to hear that J.C. is to be incorporated. If only he could be transubstantiated at the same time. Could that be made a condition?'[16]

If one could discount the personalities of the members of the committee who made these decisions, they would seem the result of an ignorant, even philistine, preference for a quiet life and little regard for quality. Kenneth Clark seems to have been uneasy; no one else. Yet everyone with any previous experience of producing opera in England had been excluded from the Opera House. While Beecham fumed, Rudolf Bing went to Edinburgh to produce an astoundingly successful Festival, and then to the Metropolitan Opera House. Ebert went to America, where Bruno Walter had preceded him.

The influence of Edward Dent, a member of the Trust, should not be underrated. A distinguished musician and musicologist, fellow of King's College, Cambridge and Professor of Music at Cambridge University, he was, according to the *Concise Oxford Dictionary of Opera,* 'an incalculable influence upon English operatic life and its relationship to the European scene'. He was also an excellent linguist and is best known to the public at large for his translations of opera libretti from Italian, French, German and Russian originals. In 1943 he became a governor of the Old Vic and Sadler's Wells, and was much concerned with operatic production at these theatres. His feeling for Sir Thomas Beecham seems to have been remarkably similar to Keynes's for Christie. The two had earlier quarrelled over a matter concerning translations of Mozart operas, and later Dent had suspected Beecham of having designs on the Sadler's Wells Opera Company: 'T.B. thinks it would amuse him to play with as a toy; we can't have him smashing it' And writing to Clive Carey he said that he always had the fear that Lilian Baylis might throw him over completely if it came to a choice between him and Beecham and 'expect us, out of personal loyalty to her, to sacrifice all our ideals on the altar of Tommy' Dent did not admire Beecham as a conductor, and told a German enquirer that 'in England we do not regard T.B.'s style as being quite the genuine article.'[17]

Although it is doubtless ironic that in decisions about appointments, members of the Trust so easily indulged exacdy the kind of subjective emotions which they were determined to avoid in those they engaged, there was an additional reason for their actions. No one can understand this period at Covent Garden unless they bear in mind that for many people, including Dent, the cause of opera in English had become a crusade. The belief that singing in English translation and the encouragement of English poets to write libretti to the music of English composers would, over the years, result in a national opera and an English 'style' was held with real fervour on both patriotic and artistic grounds.

Dent was glad to find that Webster disapproved of 'the old C.G. system of miscellaneous foreign stars all singing in German or Italian, with English singers allowed to do small parts – no proper rehearsal or production' –and he was assiduous in cultivating him. 'I am encouraging his self-confidence and love of power', he wrote to his friend, Clive Carey, 'because I want to be one of the experts whose advice he takes.'[18]

Christie could not be reconciled to the idea that he was to have no part to play at Covent Garden, however, and he persisted for several years. After the war he knew that he could no longer afford to pay single-handed for the Glyndebourne Opera Festival as he had before, but he believed that opera ought to be unified in one organization embracing Covent Garden, Sadler's Wells and the Carl Rosa, and that the work of these three units should 'boil over into Festivals' at Glyndebourne or elsewhere. He suggested that a new executive body should be formed responsible to the Arts Council for the planning and operation of the opera programme, and he was convinced that Carl Ebert was the key to success and that it was essential to have him as a permanent Director of Opera. He varied this plan slightly from time to time but pressed it, or something like it, for years.

Christie was not alone in believing that, particularly in London, there might be some advantage in pooling the limited resources in singers and musicians and for a short time some consideration was given to an amalgamation between Covent Garden and Sadler's Wells, if only through a joint committee of management. Nothing came of this (chiefly because neither side really desired it) and it was quickly decided that the two opera companies should go their own ways.

The Ballet Company was an entirely different matter. In 1939 all theatres had been closed and the Sadler's Wells companies disbanded. Two weeks later, however, the dancers were summoned to prepare for an unlimited tour of the provinces. Then, in the peace of the 'phoney war', they returned to London and opened at Sadler's Wells on Boxing Day 1940 with the new Ashton ballet, *Dante Sonata*. Early in 1940 the Government had decided to send them on the first of the many tours they would make to represent British cultural achievement to the outside world. At the beginning of May a company, including Ninette de Valois, Frederick Ashton, Robert Help-mann and Margot Fonteyn, left for Rotterdam. On 9 May Ninette de Valois was at the British Embassy in The Hague, discussing plans for evacuation in face of the German invasion of Holland. The whole company arrived in London on 14 May, but only after a difficult and frightening journey, having left behind the scenery, costumes and music for six ballets, and the manuscript and score of one other. Three weeks later they opened at Sadler's Wells with a programme which included the Ashton ballet *Dante Sonata* danced to a gramophone record.

During the blitz of September 1940 Sadler's Wells Theatre was closed as a place of entertainment and taken over for the care of air-raid victims. The Ballet Company retired once more to the country but again not for long. On 14 Janurary 1941, now called the Sadler's Wells Ballet, they opened at Bronson

Albery's New Theatre in St Martin's Lane where, apart from short spells in the provinces, they remained dancing to full houses for four years. In 1945 they were again invited to tour the Continent – this time by ENSA – and a company composed of eighty dancers and thirty musicians visited first Brussels then Paris, performing in both cities for the troops and afterwards for the public.

By 1944 the prestige of the group had grown enormously and there was very little doubt that the right place for the only national company of any consequence, either opera or ballet, was at the Royal Opera House. Since the new Covent Garden Trust had not even the rudiments of an opera company, it could hardly have opened at Covent Garden without it, certainly not in competition with it. From the point of view of de Valois, her company had earned the right to go to the most prestigious theatre in the country. Only the details had to be settled.

There was no real disagreement about the transfer, only about the terms on which it should be made, and the value of the properties, productions and so on which Covent Garden would take over. In a letter of 30 July 1945, Mary Glasgow reported to Keynes that, at a meeting between the two Boards, Sir George Dyson (for Sadler's Wells) had argued that there was no proof that the so-called 'national opera' was more than a commercial undertaking and said that he could not see why in the matter of valuation the governors of Sadler's Wells should sacrifice themselves to Messrs Boosey & Hawkes. The letter went on:

Sir Ernest Pooley [representing the Arts Council] rose in defence of Covent Garden. He said that, equally with Sadler's Wells, it had the support of the Arts Council, and that the extent of the Council aid to both must depend on

83

their actual needs – and must, therefore, be affected by their transactions.[19]

As a result Covent Garden acquired the assets of the Ballet Company on terms which in the commercial world would have been regarded as very favourable, but paid the sum of £15,000 to Sadler's Wells in recognition of loss of revenue. It was then agreed that the only way to meet the needs of the Sadler's Wells Opera Company was to set up a second ballet company. This company, which was called the Sadler's Wells Opera Ballet (the name was later changed to the Sadler's Wells Theatre Ballet) was to remain under the general direction of Ninette de Valois and to serve as a training ground for the Covent Garden Company, which would support it with guest artists. In other ways it would be independent.

Both these companies drew their dancers from the Sadler's Wells Ballet School. This had grown out of the nucleus of pupils and goodwill which de Valois had taken with her when she first joined Lilian Baylis and had been attached to the theatre since 1931. In 1945 it was recognized that the difficulties for small children in travelling about London to embark on the rigours of dance training after their ordinary school hours were too great. The governors of Sadler's Wells therefore established a self-contained school, providing general education as well as ballet training, at Talgarth Road, Barons Court – again under the general direction of de Valois.

In 1946 when the first company moved to Covent Garden the Arts Council gave a maximum guarantee against loss of £5,000 per annum for five years against the combined deficits of the Sadler's Wells Company and the Sadler's Wells School. For two years from December 1949 Covent Garden paid half the net deficit on both the Theatre Ballet Company and the School (that is net after taking account of the maximum guarantee from the Arts Council). After that the proportion to be paid by Covent Garden was limited to a maximum of £2,500 a year, the rest to be found by the Arts Council and the governors of Sadler's Wells.

Explaining in an article in the Arts Council Bulletin that the Royal Opera House would be reopened by a performance of ballet, David Webster wrote:

Those who may regret that Covent Garden is not opening with opera should perhaps reflect on two points. First, that it augurs well for the new regime at Covent Garden that its first company should be one whose dancers and choreographers are British, whose productions are largely designed by British artists, and many of whose scores are contributed by British composers. Secondly, that to prepare an opera company largely British in personnel, of a quality in any way worthy of the singing traditions of Covent Garden, takes time. It is therefore too early to talk at length on the prospects of opera given by a resident company. Other things may be said: while foreigners will not be excluded from the company, British artists will be given first chance; that the operas will be given in English; that every encouragement will be given to our own composers; and that the Covent Garden Opera Trust will on its own behalf and on behalf of opera in England combine with other authorities to set up a first-class school of training for opera.[20]

5

Ballet 1946–1949
'They are Dancing Well at Covent Garden'

Early in 1946 Arnold Haskell visited a rehearsal of the ballet at Covent Garden. Afterwards he wrote: 'English is spoken all around me and three choreographers—de Valois, Ashton and Helpmann—seated on kitchen chairs, backs to the auditorium, are watching and commenting. Three at one time and in obvious amity; the old Opera House has never witnessed such a sight.' And he added, They are dancing well at Covent Garden. They can feel the tradition and they honour it.'[1]

The amity, which Haskell found unique in a situation where three great artists sat together, was, if perhaps fitful, sufficient to ensure that the talents of this trio contributed to the whole, and grew out of the integrity and discipline, the concept of 'the company' which de Valois successfully imposed on all those who worked for her. Of the three who sat there that day, her influence was the most powerful, although Ashton was a creative genius and Helpmann had a stage presence unrivalled in ballet until Rudolf Nureyev appeared on the scene.

De Valois was extraordinary for the combination in one person of the attributes of a great administrator, an awe-inspiring, if benevolent, headmistress with the accomplishments as a dancer which took her into Diaghilev's company, a talent for choreography (her ballets *Job* and *Checkmate* remained in the repertory for many years), an instinctive and absolutely sure taste, and the gift of perceiving talent in others. She shared with Ashton the ability to recognize potential, which for more than twenty years would bring on one generation of dancers so quickly after another that the major problem for this company was the holding down of young girls ready to take over before the existing ballerinas were ready to retire. De Valois is extremely musical and Roy Strong has pointed out that all the best stage designers of the thirties and forties owed their first commissions to Ninette de Valois and Robert Helpmann.

Although Oliver Messel had worked in the theatre in the 1930s, his most important commissions had been *Comus* (1942) and *The Sleeping Beauty* (1946). Leslie Hurry was a Helpmann discovery, designing the famous wartime *Hamlet* (1942) and *Swan Lake* (1943). Osbert Lancaster began in the theatre with Cranko's ballet *Pineapple Poll* in 1951 and John Piper with Ashton's wartime ballet *The Quest* in 1943.[2]

The predominance of women is not unusual in ballet. De Valois was five years older than either of the two young men who sat beside her, while Ashton had come from the companies of Madame Rambert and Nijinska, and Helpmann had joined de Valois' school as a child. All three were imbued with the concept of 'the company', and if de Valois was a martinet, she inspired loyalty as well as fear. Margot Fonteyn is quoted as saying 'She was so hard I was frightened to go into class if I was two minutes late.' But she also said that de Valois' secret 'like that of great generals, was that she cared deeply about our lives and our personal problems as well as our careers'.[3] From the same source we learn that 'Madam', as her company soon decided to call her, also showed a certain tolerance for the gifted. 'I noticed', Fonteyn wrote, 'that new arrivals fell into two categories as far as Miss de Valois was concerned: "She's a nice child" or "She's an absolute devil, but very talented." It was the latter group that always seemed to get on.'[4]

The genius of Ashton achieved immediate recognition. Writing of an early ballet called *The Wanderer*, Beryl de Zoete spoke of his 'architectural imagination':

> Other ballets appear episodic beside his, however brilliantly worked out in detail. His design is integral so that no part could be cut away or shortened without vital damage to the whole. Allied to this is his extreme sensitivity to musical structure as well as rhythm. He composes in the round, conveying his mental design almost entire in its new medium of dancing bodies, from whom he gathers as they move, inspiration and plastic suggestion.[5]

Ashton, like Helpmann, had worked in the commercial theatre as well as with ballet companies and he was both more sophisticated than de Valois and less rigorously pure. As a result, although he derived his inspiration from the classical past, his ballets are never mere pastiche but stamped with the spirit of his age. He borrowed when he felt like it from musical comedy or revue and transformed this material by his unerring style and wit. He was as indispensable as Ninette de Valois to the sudden flowering of the British ballet because success in this field depends on the creation of new ballets. Whereas in the classical repertory of opera there are dozens to choose from, there are only about six classical ballets.* Without de Valois there would have been no ballet company, without Ashton there might well have been too few ballets to build it upon.

Helpmann's choreography has not lived as Ashton's has, and as a dancer he was not a great technician. Arnold Haskell said of him:

> Robert Helpmann . . . is a classical dancer of fluency, and great elegance of style, an outstanding partner of self-less skill, and a mime of intelligence and range unequalled in ballet today. He is the complete dance-artist; he fulfils Noverre's conception of the great dancer, as an actor in the fullest sense of the word, and his experience of drama has widened his powers both as a dancer and choreographer.[6]

Another critic spoke of Helpmann's 'small and curiously medi-aeval face, with its expressive but unnaturally large rounded eyes and parted lips. . . .'[7]

To these three was added Constant Lambert, composer and conductor, probably the most distinguished musician ever to work with an English ballet company. Nor is it possible to name the talents which constituted this first national company without including, prematurely, the name of Mar-got Fonteyn, soon to be acknowledged one of the greatest dancers in the world.

---

* *Swan Lake, The Sleeping Beauty, Giselle, Coppélia, The Nutcracker.*

Much was to be done before the company reopened the theatre with a performance of *The Sleeping Beauty*, as it had to be transformed from its wartime function as dance hall to its traditional grandeur. Two bandstands as well as the floor were taken up and the seats brought out of store, reconditioned and put back in place, while the whole theatre had to be painted. The choice of ballet was brave because Oliver Messel's four-act sets – which were to last for 22 years and in the minds of many people have never since been equalled – absorbed all the resources of the theatre. This meant that *The Sleeping Beauty* had to be danced at every performance for the first month while the sets for other ballets were prepared. And, since Fonteyn could not dance at every performance, less well-tried ballerinas had to appear.

The triumph and glory of the opening on 20 February 1946 are matters of history and have often been described. The King and Queen, Queen Mary and the two Princesses attended, along with a largely invited audience consisting of foreign ambassadors and a company of British social, musical and artistic society seldom seen together at one time. Only one thing marred the opening. While waiting to receive the royal guests, Lord Keynes had a small heart attack, and the honours were done by his wife, Lydia Lopokova, until later in the evening when he was sufficiently recovered to appear.

Congratulations were received by all, not least by David Webster who, in the circumstances of the austere post-war period, hampered by clothes rationing and other shortages, had successfully opened the house to this triumphant performance. Sir Kenneth Clark wrote to him: 'One more word of congratulation on your marvellous achievement. It was a miracle. We all basked in the reflected glory and took what credit we could, but in the end it was all back to you.'[8]

Margot Fonteyn danced Aurora at the opening and Robert Helpmann doubled the parts of Carabosse and the Prince. *The Sleeping Beauty* was given in seventy-eight consecutive performances and in these Aurora was also danced by Pamela May – 'Her dancing has poise, attack and an unforced ease of execution'; by Beryl Grey – 'Unusually tall and generously built for a ballerina, she has strength to spare and expends it on a brio that gives movement its gleam, burnishes arabesques and puts pace in the spins'; and a 'young titian-haired dancer', Moira Shearer – who caused a 'ballet sensation by her dancing of the ballerina role'. None, however, challenged Margot Fonteyn. 'I believe her to be without equal', wrote Arnold Haskell, 'in musical and dramatic range anywhere at the present time.' And he compared her to Tamara Karsavina 'who always made herself part of the poet's conception', and said she was a dancer who fulfilled 'the old poet's dictum that the great dancer is born aloft on the arms of the music'.[†9]

Caryl Brahms wrote that 'dancing with a finely-schooled perfection . . . she [Fonteyn] proved that she is one of the four greatest female dancers in the world – the other three being Danilova, Markova and Chauviré; and Baron said 'It can be said without fear of contradiction that today, outside Russia, Margot Fonteyn has no peer as an all-round performer. She excels in both the classical and the modern ballets.'[10]

Speaking of the company as a whole, James Redfern, in the *Spectator*, said it was the most considerable of all the world offsprings of Diaghilev's famous Russian Company and Philip Hope-Wallace in *Time and Tide* spoke of 'Messel's new setting,

---

[†] These quotations and those that follow are taken from ballet criticisms written throughout the season.

refulgent, plumed and gauzy', and said that 'The overall presentation . . . was quite extraordinarily satisfying. . . . How beautifully Constant Lambert conducted – there is no ballet conductor more appreciative of the enormous importance of the role; with him choreography and score always seem to flow together as if mutually inspiring one the other.'

And commenting on the difficulties of *The Sleeping Beauty*, he said: Whereas in *Giselle* you can get away with three first-rate dancers, you need a round dozen of soloists. It is *the* bravura piece.'[11]

The Sleeping Beauty should have been followed by a new ballet by Frederick Ashton but owing to an injury to Michael Somes, it had to be postponed and a Helpmann ballet called *Adam Zero* was put on in its place, without much success. Then in mid-April this was followed by the Ashton ballet *Symphonic Variations* to music by César Franck and design by Sophie Fedoro-vitch. This ballet is a suite of classical dances for six dancers and, one of Ashton's great masterpieces, it has remained in the repertoire at Covent Garden ever since. At the opening it was danced by Margot Fonteyn, Moira Shearer and Pamela May, Michael Somes, Henry Danton and Brian Shaw. An instant and immense success, it gave the company a triumphant start and established an English style. Arnold Haskell wrote: 'It was a masterpiece of pure dancing, the prototype of which is *Les Sylphides*. It was musically subtle, rich in inventive pattern and of very great complexity. . . .'[12] While Beryl de Zoete wrote:

The choreography is crystal clear in design, full of graceful, subtle invention, very musical and extremely difficult to dance. It makes the same demands upon the dancers as the works of Bach do upon instrumentalists in the way of technical control and purity of style. It is quite the most distinguished of Frederick Ashton's creations so far.[13]

The first season had to be extended more than once, and 130 performances were finally given. Short seasons were then given by a French ballet company and by Ballet Theatre of New York. In the summer of 1946 the Covent Garden Company (still called the Sadler's Wells Ballet) undertook an extended foreign tour, dancing in Brussels, Prague, Warsaw, Poznán, Oslo and Malmö. The British Council representative in Poland gave this account of its visit there.

It was an enormous success with the Polish authorities and an enormous success with the Polish people. If our own Lord Chamberlain could have seen the theatres I think he would have resigned at once. They were absolutely packed to the doors and on the last night in Poznán people were standing on the front of the boxes and holding on to the vertical pillars. The Ballet themselves were extremely good ambassadors, and that was the first occasion on which we had not only the promise of the Polish authorities to do things but their constant and active goodwill throughout, and tremendous co-operation. The Minister of Culture arranged with the Speaker of the House that the Sadler's Wells people should stay in Parliamentary accommodation and things like that went on. . . . The Russian Counsellor went to our Charge d'Affaires and expressed great appreciation of that particular Ballet. In every way it was a tremendous success and we were convinced quite worth any cost that was involved.[14]

In the three years which followed the company added *Giselle* and *Le Lac des Cygnes* to its repertoire and Frederick Ashton began a series of full-length ballets with *Cinderella,* danced at the first performance by Moira Shearer, since Fonteyn had sprained a ligament, and by Robert Helpmann and Ashton himself as the two ugly sisters. According to Alexander Bland, Ashton maintains that he was not influenced by the tradition of British pantomime but as Bland says: 'The playing of the two Ugly Sisters by male dancers lent to the work an ineradicable flavour of that ever-popular Christmas theatrical treat.'[15] When the two sisters danced the Oompah', a run against the beat first performed by Fred and Adele Astaire in musical comedy, it seemed a particularly happy example of Ashton's untroubled borrowing from other spheres to transform to his own needs.‡

In 1949 the Sadler's Wells Ballet went to America. The impresario, Sol Hurok, had seen the opening night at Covent Garden and wished to take the company over in 1948 but Webster decided to wait until the Metropolitan Opera House was available. The visit was preceded by enormous publicity, and the Metropolitan Opera House had record advance booking even before the company arrived. In America there was a tradition of dancing of a far more athletic and technically demanding kind than anything normally seen in England, and this was the most testing of all the company's undertakings. There was also some nervousness as to whether American audiences would easily accept the full-length ballets which were by now an important part of the repertory.

‡ The story is told of a ballet critic who asked Jerome Robbins who had been his greatest influence and received the reply 'Fred Astaire'. 'How extraordinary', he said, 'Balanchine came here the other day and he gave the same reply to the question.'

In an article in the *Christian Science Monitor* after the first performance – once more of *The Sleeping Beauty* – the writer said any nervousness had been unnecessary.

> Applause was recurrent, even impatient, throughout the evening. It rippled distract-ingly against some of the solos. It burst out in great tides when the scenes were finished. It rose to a roar of cheers for the curtain calls which finally ended around half-eleven. The immense garlands of flowers brought on the stage after the finale were pretty well matched by garlands of praise in the New York press.[16]

And indeed the New York press was unanimous in its praise. In the *New York Journal* Miles Kastendieck said 'It turned out to be the finest ballet company to be seen here in many years.'[17] And he reported that Margot Fonteyn 'stopped the show' in the third act. A writer in the *New York Herald Tribune* spoke of the wonders of Oliver Messel's sets and costumes, the beauties of Constant Lambert's reading of the Tchaikovsky score, the brilliance of individual performances, while the critic of the *New York World Telegraph* said 'Not since the heady pre-war days has New York loosed so much rapture and noisy applause on a dance premiere as it did last night . . .', and he remarked that the 'beautifully executed *Sleeping Beauty*' took place to the accompaniment of 'the loudest cheers ever'.[18]

Many critics spoke of the style and grandeur of this company, others of its simplicity. All gave unquestioned supremacy to Margot Fonteyn: 'As Princess Aurora she put her name firmly with such great dancers as Pavlova, Lopokova, Baronova, Toumanova, and Markova . . .' The radiant success of the company in New York was equalled in a tour of Washington,

Chicago, Richmond, Philadelphia, East Lansing and Detroit; and of Toronto, Montreal and Ottawa. Claudia Cassidy summed up the reception of this English company in every one of these towns in an article in the *Chicago Tribune* (14 November 1949) which began: 'To say that Margot Fonteyn brought the house down would not be much of a compliment. Everybody brought the house down'.[19] And, after the company had returned to England, John Martin in the *New York Times,* wrote:

> There is no gainsaying that the visit of the British organiza-tion has given us a terrific wallop in our national pride. With all our resources, which include not only unlimited material wealth but also an unmatchable supply of brilliant artists – dancers, choreographers, musicians, designers – we have never come within hailing distance of the Sadler's Wells accomplishments. Here is an organization which has really used its resources. The company is designed to be a company and not a collection of stars . . .[20]

In 1937, in a book called *Invitation to the Ballet,* Ninette de Valois has an essay on the behaviour of the audience. 'Applause', she writes, 'is another innocent or stupid example of mass psychology' and she complains that 'the stage is strewn with floral tributes of no interest to anyone but the donors and recipi-ents'.[21] Over the years Miss de Valois was to sit through more determinedly hysterical applause and watch more tributes hurled on to the stage than possibly anyone else who ever lived. Perhaps it was some consolation to her that, however unseemly their behaviour, the audiences her company attracted soon learned whom to applaud and when.

6

Opera 1946–1947
David Webster; the first season of
the Covent Garden Company

Webster's biographer tells us that 'he didn't love the ballet as he loved opera, although he couldn't *not warm* to its success.' And he adds: 'His opera, too, ultimately had to be the best; and with both together he would have the best of all possible worlds.'[1] If it were not corroborated elsewhere, it might be difficult to believe that, warmed by the extraordinary ease with which the de Valois company achieved international status, Webster so ignor-antly underestimated the difficulties of establishing a comparable opera company singing in English. Yet Lord Harewood, who later worked closely with him and came to know him as well as anyone, said: 'They had expected, I believe, nearly as instant a success with the opera company as with the ballet, taken over fully-fledged as it were from Sadler's Wells'.[2]

Webster had immense authority and the capacity to inspire

his staff with confidence and affection for him. In the early years when so much went wrong he never weakened and he acquired the reputation of being completely 'unflappable'. He used to go down on to the stage when arguments raged, dressed for the street, with muffler, hat and stick, and, with a mixture of geniality and disapproval, restore order immediately. It was said that 'he always got the curtain up', and, although this is insufficient in itself, it nevertheless requires exceptional qualities. Probably no one outside the higher echelons of politics works under so much strain as the General Administrator of an opera theatre, who is responsible at the same time for the day-to-day running of the machinery required 'to get the curtain up' and for the forward planning of the whole repertory—the engagement of singers, conductors, designers and directors – for several years ahead. Webster managed without a deputy for some time because of his ability to delegate. He had the gift of being able to leave his staff to get on with their jobs without supervision. 'I do very little', he once boasted while at Lewis's, 'besides engaging the best available staffs in each department and then I leave it to them.'[3] This and his loyalty to those who worked for him ensured that many people remember him with admiration and affection, although the same qualities led to some complacency in relation to criticism.

His first task was to follow the Sadler's Wells Ballet performances with those of visiting companies, while the preliminaries of forming the nucleus of an opera company were undertaken. The American Ballet Theatre opened on 4 July 1946 and was followed by a visit from the San Carlo Opera Company in the autumn, after which the Sadler's Wells Ballet returned for its second season. During all this time the theatre was well filled, while, for Gigli's performances with the San Carlo and the reopening of the Sadler's Wells, the seats could have been sold several times over.

The scene was thus set for a little hubris, although there were already warning voices. Desmond Shawe-Taylor in particular warned, in an article in the *New Statesman*, that the country had not the resources for the six or seven opera companies rumoured to be forming, and such talent as there was should be combined. He went on:

> The second essential is that we should swallow our national pride, admit that in this particular field we possess no solid English tradition, and remind ourselves that for a long time to come the great bulk of the repertory will continue to consist of foreign operas (mostly German and Italian) translated into English. In other words, we must make the fullest use of what little first-rate material is available, *irrespective of nationality*. What kept the artistic standard of Glyndebourne so high? The fact that Mr Christie had the sense – and the flair – to disregard 'patriotic' prejudice and engage three absolutely first-rate and irreplaceable men of the theatre: Carl Ebert, Fritz Busch and Rudolf Bing.[4]

Webster's most important task was to appoint a Musical Director. His first approach was made to Eugene Goossens, by now one of England's leading conductors, who might have been particularly suitable as he had worked at Covent Garden with Sir Thomas Beecham. He was in America, but, as early as December 1944 he cabled, in reply to an enquiry, that he was extremely interested Covent Garden and available soon if wanted'.[5]

Despite continual prompting from Ralph Hawkes, Webster

did not write to Goossens for three months. It is unnecessary to quote from his letter because Goossens' reply to Hawkes makes its contents clear. He began by saying that Webster had thrown very little new light on a scheme with the main points of which he was fairly familiar, and he suggested that if Hawkes had a copy of the letter he was probably as much surprised as he was himself "that it mentions neither the length of my proposed contract or [sic] the amount of my remuneration, both of which I specifically asked to be put in writing'. Then he went on:

The fact that any activity at Covent Garden in the matter of opera in English has to start from scratch is something no one realises better than myself. Yet Webster's own statement embodies my biggest misgiving when he writes 'Not that England is entirely devoid of good singers, but there are naturally few of them, and those few, for obvious reasons are not well schooled in Opera.' In other words unless 'those few' not 'well-schooled' in Opera prove susceptible to training and coaching, and turn into the finished article within a reasonable amount of time, either their place must be taken by the foreign artist (with imperfect English diction) – thus defeating the main idea of the project – or else the whole idea of opera in English must be abandoned. It is the prospect of shouldering the responsibility of making bricks without straw that alarms me a great deal.

I am one of the foremost champions of opera in English, but I can't agree with Mr Webster's statement that 'opera has never really prospered anywhere unless given in the language of the audience attending the performance.' The Metropolitan Opera in New York plays all its operas in their original language with the exception of about three productions per season given (excruciatingly) in English translation. I certainly think that we should all aim to keep up the good work of Ross, Quinlen, Beecham et al., but my memories of Covent Garden recall really packed houses chiefly on the glamorous nights of the 'Grand Season' (with big singers) rather than during the performances of the Beecham Opera Company and the BNOC.

Goossens made certain comments about the idea of mixing the opera and ballet evenings and a criticism of the idea (then prevailing) of giving Purcell's *King Arthur* at the opening performance. Then he went on:

> With regard to the directorial set-up, I am a little inclined to view with misgiving any divided authority. Blame for the shortcomings of a production as well as credit for its good points should fall on the shoulders of a single individual – the artistic director. . . . Differences of opinion between conductor and producer can, of course, be ironed out nine times out of ten, yet when the conception of a producer might differ dramatically from that of a musical director, and radically hamper the smooth working of the performance, there is only one court of appeal—the artistic director. . . . Mr Webster copes with this situation by acting as Chairman of the triumvirate; either with a power of ruling or else of throwing his added vote against one or other of his associates. This is not satisfactory. . . .

He says that the London project had appealed to him as much from sentimental reasons as any other but Webster's letter has finally made me realise that I cannot safely undertake the

101

responsibility for a project the artistic outcome of which I cannot foresee and consequently take full musical responsibility for.' Goossens said however that, although his contract to go to Australia would not allow him to be in London until the autumn, he would be prepared to put his services at Webster's disposal for 'part of September, all of October and half of November of this year, and from the middle of April onward for an indefinite period, next year'.[6]

When a copy of this letter was sent to Lord Keynes, he replied in a letter to Hawkes:

> This is very disappointing. Nevertheless, after reading it I am left wondering whether he is really the right man for us. He seems to me to be thinking too much along the old lines typified by the Metropolitan here, and does not, I think, grasp or sufficiently appreciate that our purpose, whilst including the traditional repertory, is something rather different, namely, to build up an English opera that has its own traditions and standards.

And Keynes wondered whether Goossens did not 'under-estimate the quality of the material we shall have at hand for our purpose'.[7] Subsequently Webster cabled: 'Delighted with Keynes' letter the view which is Clark's and mine.'[8]

Concurrent with these negotiations an approach had also been made to Bruno Walter. In March 1945, Boosey and Hawkes' representative in America in a letter to Hawkes gave an account of an interview with the great conductor who had received what is described as an offer 'of a twelve-month period of activities in England'. This offer seems not to have come direct from Covent Garden but from Boosey & Hawkes for various engagements to include work at that theatre. Walter refused the invitation on the grounds that he had become an important part of the musical life of America and felt it would be inappropriate at the age of almost seventy to 'leave all the orchestras – the Met – and the tremendous following of admirers'. However, he said that after a talk he had had with Ralph Hawkes he had been careful not to tie himself for the spring of 1946 and was willing to be in England for a period of four months, March to June 1946, 'to do during that period the type of work indicated in your cable: opera, BBC orchestra, Mahler Festival, or whatever should emerge and be acceptable to him'. Heintzheimer then gave as close an account as possible of Mr Walter's ideas on Covent Garden:

> Based on an experience of 50 years in the operatic field, and of over 30 years in a leading position, he feels that before anything definite can be said on his part, the question of singers, chorus, scenery, general organizations, will have to be clarified. 'I cannot say I will conduct *Tristan, Don Giovanni, La forza del destino*. I will have to know which cast will be available and will then determine which operas to present. . . . Who will be the chorus master? What chorus will be available. Who will train the orchestra in advance? Who will select it? Who will design scenery?'[9]

Neither Goossens' offer to come for an indefinite period nor Bruno Walter's to come for four months appear to have been accepted. The members of the Board* and David Webster may

---

* A list of all directors from 1946 to 1986 can be found in Appendix C, pp. 347–48.

have thought that it would add considerably to the difficulties of engaging a Musical Director if the work was to be shared in the first instance with someone else. However, before leaving the American scene, one more quotation from Heintzheimer to Hawkes must be given, from a letter written in March 1945:

> Let me say once more most emphatically: you will soon have to make decisions and really start signing contracts if you will require conductors and singers from this end for the spring of 1946. We must soon stop approaching people with general proposals and start engaging them for a specific period. People do not wait for us. Already now bookings are being made for the spring and summer of 1946. This is particularly important because people know, of course, of your intention to open Covent Garden after the War and will be careful to tie up artists earlier than they used to do during the past few years when there was no danger from abroad. . . . I can only warn you not to delay matters any further if you really want any large scale participation in your schemes from the American end. . . . If another two or three months elapse, I don't guarantee or promise you anything.[10]

There is evidence that Webster did see Carl Ebert, who, he said, was anxious that Glyndebourne and Covent Garden should amalgamate 'not just in a co-operative sense, but that they should join and become one entity'. Webster explained what the feeling was about Christie to which Ebert answered that it might not be necessary for Christie to come into Covent Garden but he must bring Bing: 'I was also amused when Ebert said conductors were difficult and he did not see any major reason why they should be in the inner Council . . . I am afraid I was left with the feeling that Ebert, charming as he is, had every intention of being king-pin in every way.'[11]

In his biography, Haltrecht tells us that Webster's dilatoriness was an essential part of his personality, that to commit himself to any decision was for him a form of declaring himself. But he believed that this was one of Webster's strengths, and he says that this dilatoriness was never more constructive than in the task of appointing a musical director: 'He couldn't, wouldn't move fast. The wrong choice and the whole enterprise might be in ruins.'[12] This period at Covent Garden is also discussed by Kenneth Clark, who, as we know, had been influential in Webster's appointment. In his autobiography, *The Other Half*, he says: 'David Webster didn't really know the field and would not turn to anyone who could advise him in case he would be over-shadowed. He chose as Musical Director a minor figure named Karl Rankl.'[13]

Karl Rankl, appointed Musical Director on 16 June 1946, was Austrian by birth and had been coach and chorus master at the Vienna Volksoper in 1922, Klemperer's assistant in Berlin, and Musical Director at Wiesbaden. When the Nazis came to power he left Germany first for Graz and then Prague, where he was Musical Director of the German Opera House, before escaping to England where he was at first interned. After he was released, he took British citizenship and he conducted many of the leading British orchestras. In an obituary notice, Frank Howes says:[†]

---

† Frank Howes (who wrote anonymously) was the chief music critic of *The Times* during the period under review.

Karl was a modern representative of the old German *Kappellmeister,* the all-round musician who would compose or conduct a symphony with equal competence. Such men . . . are not to be underestimated because they are neither great composers turning out immortal master-pieces nor virtuoso conductors butterflying round the world's halls and theatres. They have always been the mainstay of the German operatic set-up, and Rankl acquired experience, that was at the critical moment made available to Covent Garden, in half a dozen German opera-houses. . . . Like many another immigrant from Europe he enriched our musical life.[14]

In an agreed basis for Rankl's appointment at Covent Garden, clauses 5 and 6 are as follows:

(5) No engagement of a singer or person directly concerned with the production of Opera shall be made without the consent of the Musical Director.
(6) The choice of repertory, casting and the arrangement of rehearsals shall be made by the Musical Director subject to the consent of the Administrator on behalf of the Trust.[15]

In April 1946 Lord Keynes died. He was succeeded as Chairman of the Arts Council by Sir Ernest Pooley, and as Chairman of the Covent Garden Trust by Sir John Anderson, soon to become Lord Waverley (by which name he will be referred to here). Of all the appointments made at this time, this seems in retrospect the strangest. Waverley's eminent biogra-pher, Sir John Wheeler-Bennett, says: 'The association of John Anderson with the world of arts is not one which springs immediately and spontaneously to mind.'[16] And he tells us that, although it was agreed between Webster and the members of the Board that he was the one man 'who could fulfil all the requirements of a chairman of the Trustees', Waverley himself took time to reflect: 'This was a new world to him, a world different in many respects from any that he had moved in before.' And he adds that Waverley's wife, Ava, was immensely anxious that he should accept the invitation: 'He realized how much his acceptance would mean to her and what a fortunate medium of expression Covent Garden would afford her social talents and aesthetic sensibilities.'[17] In fact, although Lady Waverley's social talents may well have matched those of her predecessors, Lady Ripon and Lady Cunard, she had not the passionate devotion to music of either. There is no evidence that she attempted, as they had done, to exert an influence on the course of affairs, except possibly in matters which touched social life, such as the choice of members of the Board.

Before agreeing to accept the appointment as Chairman of the Covent Garden Trust, Lord Waverley wrote to the Chancellor of the Exchequer, Hugh Dalton. In this letter he said that he would not feel justified in accepting the appointment unless he was assured that the project had been placed on a sound financial basis. The key sentences in this letter were as follows:

I want to be assured on two points in particular – First that in expressing your offer in terms of so much a year 'for the quin-quennium' you do not in any way rule out the possibility of a larger payment in certain contingencies before the end of that period, and, secondly, that you recognise in the arrangements now contemplated that the State will be assuming a definite obligation to see to it that, subject to others playing their part, Opera is not let down.[18]

Dalton replied that in general he would wish the Arts Council to feel themselves responsible for the allocation of the funds which Parliament puts at their disposal and to be able to plan ahead in expectation of an assured but limited grant. Then he said:

> I recognise, however, that the magnitude of the Covent Garden undertaking and the difficulty in present circumstances of estimating its future needs places it in a special position, and that the State will be assuming a definite obligation to see to it that, subject to others playing their part, Opera is not let down. I do not therefore rule out the possibility that the fulfilment of this obligation might in certain circumstances make it necessary to increase the Treasury grant to the Arts Council still further than I undertook in my letter of the 15th July. It would, I think, be agreed that these circumstances would not be held to have arisen unless in any year the Trust could show a need for a grant from the Arts Council of an amount exceeding £60,000.[19]

It is said that Lord Waverley carried this letter about and showed it to people, and that he believed that the agreement expressed in it was binding on future Chancellors. Rankl and Webster began immediately to hold auditions. They had less difficulty than might have been expected in engaging a chorus, while Douglas Robinson, who was to remain at Covent Garden for twenty-seven years, was immediately appointed chorus master. When Rankl introduced the chorus he had engaged to their new chorus master, he demonstrated, by making them sing scales, that all the first sopranos and tenors had top Cs, and he said to them: 'You have the finest collection of voices in the world. It is up to you to make them into a chorus.'[20]

Principals were more difficult, and all through 1946 Webster and Rankl gave auditions all over England and in America.

The original intention was to open with Purcell's *The Fairy Queen*, but, as this production took shape, it became clear that, having more the quality of a masque than an opera, it put emphasis on spectacle, ballet and mime rather than on singing, and it was finally given on 12 December 1946 between the season of ballet and the first production of opera. The sets and costumes were by Michael Ayrton, Robert Helpmann mimed the part of Oberon and Harold Rosenthal speaks of 'the magnificent singing of the chorus'.[21] Nevertheless the most notable thing about this performance of *The Fairy Queen* was the non-appearance of Joan Cross, one of the very few singers of the first quality England possessed who had sung the role before. Haltrecht says:

> Not till cast-lists were pinned on the notice-board was it learnt that she'd been overlooked, and this perhaps gives a measure of the chaos out of which was to emerge order of a kind; also, perhaps (she was a very outspoken lady), it gives the measure of Webster's nervousness at this time of people with pre-war experience of opera.[22]

And in the files at Covent Garden there is a letter from Leslie Boosey to David Webster in which he says: 'Joan Cross went to try on her dress for *The Fairy Queen* and was informed that there was no dress for her. This was her first intimation that she was not going to sing'.[23] *The Fairy Queen* was only moderately successful and not revived until 1951. On 14 January 1:947 the opera season of the new company opened with the production of *Carmen*.

History must largely be drawn from the preserved accounts of contemporary writers, yet the history of opera does not consist in the record of dates, names and sundry events, but in descriptions of quality. The difficulty here is that the accounts which remain are almost exclusively those of professional critics, and these have a bad name. Not only are they often wrong and quirkily harsh, but they too often disagree with one another. Yet, when the views expressed are those of the very few who at any given time have both the knowledge and the capacity to experience real delight in the presence of musical talent, and when in addition their accounts agree, they are, though subject to human error, the best we have. For the period under review Ernest Newman, Desmond Shawe-Taylor, Philip Hope-Wallace, Martin Cooper, and later Andrew Porter, Peter Heyworth, David Cairns and Rodney Milnes will be chiefly relied upon although other accounts will be given where they differ in any important particular or when the writer has something special to say.

It is hardly possible to question that the performance of *Carmen* was a disaster. Philip Hope-Wallace began an article in *Time and Tide* as follows:

> We all wish the new Covent Garden Trust success, but that must not stop me from describing their first effort, a *Carmen* in English, as a dire penance for any one who really loves this epitome of the Gallic spirit, this gem of the French lyric stage. . . . Why, dear Trust, pick *Carmen*? It is the most difficult of operas to sing in English, and indeed is difficult in any language other than French. . . . Assets here are a good

chorus and a responsive if coarse orchestra; a handsome production by Henry Cass, which is marred only by some fearsome musical-comedy touches, and vivid if rather too arty decors by Edward Burra.

I thought Karl Rankl handled this adorable score with, at the best, a sort of cavalier efficiency. Delicacy? there was none. . . . *Sur la place* quite missed the feeling aimed at; the point is to suggest atmosphere, it is not the opening of a jolly revue. That little miracle, the quintet was the merest sea-shanty, and as for the way he steered into *Ha-bas, la-bas dans la montagne'*, one of the most magical moments of all, it was sheer bull-dozing. . . .

But the most serious fault to be found by almost every critic was the casting. Edith Coates, in fact one of the best of our native singers, was hopelessly miscast as Carmen. Speaking of her performance, Hope-Wallace said that she was a good Verdian, but went on:

A hard worker with plenty of power and temperament, she did not spare herself. There were moments when one rather wished she had. . . . Not the sternest critic could fault Miss Coates on sauciness . . . there were moments when one feared she might fall down from sheer sauciness. Sometimes she was able to let fly in her best style, but the passages needing above all neatness seemed to me very heavy going. . . .

And he ended his review by saying:

The agreeable José was Kenneth Neate, with pretty tenor

111

and nice looks but not much pathos. Dennis Noble's Escamillo is experienced. Everyone had obviously worked like Trojans. Better luck next time.[24]

With the production of Massenet's *Manon* the company had only marginally better luck. The critic on *The Times,* who had been kinder than many about *Carmen,* praised the imported American soprano, Virginia McWatters and the conductor, Reginald Goodall, but Desmond Shawe-Taylor said the singers were frankly inadequate, and Philip Hope-Wallace that the 'pretty and vivacious little soprano from America was just not big enough to get the pathos across'.

'Heddle Nash', this critic went on, 'though phrasing with the experience born of years, frankly sounded dull and foggy in his more ambitious flights. No one else, vocally, matters and it is typical of the present set up at Covent Garden that all the minors sang louder than the principals.'[25] But he did praise the work of the producer, Frederick Ashton, and the conductor, Reginald Goodall.

The production of *The Magic Flute* was no luckier. This had marvellous sets by Oliver Messel but Desmond Shawe-Taylor complained of the director, Malcolm Baker-Smith, who, he said, had turned Papageno's share of the dialogue into a kind of stage Irish: 'Sure, if it was wings and not feathers I had, it's after flying I'd be . . . until it's turning in his pauper's grave that ould Mozart must be and looking at its watch, begorrah, the long-suffering audience.'[26] Philip Hope-Wallace, having said that he reckoned he suffered less than many Mozartians at the Covent Garden revival of *The Magic Flute,* nevertheless compared it unfavourably to the pre-war Sadler's Wells production with Joan Cross, and said that frankly he had heard not one really beautiful moment.

He compared the performance of the overture to 'the town-band in a hurry to get home to tea'. Everyone praised Oliver Messel's sets.

The one success, even if of a modest kind, was the production of *Der Rosenkavalier* by Joan Cross with designs by Robin Ironside. For this the Marschallin, Doris Dorée, was imported from America as also once more Virginia McWatters the Sophie. A young English singer, Victoria Sladen, sang Oktavian. Desmond Shawe-Taylor said that this was much the best performance the new regime had given and this was the general view. Shawe-Taylor went on to say that he did not intend faint praise, 'though, looking back on the really rather miserable *Carmen, Manon* and *Magic Flute,* I fear that it will sound so'.

> The new *Rosenkavalier,* however, is a thoroughly studied, professional, on the whole well-cast affair, roughly compara-rable to a performance of the same work in Paris, and that I suggest, is the proper sort of comparison to make, and not one which involves Lotte Lehmann, Elizabeth Schumann and Richard Mayr. . . . The three female principals are all good, one of them outstanding. Victoria Sladen catches all the essentials, Doris Dorée's Marschallin has dignity of movement and an excellent musical style, and she really rose to the emotional level of her big scenes in the first act.[27]

Philip Hope-Wallace began his article, 'What an exhumation devoutly to be wished was this and how faded the roseleaves might have seemed. But beyond all expectation it was good and moving. . . . The accents on the stage were mostly American or Welsh, but in the stalls we were nearly all Viennese and nearly all in tears.'[28] And he went on to praise all three singers. No one praised the Baron Ochs.

In the following week Ernest Newman in the *Sunday Times* summed up a more or less general feeling. He had been out of England when *Carmen* and *Manon* were given, but he said: 'After seeing *The Magic Flute* of a few weeks ago and *The Rosenkavalier* of last Tuesday I cannot help asking myself whether the people in charge there are not making the mistake of flying too high on their trial trip.' He would be told, he thought, that the singers were young and inexperienced and that allowances should accordingly be made, but with every sympathy for young singers he believed they came only into the third line of consideration:

The first thing to be considered is the work: if that is treated in a way that does it less than justice, or positive injustice, it is no mitigation of the offence, in my eyes, to say that the performers were inexperienced but did their best. The second object of my consideration is the public. If the audience at a mediocre performance happens to be a seasoned one, it has a right to expect something better at Covent Garden than the second-rate: while if it is comparatively fresh to opera . . . it is not right that it should receive its first impressions of a masterpiece from a performance that hardly anywhere rises to the height of the work. What seems to me principally wrong at Covent Garden is the low over-riding standard of taste in the productions: only taste of the worst kind could have made possible some of the inanities and vulgarities plastered on a performance of *The Magic Flute* which, apart from these, had many real excellencies. . . . And only imperfect taste on someone's part can account . . . for the complacent tolerance of the faults that made a great deal of *The Rosenkavalier* so depressing an experience for those of us with memories of Covent Garden in its great days.[29]

He went on to praise all three leading singers and also the Annina of Constance Shaddock.

Desmond Shawe-Taylor also summed up his impressions of the Covent Garden Company's first season. The ensemble and orchestra, he thought, had generally been good, 'the chorus fine, and the designs (a welcome novelty) entrusted to artists of some repute'. Yet he said:

One deficit has so far outweighed all these qualities: with few exceptions, the solo singing has been sadly inadequate . . . the impression persists that the authorities at Covent Garden are curiously indifferent to the actual sound made by the human voice; and curiously unaware of where to look for English singers. . . .[30]

The first season of the Covent Garden company was followed by a short season of the Vienna State Opera and then by one even shorter of the English Opera Group. Following Shawe-Taylor's remarks, it is perhaps apposite to mention that in the ten days' season of the English Opera Group the singers heard were: Joan Cross, Kathleen Ferrier (who sang also at Edinburgh in these years), Peter Pears, Richard Lewis, Denis Dowling and Otakar Kraus.

7

1947–1950
The Age of the Producer

The second and third seasons of the Covent Garden Opera Company (31 October 1947 to 5 June 1948; 29 September 1948 to 5 March 1949) were hardly more successful than the first – except that by all accounts the Rankl-trained chorus now sang superbly. A concession to the need for improvement in the solo singing had been made by the engagement of foreign singers, including Kirsten Flagstad and Elisabeth Schwarzkopf, but these were at their best when, as with Flagstad in *Tristan und Isolde* and *Die Walküre,* they sang in the original language. Schwarzkopf, who sang Pamina, Sophie and Violetta (in a new production of *La traviata)* managed well in the unaccustomed English version, but, although Flagstad bravely learned to sing in translation for Eva in *Die Meistersinger,* and Silveri 'gave a powerful interpretation of the title role in *Rigoletto* the compromise whereby foreign singers were forced to relearn their parts in

English often achieved the worst of both worlds. 'Our visitors seldom succeed in making their words intelligible (audibility after all is the sole excuse for the whole proceeding) and they arouse in us a suspicion that they are capable of better things in their own language.'[1] However Flagstad who sang magnificently always filled the house.

The production best received by the critics was *Peter Grimes*, sung chiefly by members of the original cast including Joan Cross, Peter Pears, Edith Coates, Blanche Turner and Owen Brannigan.* When Eva Turner sang *Turandot*, Desmond Shawe-Taylor complained that while for some twenty years she had been the best in the world, and there were still moments which recalled the old magnificence, 'elsewhere the sense of strain was too pronounced and too continuous for comfort.'[2]

But the chief criticism was that, unable to present first-class singers, the management at Covent Garden attempted to make good the deficiency by the splendour of the productions:

> It may without injustice be said that the productions thus far of the Covent Garden Trust have been notable for stylish, often sumptuous mounting and dressing and for a high proportion of merely passable or indifferent singing. Undeniably the tendency has been to put the cart before the operatic horse; it is not to be wondered at that the

---

* *Peter Grimes* was first produced at the reopening of Sadler's Wells Theatre on 7 June 1945. Rosenthal who said of the performance at Sadler's Wells Theatre that a new chapter in the history of British opera had begun went on to say: 'At Covent Garden after a few performances Richard Lewis took over from Peter Pears and Reginald Goodall from Rankl, who was out of his element in this music'.

117

poor beast should whinny.[3]

And 'most necessary of all at Covent Garden is a change of heart on the part of the management as to the relative importance of fancy production and sound singing.'[4]

Today these remarks have the ring of ingratitude, for in this period, in all branches of theatrical art, direction was given a new status. In opera, where previously this had been little more than the indication to singers of their position on the stage, there was a degree of trial and error, due usually to neglect of the first importance of musicality in this multifarious art. But here the writers are speaking of design and, although again there were notable exceptions, the distinguished artists engaged at Covent Garden often produced sets that were very beautiful and also dramatically practical. A ten-year report issued by the Covent Garden authorities in 1956 mentions that the sets for *Bohème* and *Tosca* were those made for the original Covent Garden productions half a century before, while *Fidelio* was played in sets designed by Rex Whisder before the war, and then goes on to list the designers of the last ten years: Leslie Hurry (for *Turandot* and *Der King des Nibelungen)*, Oliver Messel (for *The Queen of Spades* and the first production of *The Magic Flute)*, Georges Wakhevich (for *Boris Godunov, The Tales of Hoffman, Otello* and the revised production of *Carmen)* and Casper Neher (for *Wozzeck)*. It seems merely carping to complain that one element of opera is too good because another and more important is not good enough.

It was inevitable that the whole policy of singing in English, particularly with foreign singers, should now be questioned. Ernest Newman, speaking of a performance of *Bohème* remarked: 'Not much in the way of subdety or even unity of style could reasonably be expected of a performance in which the principals of various nationalities (Welitsch, Schwarzkopf, Schock, Silveri) sang this Italian work in the English language.'[5]

About the same time a writer in a Manchester paper drew attention to the fact that the BBC Third Programme was accustoming listeners to the singing in the leading opera houses of France, Switzerland, Italy, Germany and even Czechoslovakia.

> If one result of all this diffusion familiarises the big public with the sound of operas in their own language, another has been to acquaint it with Continental standards of singing.
>
> It is asking a great deal of expert musical people with singing of this order uppermost in their minds to go the next night to Covent Garden and sit politely through Mr Carron's Manrico or Mr Clifford's Papageno. The drop is simply too steep.

And this writer went on to question the whole policy:

> It would be interesting to discover, by means of a referendum, what proportion of Covent Garden audiences would prefer to hear some English soprano as Briinn-hilde and Isolde; what proportion cares about the language question one way or the other; and of those who do, how many will not positively prefer the original German.[6]

A writer in the *Nottingham Journal* went further: 'The real objection . . . is against most English librettos. We would rather not understand the words than have to listen to a banal translation.'

David Webster, announcing the 1947–8 season, was unrepentant: 'One of our biggest drawbacks appears to be that we are performing in English. . . . The box office reports that the higher priced seats are not always filled. . . . It seems incredible that certain sections of the public view opera in English as inferior to opera in foreign languages.' Probably the lack of acclaim by the critics was not given as much weight at Covent Garden as it might have been. This was partly because the critics, being so highly fallible, must always be largely ignored by people trying to do creative work, but also because, although many of them had warned that the Covent Garden authorities were embarking on an enterprise which was not really viable, there was anger that they did not nevertheless give it more support in its early days, even at some cost to their professional integrity.

However, the professional critics were not alone in thinking all was not well at Covent Garden. John Christie had never renounced his belief that the right way to achieve great opera in England was through combining the three opera companies – Covent Garden, Sadler's Wells and the Carl Rosa – under one Advisory Council. In pursuit of this object he had in 1947 sent a memorandum to various people including Sir Ernest Pooley, the civil servant at the Treasury concerned with the Arts, and the Chancellor of the Exchequer himself (by now Sir Stafford Cripps). In this he said that the opera companies were at present so separated that the Arts Council had to concentrate on preventing them all performing *Rigoletto* on the same day. Then he went on:

The English artists have not worked with great producers

nor with famous conductors. When they have worked with foreign singers, these singers have been struggling with the difficulty of singing in English— In these circumstances, it is difficult for the great foreign singer to inspire his English colleague. . . . The essential opportunity for the singer, experienced or inexperienced, is to work with great artists under ideal conditions, conditions when the great artist is inspired and extended. . . .[7]

In analysing the causes of failure at Covent Garden, Christie said that the premature insistence on the English language was a large contributing factor. He gave an outline of his own ideas for an expert executive under a governing body and for opera which 'boiled over into Festivals' whether at Covent Garden, at Glyndebourne or at Edinburgh.

From a letter written to Sir Ernest Pooley by P. D. Proctor of the Treasury, dated 29 June 1948, we know that Christie later gained access to the Chancellor of the Exchequer. Proctor, who obviously had some sympathy with Christie, said that at this meeting he had kept Glyndebourne right out of it: 'His main point is that the present management organisation [at Covent Garden] is not delivering the goods.' Christie had said that there ought to be somebody in charge of opera of really high calibre and 'soaked in the main stream of opera tradition'. 'As it is, the man in charge is David Webster, the Manager, and he does not know anything about opera. Christie also thinks that Rankl is second-rate, though he thinks he would be well worth his place in the team if there were a first-rate man in charge.'[8]

Following this the Chancellor called a meeting with Sir

Ernest Pooley, Sir John Anderson, David Webster and James Smith.[†] This meeting took place on 9 September 1948. In a note of a discussion which he had with a colleague previously, Proctor says that Sir Ernest Pooley had taken soundings with a view to the meeting and 'there is a general agreement that the Covent Garden Opera has not yet arrived at first-rate quality, and there is a large and growing body of opinion that it will never do so as long as the artistic direction continues to be in the hands of David Webster.' He then says that there seem to be two alternatives. The first (favoured by Christie) was to appoint a new musical and artistic director who, in Christie's view, should be Ebert.

> The alternative solution, which is favoured by Sir Ernest Pooley, is to appoint a Panel, under the Chairmanship of Rankl, who would be responsible to the Trust for the whole of the artistic side of the productions, including the choice of operas and the choice of singers. Webster should *not* be on the Panel. The Panel would invite guest conductors from time to time. This solution is strongly favoured by William Walton. Suggestions for the membership of the Panel under Rankl are Walter Legge (who is held in very high regard by singers), Braithwaite (already serving as conductor at Covent Garden) and one of the Trustees, probably Walton or Smith.[9]

[†] The Hon. James Smith was on the Covent Garden Opera Trust from 1946–50 and remained as a director when the constitution was changed from 1950 to 1961. He is an important figure as he was also a governor, and in 1947 Chairman of Sadler's Wells and first Chairman of the Co-ordinating Committee between the two theatres.

A copy of this note reached the Secretary of the Arts Council, Miss Gladstone, who, having expressed the view that it was inevitable that Covent Garden had not yet arrived at first-class quality, made the following comments:

> The composition of the Opera Trust, for instance, may not be ideal but the addition of Mr Christie suggested by Proctor would finish it.
>
> I wish he had said something about keeping David Webster as *Administrator* of the Trust. Or is it proposed to throw him out altogether—I have forgotten where he gets his information from about Walter Legge. My information is that, while he is a good musician, his name is anathema to the bulk of the profession![10]

At the meeting with the Chancellor, Sir John Anderson gave an example of political experience and skill in blocking discussion. Having said that the most important object was to nurse the growth of Covent Garden as an institution, inevitably a slow matter, he went on: 'Its future health . . . is far more important than any temporary fluctuations in the standard of individual performances.' Mr Webster, supporting this view, pointed out the difference between the work of a permanent opera company and seasons given under special festival conditions, and said that to bring in guest conductors at this stage could only have a disturbing effect. The important thing was to find the right man for any new appointment. At the conclusion of the meeting Sir Stafford Cripps asked the trustees to think the matter over and make recommendations in the fairly near future, and as a result a subcommittee was appointed to examine the criticisms and report to the Board on the questions raised. The main criticisms were that there was a lack of knowledge of singing and of the ability to select singers among the staff of Covent Garden, that bad selections had been made, that the standard of production was low, that the standard of conducting was low.

The sub-committee felt that some of these criticisms came from lack of appreciation of the aims of the Trust. 'To ask a beginner like Sylvia Fisher to take such an important role as Fidelio might be considered too great a risk for a Covent Garden performance, but it was inevitable at the present stage of development of the company.' Perhaps, the report went on, too much reliance had been placed on British singers, but initially it was not possible to employ singers from Austria or Germany: 'The opera houses of Europe and America are all extremely short of good talent. There is probably not a first-class halden tenor in the whole of Europe, nor a first-class soprano for Wagnerian roles. Italy has not a first-class Radames, Manrico or Otello.'

The sub-committee also felt that some of the criticism was out of date: 'The standard of production in *Turandot, Peter Grimes, La traviata* and *Boris* was as high as could be found anywhere, and the general production standard, low in *Carmen* and *The Magic Flute*, had shown a very considerable improvement.'[11] On the question of an artistic director, it was felt that such a director should be British, but even were a foreigner a possibility, no recommendation of a suitable person could be made. It was agreed that some assistance for the General Administrator was essential and should be found as soon as possible and that the Trust should continue the search for an Artistic Director.‡

---

‡ In relation to the last recommendation, the terms of the renewal of Webster's contract in 1949, at the end of his first period of five years,

The report of the sub-committee in answer to criticisms held much truth and seems at least temporarily to have satisfied the Chairman of the Arts Council and the Chancellor of the Exchequer, although others were more difficult to satisfy. First, and most dangerous, was Jay Pomeroy, a man who had the distinction of having given two years of opera sung in Italian at the Cambridge Theatre during the precise period 1946–8 which had proved so disappointing at Covent Garden. He had brought Dino Borgioli and Alberto Erede to London, as Artistic and Musical Director respectively, and such singers as Stabile, the dramatic baritone Marko Rothmuller, and a younger generation which included Giuseppe Taddei, and had presented performances which had achieved critical approval and given opportunities to several British singers afterwards of note. Pomeroy is stated to have lost £200,000 over the two years (less however than the total of the Arts Council grant to Covent Garden during the same period). Undaunted, in 1948 he made a bid for the lease of the theatre at Covent Garden.

The lease given to Messrs Boosey & Hawkes in 1944 had

---

suggests the power of the position he had by now achieved. In a first draft of the new contract, clause 3 appointed him chief adviser to the Trust with responsibility for the administration of its affairs, and an additional clause 3a declared the intention of the Trust to appoint 'a suitable person as Artistic Director who will be primarily responsible through the Administrator for the artistic side of the Trust's activities'. In the final draft dated 20 May 1949, these two clauses had been replaced by one clause 3 which, after saying that the Administrator would be chief adviser to the Trust and responsible over the whole range of its administration, went on: 'In particular he will be responsible for all the financial and business operations of the Trust and for the co-ordination of the artistic work of the Trust.' (Royal Opera House archives, 20 May 1949) been for a period of five years, expiring in December 1949. In May of that year the Chairman of Covent Garden Properties Ltd (Louis Nicholas had succeeded the late Philip Hill), without mentioning Pomeroy's name, told Leslie Boosey that they had received an offer for a forty-two-year lease following that date, but that the directors of the company were prepared to accept a similar offer from Boosey & Hawkes or the Arts Council. Because it was necessary to get permission from the Treasury before entering into a commitment of this length, the whole matter was taken over by the Ministry of Works, who failing to agree terms with Covent Garden Properties Ltd, then decided to buy the theatre. A compulsory purchase order was put upon it. In this way the future of the Covent Garden Trust was made safe, although there was some indignation, both from the people who saw it as an act of nationalization by the Labour Government, and also by people who were dissatisfied with the standard of performances given there. Pomeroy said that his intention in making an offer for the lease had been to restore Covent Garden to its pre-war eminence: 'I and my associates are anxious to lift it from the quagmire of dull mediocrity into which it has been allowed to sink.' And an article in the *Spectator* protested that 'The result [of the existing arrangement at Covent Garden] has been only too often a vast expense of money in a waste of splendour which could not disguise the musical inferiority of the performances.'[12]

Last, but by no means least, there was Sir Thomas Beecham. Speaking to a conference of the Incorporated Society of Musicians on 5 January 1949 he made operatic policy his subject. He asked for an inquiry into the work and composition of the Covent Garden Opera Trust, and in the speech which followed he managed a unique combination of criticisms, both informed and ignorant, often libellous nonsense. He complained that no member of the Trust 'knew anything about opera or had any practical experience of it' and pointed out 'a total absence of the name of any British musician ever associated with opera over a lengthy period of time'.[13] He made a completely unjustified attack on Messrs Boosey & Hawkes, asking how it came about that two publishers were included among the trustees, and also complained that a journalist, a music critic, was included in the list of trustees (Edward Sackville-West had joined the Trust in April 1950). Referring to Dr Rankl, he said that the appointment of an alien, and especially one bearing a German name, to the post of Musical Director of the British National Opera was so incredible that he had to remind himself that it had actually happened and was not a dream.

Sir John Anderson had no difficulty in dealing with these complaints. The names of those on the Trust included Sir Stanley Marchant, Sir Steuart Wilson, Dr William Walton, Professor E.J. Dent, Mr James Smith – a former colleague of Sir Thomas's – and Sir Kenneth Clark. Particularly deplorable he said was the attack on Messrs Boosey & Hawkes, who, as lessees of the theatre were 'out of pocket to the tune of thousands of pounds', while the Trust had the highest admiration for the manner in which Dr Rankl had addressed himself to his task. Nevertheless, Sir Thomas had succeeded in giving a great deal of publicity to the shortcomings at Covent Garden, and an opportunity (of which John Christie was quick to avail himself) for other people to take the matter up in the press.

What finally brought matters to a head, however, was not these criticisms but a new production of the opera *Salome*.

One of the most adventurous of Webster's actions at this time had been the appointment of the young Peter Brook as Artistic

Director. Brook was then twenty-five, but had made an enormous success with a production of *Romeo and Juliet* at Stratford,
and it was a bold and imaginative appointment, which in the
event proved disastrous. Brook had little or no musical experience and was more interested in what he termed 'good theatre'
than in the composer's intentions. He began with a production
of *Boris Godunov* which was full of theatrical tricks, and which
drew from Ernest Newman the comment that the production
'touched for the most part the lowest depths to which Covent
Garden has yet fallen'.[14] Opinion on this production was,
however, divided. Thus Desmond Shawe-Taylor said the designs
struck him as 'the boldest and most successful yet seen at Covent
Garden outside the ballet' and went on: With its mobs, its proces-
sions and proclamations *[Boris]* is very much a producer's opera,
and Peter Brook has seized his chance with both hands'.[15] There
was sufficient agreement with this point of view for the production of *Boris* to rank as one of the successes of the management at
Covent Garden.

There followed a lavish production of *The Olympians,* a new
opera by Arthur Bliss with a libretto by J.B.Priesdey (all the Brook
productions were extremely expensive), and one of *Figaro* which
was successful and remained in the repertoire. Then came *Salome,*
for which Brook chose Salvador Dali as designer. Even before
the professional critics had a chance to give their views of this
production, Rankl had stormed out of the theatre in protest and,
although persuaded back, had refused to take a call on the first
night.

Ernest Newman was the first to protest. In a review largely
devoted to other matters, his last paragraphs read:

Salome on Friday night was alleged to be sung in English

and what English some of it was, particularly that of Franz Lechleitner as Herod! Apart from ten minutes of good singing by Mme Welitsch in the closing scene, the performance both vocally and orchestrally was the most miserable one of *Salome* I have ever heard, while the production beat even the present Covent Garden's latest record for inanity.

I shall go into the whole subject more closely next week; meanwhile I ask myself despairingly how much longer the London opera public will be expected to tolerate performances and productions at Covent Garden that are for the most part an affront to its intelligence. How long, O Lord, how long, we ask.[16]

And the following week he said:

Of the production in general it is difficult to speak in the restrained language appropriate to a Sunday paper.

One absurdity followed fast on the heels of another; space fails me to deal with all of them.[17]

Newman's protest was the signal for virtually every critic in London. In the *Observer* of the following week, Eric Blom, having said that the daily and weekly critics had been in surprising agreement – 'Reluctantly they all declared that there is something distinctly rotten in the state of things at the Royal Opera House on the side of production' – went on:

There can be no beating about the bush: the present goings-on simply will not do. Audiences are asked to pay a good deal both directly by buying high-priced tickets and indirectly with public money that goes to the Opera through the Arts Council. The august establishment must thus be subject to sharp criticism until one notices improvements.

Blom made a comparison with a *Don Giovanni* at Sadler's Wells – 'where, whatever incidental faults were found, it was evident that it had been planned with a continual regard for Mozarf, and with a production of Britten's *Let's Make an Opera,* 'which, light and slight as it is, has been delightfully staged'. And then he went on:

> At the same time, in the very centre of London, at a venerable opera-house laden with history, a great and coveted scene for the masterpieces of a particular and important species of the art of music, that art is now perpetually – one may almost say systematically – misunderstood or disregarded.

Blom particularly disliked the lighting, as did very many other critics:

> The switchboard is rarely left alone for five minutes together. The sun rises, night falls, a moon appears and disappears (sometimes several moons at the same time), all within one short scene and in no natural sort of order. . . . As for spotlights, they could not behave more vulgarly or irrationally at a music-hall than they do nowadays at Covent Garden.[18]

A young critic on *The Isis,* named Peter Heyworth, ended his complaints by saying:

Mr Brook may think what he has achieved is, at any rate, good theatre.§ Good theatre it may be, but it is exceedingly bad opera. In the improbable event of my being asked to dance for the General Administrator of Covent Garden, it will be the head of Mr Peter Brook I shall demand on a silver charger.[19]

The critics were not alone in condemning this production, and members of the public also wrote to the press about it. Perhaps the most damning of all, however, was Philip Hope-Wallace in *Time and Tide*, who said in a generally highly critical review:

I will not say I have had no pleasure in Covent Garden since its partial nationalization; there was Flagstad, and some fine Wagner. One could count at least five artists who have given active pleasure besides, in perhaps three or four productions. But as a whole it now seems not only fair but absolutely urgent to say, that neither the musical nor the production side of Covent Garden can much longer be tolerated. To reply that it is this or nothing may well be the truth; if that is so, let us give all the public money to Sadler's Wells instead and turn the Royal Opera House once more into a dance hall. The cause of opera will not be furthered by asking people to pay prices such as are obtained here for continual disappointments.[20]

And Ernest Newman asked the following pertinent questions:

---

§ Brook had made this answer to the criticisms.

We ask ourselves once more how some of these people who are running opera . . . ever came to occupy the positions they now do. Who appointed them, who gave us and opera into their keeping, and in virtue of what supposed qualifications? What were *their* qualifications for exercising so powerful a hand in the shaping of the destinies of opera in this country?[21]

8

1950–1954
Financial Crisis

In 1950 the Festival Theatre at Glyndebourne reopened, a measure of security having been achieved through the formation of a Trust. Both Busch and Ebert returned. 'I never remember enjoying a *Cosi fan tutte* more than this', Philip Hope-Wallace wrote of the opening performance, 'The orchestral playing under Fritz Busch is of a precision and vivacity which nowadays seems like a miracle and brings tears to the eyes before the end of the overture.'[1] And Desmond Shawe-Taylor said: 'There is a tendency to take Glyndebourne for granted. But it is always a miracle; and to have restored pristine standards in 1950 is hardly less miraculous than Mr Christie's original achievement.'[2]

In 1951 Norman Tucker was appointed sole director of Sadler's Wells, with Stephen Arlen as general manager, and a period of expansion began in which productions of operas by

Stravinsky, Prokofiev, Bartók, Ravel, Smetana and Dvorak were given, as well as operas by Mozart and much of the Italian repertory including the first performance of *Don Carlos* since 1933, all sung in English. Performances of modern British works included *The Mines of Sulphur* by Richard Rodney Bennett and *Our Man in Havana* by Malcolm Williamson.

In March 1950 at Covent Garden, David Webster wrote a letter to Dr Rankl which, wrapped up in great courtesy and some unconvincing logic, contained the information that his appointment as Musical Director would not be renewed after the 1950–1 season. Webster began with the assurance that they had come a long way since 1946, one of the most remarkable features being the rise in subsidy from £25,000 a year to £145,000 a year. They had been lucky, he thought, in having Cripps at the Treasury and Anderson, who knew public life so well, as Chairman. Then he said: 'It is even more remarkable that Cripps has been prepared to back Covent Garden so strongly in the teeth of considerable critical opposition. Deserved or undeserved, generous or ungenerous, knowledgeable or unknowledgeable, the criticism itself is a fact.' Webster went on to say that the vote of £145,000 or more was by no means established and that Anderson and the Arts Council were apprehensive of a change at the Treasury.

No one, he thought, knew better than Rankl how far they had come, partly through the passage of time spent in performance, but chiefly through his (Rankl's) own work. Everyone in the theatre gave him the fullest credit and all were grateful:

But we have asked so much of you that we cannot go on making such full demands. We have failed to find a conductor of sufficient ability in this country to support: you in any reasonable way. The job you have done is at the turning point. With another gigantic effort it can quickly be turned into the great company we want it to become. To do this well you need direct conducting help and you need freeing of some of the almost intolerable burden of work that has been placed on you.

After several more professions of the benevolence of his intentions, Webster returned to the criticisms. You could say, he wrote, that the critics were snobs, or that there was a great deal of ignorance among them, and he personally thought they had been less than generous. Nevertheless, 'The fact is that the criticism is there and it is a factor which has to be dispelled because while the Trust can point to good audiences its opponents can point to a very critical press as a fact.'*

All this and a good deal more of the kind was preliminary to informing Dr Rankl that Erich Kleiber had been appointed for three months in the autumn as guest conductor 'to do some works out of the repertoire and one new production', and that he hoped Rankl would stay on as one of 'two first class conductors . . . each responsible for his own productions, entirely in control of them. . . . In other words, your directorial but not your conducting function would lapse.' In the same letter Webster told Rankl that Steuart Wilson had been appointed deputy general administrator, to assist himself.[3]

Rankl replied to this letter: 'Are you,' he asked, 'presenting me with a *fait accompli* or are your proposals still open to discussion

---

* Attendance had been good in the cheaper seats, but poor in the more expensive ones which, whether or not occupied by 'snobs', were financially the most important.

between ourselves?"[4] To which Webster answered:

> The principles in my letter are beyond discussion. They
> are:
> (a) Two principal conductors for the company.
> (b) A Deputy General Administrator with special duties on
> the operatic side.
> (c) The divorce of directorial function from the executive
> artistic function i.e. from actual conducting.[5]

Sir Steuart Wilson, a distinguished professional singer, had been appointed Overseas Musical Director of the BBC in 1942 and held this post until March 1945. He also served the BBC as Head of Music from 1948 to 1950. In between these two appointments he had gone as musical director to the Arts Council. He therefore had considerable administrative experience when he joined the Covent Garden Trust in 1946. He had also some experience in producing and conducting opera. When he was invited to leave the Trust and take up the post of assistant to David Webster he seemed an obvious choice.

After the production of *Salome,* Peter Brook left Covent Garden for good. Christopher West, originally engaged as his assistant, remained as resident producer. There was no disagreement between the Trust and their General Administrator as to the absolute necessity to import a conductor of higher quality than Dr Rankl, although it was hoped that he could be persuaded to remain as one of two. The difficulty in this case was not only that he knew and disliked Dr Kleiber, but also that Kleiber would wish to conduct operas such as *Der Rosenkavalier,* which Rankl had made particularly his own. Rankl however agreed to accept the new arrangement.

The appointment of Steuart Wilson was a different matter. According to Montague Haltrecht, at the time that the Ministry of Works took over the theatre, a sub-committee, consisting of David Webster and some members of the Trust, drew up a memorandum on future policy. Haltrecht writes:

> Among other things it was decided—certainly not by Webster himself—that an Artistic Director must be found for the House. Webster considered himself well able to absorb the duties of Artistic Director into those of General Administrator and he expertly delayed, suggesting that Ian Hunter, who was to follow Bing as Director of the Edinburgh Festival, should come as his assistant. . . . The appointment was intended to be an alternative to having an Artistic Director—but this particular threat was averted finally when not Ian Hunter but Sir Steuart Wilson was appointed Deputy General Administrator.[6]

There is invariably some uncertainty about the justice of quoting Webster's biographer, since Haltrecht is so often most admiring when Webster is at his least admirable. He actually boasts of matters most biographers would treat with discretion. There is however some support for his remarks in the following record of a Board meeting at Covent Garden on 26 January 1950:

> Mr Webster said that the proposal which he had discussed with Sir Steuart Wilson was that Sir Steuart should be appointed Deputy General Administrator, and should not receive the title of Artistic Director, as originally suggested. The public announcement would explain that the

137

appointment had been made because of the pressure of work on the General Administrator, who at present had no assistant.[7]

Sir Steuart would be primarily responsible for the Opera Company, administering its affairs, chairing its committees, being responsible for auditions and the development and well-being of singers. He would supervise the staff of répétiteurs and arrange for close co-ordination between the orchestra and the stage. His experience of the English language in song would be of great value to the chorus.

In November Rankl again received a letter from Webster, ostensibly about the arrangements for Kleiber, but also containing the news that Webster had heard from Sir Thomas Beecham who asked if there were anything he might do at Covent Garden in 1951. Webster went on:

> Beecham has said all sorts of things against this institution and will doubtless say them again. I am acutely aware that he specifically singled you out and that was very unpleasant for you. Slanging is and always has been part of Beecham, I almost said part of Beecham's fun, and has little or no actual meaning. . . . But whatever his character or his behaviour one thing is undoubted and that is his musical ability. He is the finest conductor we have produced and he has something of a flair for opera.

Webster then said that Beecham would like to do *Die Meistersinger*, and that it would be possible if three or four extra performances were put on after Rankl had done *Parsifal*. Then he reminded Rankl that there was an agreement that Covent

Garden should be kept open in August – the peak tourist season – and that Rankl had suggested that *The Gipsy Baron* would be suitable. However, Beecham had been asked to put on something light in Liverpool for their festival and would like to combine with Covent Garden in doing this. 'It seems a really good notion', Webster said, 'that if we do combine to do this that we should then bring the show from Liverpool into London' – in other words that Beecham, not Rankl, should conduct the 'something light'.[18] In writing thus to Rankl, Webster did his best to present without too much offence decisions agreed by the full Board, by now well aware that some change must be made. Rankl accepted the conditions imposed upon him.

Kleiber's reception at Covent Garden was immediate and dramatic. 'Are things really on the mend at Covent Garden?' Shawe-Taylor asked, speaking of Kleiber's first appearance to conduct *Der Rosenkavalier*. 'The cheers which swept round the house when the famous conductor made his appearance were more than a welcome to a distinguished visitor. 'They sounded uncommonly like the cheers of a beleaguered garrison at the sight of the rescuing force.' Shawe-Taylor went on:

> Not for a long time . . . have we heard at Covent Garden orchestral tone so smooth and rounded, or an ensemble so consistently easy and unruffled. . . . By and large this is the kind of sound, and this the rhythm, which Strauss surely

---

[†] At Beecham's suggestion, *The Bohemian Girl was* given instead of *The Gipsy Baron* (see p. 75).

intended. In a score commonly regarded as heavy, the lightness and clarity of the orchestral texture enabled us to enjoy innumerable fine points of detail which are usually muddled or lost. Still more important was the effect on the singers.

Although a famous exponent of modern music, Shawe-Taylor continued, Dr Kleiber 'never lathers his orchestra into a voice-drowning frenzy'. And,

No one benefited more from the new lightness and flexibility of the orchestral playing than Sylvia Fisher. Since she first sang the Marschallin, she has progressed amazingly; and her performance is now, both vocally and dramatically, most distinguished. She handles the complicated stage business with finesse and composure, and her attractively poised soprano tone commands many fine shades of tenderness, humour and resignation. Most remarkable of all is the clarity of her enunciation, achieved without distortion of the vocal line; she treats the English text, not as so many particles of necessary information, but as something to be turned to aesthetic account. The result is that we find ourselves savouring her beautifully inflected phrases for their own sake, almost as we can savour those of a fine performance in the original language. When this rare result is achieved . . . the policy of opera in English is justified on quite another plane from that of the crude utilitarian arguments usually advanced in its favour.

However, Shawe-Taylor said that 'like Hamlet confronted with assurance of partial reform', the critic cannot rest content; his

140

cry must be: 'O reform it altogether,' and he went on to make various criticisms.[9]

Eric Blom said that on the evidence of one's ears alone one would 'have sworn that Dr Kleiber had brought some fine and assiduously drilled orchestra with him, from goodness knows where'.[10] And Martin Cooper said: 'Those who think the role of the conductor greatly exaggerated would be hard put to it to find an explanation of the vastly improved finish, resonance, balance and vitality.'[11]

Beecham was also received with joy. 'It is a long time', Newman wrote, 'since we heard a *Meistersinger* so pressed down and running over with all that makes orchestral listening a delight – ardour, passion, beauty, tenderness, thoughtfulness.'[12] And speaking of a later performance, the *Times* critic said: 'Now as in June the orchestra poured out a golden stream of tone in which the intervening phrases were moulded with a delicacy and a significance which revealed a thousand beauties within the one beauty of the most humane opera ever written.'[13]

However, while the Board and management of Covent Garden had acted with a kindly motive in appointing Rankl as one of two principal conductors, their decision took no account of the fact that it was in this department, and really only in this, that he had failed. The critics continued to castigate him to the end. 'I ask myself glumly', Newman wrote, 'what notion people can possibly get of the grandeurs and subdeties of the *Ring* who are making its acquaintance for the first time at Covent Garden.' He praised the physical beauty and splendour of Flagstad's voice and spoke of her 'flood of brilliant tone', but went on to say that 'until the Covent Garden management has become considerably more enlightened we shall have to put up, I suppose, with the normal seventy per cent of poor singing in the *Ring*' And a critic in the *Gramophone Record* remarked 'Unfortunately the orchestral playing throughout was lamentable. . . .'[14]

Members of the Board were no less astonished than the critics at the transformation of the orchestral playing under Kleiber. James Smith and Edward Sackville-West among others were passionately devoted to music and quite selfless in their desire to improve performances at Covent Garden. In the spring of 1951 it was agreed that to start another season under the leadership of Rankl would be 'disastrous'. Complaints were also made at this time about the General Administrator's 'dilatoriness' in signing up singers and of a general tendency to leave everything to the last moment 'so that we often have to make do with singers inferior to those we might secure.'[15]

Rankl resigned at the end of the 1951 season, when his contract expired. Before he left he sent David Webster a record of his period at Covent Garden. In 1946 seventy people without experience in choral singing or acting had been engaged and these now formed one of the best opera choruses in the world. They had started with an orchestra completely inexperienced in opera, 'nor were they first class players.' This was now 'quite a good orchestra' with a repertory of twenty-seven operas. With only one répétiteur with prewar experience, they had built up a musical staff. He then gave a list of singers who had been 'picked up' with little or no operatic experience and trained. These included Geraint Evans, Constance Shaddock, Sylvia Fisher, Adele Leigh, Monica Sinclair, Edith Coates and Edgar Evans.‡[16]

Dr Rankl's work was perhaps given insufficient credit during

---

‡ Although he does not mention it, Rankl also introduced the young conductors Reginald Goodall, Warwick Braithwaite and Edward Downes.

his time at Covent Garden but it has been fully acknowledged since. In his obituary notice, Frank Howes (critic of *The Times)* said: 'He had a place in English musical history, comparable to that of Charles Hallé a century ago, in that he established our national opera, just as Hallé established the idea of a permanent orchestra.'[17] Nevertheless, without necessarily detracting from Rankl's services, speculation is inevitable as to why the Covent Garden authorities thought it necessary to fill the places in chorus and orchestra, as well as the ranks of the soloists, only with people without pre-war experience in opera.

For the Ballet Company the main feature of the early fifties was the extensive American tours. In the autumn of 1950, after opening in New York, the company 'carried the flag of British culture . . . over twenty-one thousand miles of the North American continent, starting on 10th September and finishing in Quebec at the end of January 1951, travelling in a special train made up of six sleeping-cars, four scenery wagons and a restaurant car'.[18] This was financially the most successful of all the tours and the company returned with a profit of £50,000. In the New Year's Honours list, Ninette de Valois was created a Dame Commander of the British Empire and Margot Fonteyn received the CBE.

This was the first of many tours all over the world and our ambassadors, wishing to show 'the flag of British culture', invariably asked first for the Sadler's Wells Ballet. In 1952 the company danced in Portugal and Berlin, in 1953 again in America and Canada, a tour lasting from the beginning of September until the end of January 1954. Then in June 1954 they visited Holland, danced in Paris in September–October, and at Milan, Rome, Genoa and Venice in October–November. For nearly thirty

143

years they would be seen in the USA and Canada nearly every other year and in the intervening period in most of the countries of Europe and South America. Margot Fonteyn and her partner, Michael Somes, danced as guest artists all over the world.[§]

In the early fifties the company was less successful in England. Robert Helpmann resigned while in America in 1950. On their return, the whole company were very tired. There was a creative pause, and a more severely critical attitude on the part of the critics. None of the new ballets was very well received, although Ashton's *Daphnis and Chloé* remained in the repertory and grew in popularity, as also his new version of *Sylvia*, which was more immediately successful. Moira Shearer, second only to Fonteyn in public favour, left the company, although Nadia Nerina (from South Africa) and the exceptionally gifted Svetlana Beriosova (from Lithuania) now joined. Nerina, partnered by a young dancer from the Sadler's Wells Theatre Ballet named David Blair, made a great success in a new version of *Coppélia* with designs by Osbert Lancaster, and Beriosova made a sensational debut in *The Sleeping Beauty*.

Since there were resident companies for both opera and ballet, if singers and dancers were to be fully employed, both companies had to spend a good deal of time on tour. This also complied with the policy of the Arts Council. The Opera Company went to Birmingham, Cardiff, Coventry, Croydon, Edinburgh, Glasgow, Leeds, Liverpool and Manchester.

The year 1952 saw the first of the financial crises in the arts which were to become almost an annual feature. Webster's

---

[§] A list of the foreign tours of both Royal Ballet companies will be found in Appendix A, pp. 343–44.

expressions of insecurity in his letters to Rankl had not been without cause, nor his fears of a change of Chancellor. In the estimates submitted by the Arts Council to the Treasury early in 1952 for the year 1952–3, a figure of £190,000 was included for Covent Garden. The Chancellor felt unable to increase the Arts Council grant, and in consequence that of Covent Garden had to be cut back to the level of the previous year: £150,000. Yet, after severe pruning of the estimates including cutting 50 per cent on new productions, there was a shortfall of £70,000 on 'next year's working'. In addition there was an overdraft of £100,000 – a figure which would have been higher but for a nonrecurring windfall from the ballet tour of America. The management were responsible to the Ministry of Works for heavy dilapidations as well as for the mounting cost of maintaining the large and uneconomical building. Seat prices were to be raised and, if the existing level of attendance were maintained, this would reduce the estimated deficit to £44,000, taking no account of the existing overdraft.

Three courses were discussed: abandon Covent Garden altogether; abandon opera entirely and retain Covent Garden for ballet; cut out the tours. In the course of well-argued objections to all three possibilities, consideration was given to 'what other nations think fit to spend upon Grand Opera'. France subsidized its Opera with a sum equivalent to £800,000 a year; La Scala, Milan to 50 per cent of gross expenditure (as against less than 25 per cent for Covent Garden). The subvention to the Argentine opera was roughly twice as much as that to Covent Garden and the subvention to the small-scale opera house at Stockholm about the same.

In July of that year Parliament approved a supplementary grant of £90,000 to the Arts Council for Covent

Garden – £40,000 being for 'bricks and mortar' and £50,000 towards paying off the overdraft. The Chancellor described this as a 'rescue operation', but in a memorandum addressed to him the Arts Council gave the opinion that a similar figure would be required in the following year:

> The expectations of attendance on which Covent Garden has been budgeting leave no margin for mischance. In 1953–54, the Ballet Company will again visit America and is expected to bring back a profit of over £100,000. A similar windfall two years ago, however acceptable, has served to conceal the precarious financial foundations on which Covent Garden is built. These are lottery economics—betting on a 90 per cent attendance and betting on American tours. We should like to see our national home of Grand Opera secured on a less sporting basis.[19]

For three years after Rankl resigned there was no Musical Director at Covent Garden. An approach was made to Sir John Barbirolli who was too heavily committed to the Hallé Orchestra to accept a full-time appointment.[¶] He was willing to conduct, however, and in the seasons 1952–3 and 1953–4 he conducted performances of *Aida, La Bohème, Orphée* (with Dunne, Leigh and Ferrier), *Tristan* (with Fisher and Shaddock) *Turandot* and *Madam Butterfly*. Kleiber continued for two seasons as principal conductor and gave performances of *Le nozze di Figaro, Der Rosenkavalier,*

¶ According to Harold Rosenthal, there was also 'a certain amount of opposition in official circles', presumably Covent Garden official circles. *[Opera at Covent Garden*, p. 261.]

Tristan and *Wozzeck*. In 1953–4, Rudolf Kempe conducted performances of *Der Rosenkavalier* and in 1953 of *Elektra*.

The high spot of these performances was the first production of Alban Berg's *Wozzeck*, an opera which had had its first performance, also under Kleiber, twenty-six years before, and which is described in the *Concise Oxford Dictionary of Opera* as 'among the most powerful and original music dramas of this century . . . expressing in its way Berg's profound compassion for the lowest in humanity'. Rosenthal also says elsewhere that the production of *Wozzeck* 'was one of the greatest achievements of post-war Covent Garden . . . [and] certainly Kleiber's most memorable contribution to post-war opera in London'.[20] *Wozzeck* is extremely gloomy – Martin Cooper described it as 'the illustration of a nightmare'[21]—and not an obvious box office draw, but, with Marko Rothmuller in the tide role and Christel Goltz as Marie, it was treated with respect by the critics, who agreed the production did much credit to Covent Garden. It has been revived eight times, notably with Geraint Evans in the tide role and Marie Collier as Marie.

But in the nation's leading opera house, probably the greatest event of those years was the first performances of Britten's *Billy Budd* conducted by the composer. This opera had a mixed reception, Newman saying that Britten had been ill-served by his librettists – E.M.Forster and Eric Crozier – and that he 'could see no such musical advance . . . as I had hoped for',[22] while the critic of *The Times* wrote two columns of praise for the text of the opera and said:

An anxious lingering, a sense of horror and defeat, has been drawn from the text here and there by a musical imagination which moves among the shadows with a sensibility

147

which sometimes recalls Mahler's; yet this rather uncomfortable impression is not diffused by the plain words sung. These perform the true function of an opera libretto. They build a firm dramatic scaffolding, and then, without ostentation, allow the poetry to flow round firm points of suggestion, so that words and music form the strands of a single web.[23]

Desmond Shawe-Taylor, who felt that the opera fell some way short of success as an integral work of art, nevertheless said that the composer showed 'his old unfailing skill in establishing and sustaining atmosphere—Throughout a long evening, the immediate theatrical effectiveness of *Billy Budd* was never in doubt. . . . The audience was gripped, surprised, stirred; at moments deeply moved.' He also said that no scene quite lacked the impress of genius; 'and one whole act—the second—strikes me as a masterpiece of dramatic veracity going hand in hand with musical beauty'.[24]

On the whole, the opera was recognized immediately as a work of such dramatic and musical worth as would ensure it a place in the repertory of modern opera. Not so, *The Pilgrim's Progress* with music by Vaughan Williams, which failed not so much through the musical score as in dramatic tension, and was considered more suitable for a cathedral than a theatre.

Another important innovation was that of Tchaikovsky's *The Queen of Spades*, with a production by Oliver Messel of which Andrew Porter, in the *Financial Times*, said it looked 'grand and elegant' and that Messel's vividly imagined progress from the realistic to the exaggerated proceeded so cunningly that we might be looking through the eyes of Hermann himself. And he said: 'The central scene was a gripping theatrical experience, chiefly because of the wonderfully telling performance of Edith Coates as the Countess. As she reminisced over the bright, departed days, or mouthed a wordless terror, she held the house breathless.'[25]

Gloriana, to a text by William Plomer after Lytton Strachey's study of *Elizabeth and Essex*, was performed to celebrate the coronation of Queen Elizabeth. Conducted by John Pritchard and with designs by John Piper, it was nevertheless a disaster at its first performance in Her Majesty's presence. The comments of the critics and of those present were extremely bitter and, although the Royal Family sent conventional messages, it was widely rumoured that they thought the story of the ageing Queen inappropriate. At performances by the ENO in 1966 the opera had more success.

The administration of the Opera House continued to give every opportunity to British composers of opera, and to believe in the virtue of singing in English translation with almost as much fervour as before. Yet this policy now became considerably dented in practice. The attempt to sing the *Ring* in English had been abandoned, the explanation, according to Philip Hope-Wallace, being 'that it is far more tiring to sing Wagner in another language, since only with his consonants can the singers get the purchase on the notes they require.'[26] Even more important, leading European singers showed themselves unwilling to learn English translations in order to sing them a few times at Covent Garden. Even Schwarzkopf, when she sang the Countess instead of Susanna in *Le nozzi di Figaro*, would not learn the new role in English. Victoria de los Angeles sang Manon, Elsa and Mimi in 1950–1, each in the original language, and Philip Hope-Wallace, who said she sang 'with warmth, a natural . . . legato and great musical interest filling every phrase' thought that she made nonsense of the whole policy of singing in English at Covent Garden.

Then in 1952 the great Callas appeared in *Norma*.** The house could have been sold several times over, and on that night people stood all along Bow Street offering money in the hope of buying seats off the lucky ones. Callas was recognized as an extraordinarily gifted singer, vocally and temperamentally, but critics were still uncertain how to evaluate a performance with so much to praise and yet such obvious faults. Richard Capell said that she did not pass the great test, namely the cavatina 'Casta Diva', where the flaws were 'a broken, aspirated performance of the *gruppetti* at the beginning of the melody' and later on an occasional loss of roundness 'not to say shrillness' on high notes.[27]

Since there would be a continuing difficulty in assessing the genius of a singer generally thought the greatest performer of her age, Desmond Shawe-Taylor's review of her performance at a revival of *Norma* five years later is interesting here:

> And when at last the Druid princess made her majestic entry, all was instantly explained; let cynics say what they would, this was something far above the world of publicity and ballyhoo; it was a glimpse, in our day almost unique, of what is meant by the grand manner. Mme Callas . . . is now immeasurably more noble and poetic than before. Gone is the slight suggestion of an athletic campus girl with

---

** This performance of *Norma* was conducted by John Pritchard, admitted by everyone to be one of the English operatic finds of the day. Schooled by Fritz Busch at Glyndebourne, where he has since conducted regularly, he conducted first at Covent Garden in 1952 and has appeared there regularly since.

purposeful stride and brawnily folded arms; gone, too . . .
several stone –so we are authoritatively told – of superflu-
ous flesh. What we see now is a classical heroine lithe as a
ballerina, with arched brows, burning eyes and a somewhat Oriental profile, such as might be found on a Greek
coin or a Minoan fresco. . . . The role of Norma calls for an
immense range of emotions—imperious, tender, amorous,
scornful, pitiful, exalted; all these she composed into a
portrait of harmonious beauty and theatrical force. Also
she can sing.

Shawe-Taylor admitted that here controversy began, and, to the
question how good is her singing:

Sour, uneven, unsteady, says one faction; shapely, grand,
classical, says the other—Absurd as it may seem to admit it,
both are right. The man who thinks Mme Callas a perfect
vocalist has no ear; the man who fails to see that she is one
of the supreme artists of our day has no taste; I find myself
equally impatient with both.[28]

Kleiber did not return to London after the 1953/4 season.
From the beginning his fees had been higher than Covent
Garden could properly afford to pay (originally £150 a performance, they had been increased to £250, and in 1953 the Board
refused to add to this a further £150 a week.) However, although
his biographer says that money was the outward difficulty, he
goes on to say:

I don't myself feel that money was the real obstacle: I think
that it was that he didn't sense at Covent Garden what he

had sensed at the Berlin Staatsoper and the Teatro Colon (Buenos Aires) – the determination to put art first, *at whatever cost*, and with no sidebets on friendship or social position, or safety of one kind or another.[29]

In October 1954 it was announced that the Czech conductor, Rafael Kube-lik, had been appointed Musical Director at Covent Garden, the appointment to take effect from October 1955.

Two other appointments were made in the early fifties, both to a sphere more often than not ignored in discussion of the artistic standards of state-aided theatres. The Earl of Harewood was appointed to the Board of Covent Garden in 1951, and the Viscount Moore, son of the Earl of Drogheda, in 1954. Both appointments were of surprising importance to the future of British opera.

9

1954–1958
Rafael Kubelik

Lord Harewood is not an instrumentalist but music is so central a part of his life that, although classed as an amateur when he joined the Board at Covent Garden, his knowledge and experience of opera were probably greater than that of anyone on the administrative staff. It is said that as a prisoner of war he read right through *Groves' Dictionary of Music,* and he certainly revised and edited a new edition of Kobbé. His first wife, Marion Stein, came from a family of musicians and had, so he tells us, 'a real talent for travel'.[1] When they were first married most of the travelling the Hare-woods did took them to the opera houses of Europe, and by the time Lord Harewood joined the Board at Covent Garden, his knowledge of individual singers, conductors and producers was at professional standard.

Webster met Lord Harewood while he was still in Liverpool, and it was he who suggested him for the Board. Lord Harewood's emotional commitment to any cause he personally supports is equal to his commitment to music, and Webster must have recognized him as potentially a valuable ally. His term on the Board lasted only two years, after which he accepted an appointment to the staff of Covent Garden, but from the time he joined the Board he wrote long letters to Webster from his travels, describing the work of leading European conductors, producers and singers, and he continued to write these even after he left to go to Edinburgh in i960. In one he described a young soprano as 'absolutely third-rate as Amelia, shrill and skating over the difficulties . . . ugly, fat and uninvolved in the drama'. In the margin of this letter there is the note We have just engaged her.'[2]

Lord Harewood has told us that he was asked to go on the staff of Covent Garden in a kind of general capacity and to find his own level. Although he received the tide Controller of Opera Planning only in his last year at Covent Garden, he was directly concerned with this aspect of the work from the beginning. Lord Drogheda, who was on the Board during the whole of this time and chairman for the last few years, says:

> It was certainly true that he [Harewood] played a more important part in the operatic side of the work of Covent Garden than any other single individual. He established links with several of the leading conductors, notably Klemperer, Giulini and Kempe. . . . There is little doubt that David Webster leant on him heavily, although not always giving credit where it was due.[3]

In his own memoirs Lord Harewood makes plain his attachment to the policy of singing in the vernacular and of the ensemble as a basis for an opera company. 'The possibility of an

154

alternative system did not occur to any of us', he wrote, 'although it was assumed that the existence of an ensemble did not at all preclude guests from being invited from time to time to take part in performances.' And: 'I have always believed in an ensemble as the basis for opera, in other words in a company.'[4]

The appointment of Lord Harewood to the staff probably contributed to the debacle of the relationship between Webster and Steuart Wilson, one of Wilson's complaints being that he had not been informed of this until after it had been made, while he must have seen Harewood as a probable rival. In any case, a powerful antipathy had already developed between himself and Webster, partly because Wilson felt himself more suitable to be General Administrator than the occupant of the post. 'He wanted my job', Webster said.[5] Soon after his appointment as deputy general administrator, Wilson saw Lord Waverley and made criticisms of the running of the opera house, and two years later he circulated a highly critical memorandum to members of the Board. All copies of this memorandum are said to have been destroyed but it is known to have contained complaints about a homosexual ring which allegedly held power in the Opera House. Lord Waverley ruled that it would not be proper for Wilson to appear before the Board to discuss the administration, although he was prepared to see him himself. The upshot was that in April 1955 Wilson left on salary four months before his appointment naturally terminated.

The choice of his successor was to be even more important to the future of Covent Garden than that of Lord Harewood. Eric Cundell, head of the Guildhall School of Music, suggested that his assistant, John Tooley, might be a suitable replacement and, after both David Webster and Lord Drogheda had interviewed him and reported favourably, he was appointed – 'Not', Lord

155

Drogheda says in his memoirs, 'be it noted, as assistant general administrator, but as assistant *to* the general administrator.'[6]

Although to some extent achieved by the engagement of foreigners at the expense of the proclaimed policy, the fact of several genuine successes had reduced tension. Most encouraging of all at this time was that, however inappropriate for singing, English is the first or second language of half the world, and it was therefore natural for young dancers and singers from the Commonwealth, seeking a career, to come to London. In addition to Amy Shuard and Josephine Veasey (both English), Covent Garden's young singers included Elsie Morison, Marie Collier and Joan Sutherland, all Australian, while Geraint Evans (Welsh) and Michael Langdon were now joined by the Canadian Jon Vickers. Vickers is claimed as 'a Webster discovery', but, a world star of the first quality, it was really a question of who had the luck to get him first. In the very week he was engaged at Covent Garden, he received several other invitations.

The General Administrator had never lacked confidence, but he gained now in geniality and charm and began to impose himself upon the public. When dealing with members of the Board or anyone except his own employees, Webster played his cards very close to his chest, but in the Opera House there had grown up a team he felt he could trust. This included both Muriel Kerr (his secretary) and John Tooley (his new assistant), Morris Smith (the orchestral manager), Edward Downes (the young and successful conductor) and Lord Harewood. The latter wrote:

> David Webster himself was a remarkable chief to work for, easy to criticize because he wore his faults on his sleeve, more difficult to praise as his greatest virtues were plainly visible only to those who worked with him. . . . Scrupulously

156

loyal to his subordinates, he had little trouble in inspiring a reciprocal loyalty, even devotion – rare emotion! – inside the company.[7]

Among the musical events of the mid-fifties were the first performances of *The Bartered Bride*, conducted by Kubelik before he actually took over as Musical Director, a new *Ring* and the first production in England of William Walton's *Troilus and Cressida*. *The Bartered Bride* received a mixed reception, being thought more suitable for Sadler's Wells Theatre and promoting a further discussion of the whole question of duplication between the two opera houses. Nor was it immediately popular with the public. The new *Ring*, conducted in its second season by Rudolf Kempe and with an international cast of singers, was received with joy.[*] Andrew Porter wrote after the performance of *Das Rheingold:*

> The *Ring* is the most important production an opera house can undertake and Covent Garden has assembled a cast which could scarcely be paralleled outside Bayreuth. Hans Hotter's Wotan, perhaps the noblest and most affecting performance in the theatre today, needs no further superlatives at this date. He was in majestic voice.

He went on to praise the Fricka – Maria von Ilosvay – Otakar Kraus's Alberich and Peter Klein's Mime. 'Eric Witte's impersonation of the fastidious, sophisticated intellectual [Loge] is a

---

[*] The new production of the *Ring* produced by Rudolf Hartmann and conducted by Fritz Stiedry with sets by Leslie Hurry had been given first in 1954.

brilliant tour de force and brilliantly sung.' The rest of the cast all maintained 'this international level'.[8] There was little disagreement with this view. Philip Hope-Wallace summed up the general opinion when he wrote: 'Incontestably the finest performance *of Das Rheingold* we have heard since the war.'[9]

Enthusiasm was maintained throughout the cycle. The level of acting as well as of singing was high and the production by Dr Hartmann and the lighting 'admirably clear and convincing'. Andrew Porter quoted Richard Strauss as saying that 'many of the inexhaustible riches of the score are lost at Bayreuth. . . . On the whole I am more in favour of the old Italian theatre', and went on 'in such a theatre Mr Kempe has been giving us performances of chamber-music subtlety.' Shawe-Taylor said that although the main credit for the success of the performance belonged to Rudolf Kempe, the Wagnerian tenor was a 'far rarer animal' than the Wagnerian conductor. He doubted if a more satisfying Seigfried than Wolfgang Windgassen had been heard since the war, 'which means, in effect, since Lauritz Melchior'.[10] Ernest Newman devoted several articles to it, in one of which he said: 'In a word, the greatest musical-dramatic work of all time is on one side of the footlights being performed, and on the other apprehended, as it really is, a work in which the musical and dramatic elements are simply two facets of the one great edifice of thought.'[11]

To set against these performances, sung in German and mostly by German singers, 1954/5 saw the performance of *Troilus and Cressida* and 1955 the first performance of Michael Tippett's *Midsummer Marriage*.[†] Lord Harewood has told us that

---

[†] *Troilus and Cressida* was conducted by Malcolm Sargent with designs by Hugh Casson and *Midsummer Marriage,* conducted by John Pritchard had designs by Barbara Hepworth.

in the opera house sides were taken by the staff producing these operas, some preferring one, some the other.

> The works could not have been in greater contrast, Walton's is the operatic equivalent of a 'well-made play', modelled carefully on what he personally liked best in the operas he knew well; Tippett's a long occasionally sprawling compendium of the many philosophical ideas and trends which he found appealing at that time.

However, he goes on to say:

> Looking back, I am quite sure that *Midsummer Marriage* is the masterpiece we then sensed it to be, a work for all time. But a subsequent revival of *Troilus* has convinced me that this too is a rewarding work, on any terms a successful opera, and a bit unlucky perhaps in its initial timing in that it was born under what amounted to a low-brow star.[12]

Neither opera has achieved sufficient popularity with the public to be given regular performance at Covent Garden.

One may wonder whether the management at Covent Garden could have survived the desolating reception given the Opera Company for the first ten years of its existence without the exertions of the Ballet Company. The contrast between the two companies was extreme – the one achieving not merely profits from its foreign tours but a cultural prestige hardly ever equalled by a British company, while the other made one forlorn attempt after another to achieve standards worthy of the great theatre which sheltered both. Yet as Lord Drogheda wrote:

159

Despite the valuable, indeed vital part played by the ballet in the affairs of Covent Garden, the members of the Company always had the feeling that they were being treated like poor relations. They believed that without their exertions Covent Garden's state would be extremely parlous. And yet when it came to the use of the orchestra and the stage for rehearsals, consideration of their needs always came second.[13]

Lord Harewood, now responsible for the planning, says that Webster believed that the ballet, which did not rely on guest artists, was more flexible than the opera, while ballet required less scenery and could rehearse in a studio of appropriate size – 'or so David led me to believe, and so I still think in essence it was.'[14] The doubtful tone of these remarks is partly explained by Lord Harewood's statement that, because Webster would not delegate authority to him, he had no direct contact with de Valois.‡ Yet he also says that, although everything possible was done to change plans which did not suit the ballet, there were times when this was impossible. Difficulties of this kind are inevitable in a theatre housing both opera and ballet, but it may have been exacdy because the ballet could be trusted to enhance the prestige of the house that Webster's ambitions were more closely bound to the Opera Company. His biographer tells us again and again that he regarded the great theatre, with its long tradition, as 'his' theatre and the Opera Company as 'his' opera. By no stretch of the imagination could he have

___

‡ See p. 99 for Webster's own view of his power to delegate. He seems to have delegated jobs but not authority.

regarded de Valois' company as 'his' Ballet.

The mid-fifties was in fact a time of change and progress for the ballet companies. During the first ten years of its life the company now known as the Sadler's Wells Theatre Ballet had thrived almost as strongly as that of Covent Garden. Several of the classics had been added to its repertory, notably *Les Sylphides* and *Le Spectre de la rose,* and later *Swan Lake,* while it had acted as a nursery for young choreographers and had successfully performed new ballets, the most successful being *La Fête étrange* by Andrée Howard (based on *Le Grand Meaulnes* by Alain Fournier) and *Pineapple Poll* by John Cranko, both of which went into the repertory at Covent Garden.§ Dancers included Kenneth MacMillan and (still in the *corps de ballet)* Lynn Seymour and Donald MacLeary.

The Sadler's Wells Company had spent much of its time on tour while, because of its size and its other commitments, touring had become progressively more difficult for the company at Covent Garden. In 1955 Peggy van Praagh resigned from the directorship of the Sadler's Wells Theatre Company and was succeeded by John Field, while Kenneth MacMillan took over from Cranko as chief choreographer. It was then decided to change the tide of the second company which became the Touring Company and to set up a special new group to appear with the singers at Sadler's Wells. Peter Wright came from the Ballet Joos to run this company.

Alexander Bland has already given a full description of what happened next. He says the first tour under John Field's

---

§ *La Fête étrange* was designed by Sophie Fedorovitch, *Pineapple Poll* by Osbert Lancaster.

direction was extremely successful and the company very well received when it appeared at the Santander Festival in Spain, giving *Giselle* with Nadia Nerina as guest artist. Then he goes on:

> But complications – indeed disaster – threatened. . . . Funds, as usual, were alarmingly low . . . [and] early in 1956 Sadler's Wells, which was going through a financial crisis, decided that it could no longer afford to maintain the Ballet Company, which was losing £6,000 a year. Covent Garden acted immediately. 'Come back to us and bring all your dancers with you', Webster telephoned to Field. 'I don't know how we'll raise the money; but let's try.'[15]

There was no difficulty in raising the money, because the Arts Council, anxious that the Touring Company should remain in being, agreed that Covent Garden should be recompensed for any additional financial burden.

The financial crisis at Sadler's Wells also precipitated changes at the ballet school. With Arnold Haskell as Director, it had begun at Talgarth Road in 1947 with fifty-five girls between the ages of ten and eighteen, and had received its first boys a year later; then grown rapidly, with many students entering from overseas as well as from all over Britain. In 1953 the governors of Sadler's Wells could no longer bear the expenses of this school, and indeed were seriously embarrassed because of the large capital tied up in its buildings. It had also become evident, in the words of Ninette de Valois, that in order to receive and develop the maximum talent a scheme of expansion was urgent. The major problems were that since Talgarth Road was not a boarding school, only children whose homes were in London were adequately housed, and it was impossible even to tap the talent in the Midlands, the North or the Dominions. In addition, because the existing staff could have dealt with more than the number of children for which there was room 'expenses mount while income from fees remains stationary'. There were no resting facilities nor proper provision of meals for the senior students, who also had to attend rehearsals outside the building, and who often left their homes at nine in the morning and did not return until midnight. For all these reasons, Ninette de Valois suggested to the Board at Covent Garden that a large coeducational boarding school should be opened as a junior school. This should be within twenty-five miles of London and capable of taking up to a hundred boarders and fifty day boarders.

The house finally acquired for this purpose was White Lodge, the Royal Hunting Lodge in Richmond Park, built for George I and subsequently lived in by various members of the Royal Family, the last of whom were King George vi and Queen Elizabeth when Duke and Duchess of York.¶ The aim at White Lodge was, and still is, to provide a balanced education with ballet as an important but not a dominant part. In the upper school ballet dominates but the prime academic objective is to provide as wide a range of skills and qualifications as possible as a precaution against inability for any reason to continue as a

---

¶ A lease was acquired from the Commissioners of Crown Lands and the necessary initial capital of about £60,000 was borrowed and refunded by the Arts Council over a period of years. The schools were eligible for grants to pupils from local educational authorities, and it was assumed that both branches would be self-supporting for revenue. The Arts Council urged the Covent Garden Board 'to make available to the School some part of the profits on any future tour of America by the Sadler's Wells Ballet' (Arts Council Minutes of 55th General Meeting, 13 October 1954).

dancer. Music and languages are very important in both schools.

Each year the directors of the two companies select students to form a graduate class from which any vacancies can be filled. Thus they ensure first choice although there is a wide demand from other companies. In this way style is maintained. 'Even an untrained eye can spot at once the uniformity of style which no amount of rigid drilling can replace – timing, the angle of the head, the emphasis in a dance-phrase, the line of arms and legs. This is the seamless material from which individual artistry can be shaped and cut.'[16]

The value of the new arrangement was immediately apparent. Moira Shearer had left the company as also had Beryl Grey, and in 1956 Violetta Elvin (the Russian-born dancer) retired. Their places were easily filled by dancers from the second company or from the schools. Svetlana Beriosova and Nadia Nerina (both from Sadler's Wells) had previously joined the Covent Garden Company and these were now followed by a proliferation of marvellous young ballerinas from the schools – Annette Page, Anya Linden and Merle Park, Doreen Wells and Lynn Seymour (whose careers initially lay with the Touring Company) and later, Antoinette Sibley. Dancers such as Helpmann, Harold Turner and Alexis Rassine had all gone, but for the first time a strong contingent of male dancers was ready to take their place – Alexander Grant, David Blair, Graham Usher and Ronald Hynd.

By 1955 a change of title for the Ballet Companies and School was felt necessary, both in the interests of identity in the public mind and in recognition that the companies had achieved the status of British National Ballet in all but name. In addition de Valois was disturbed that the financial grants on which her Companies depended were tied to the theatres on which they were based, and she wished to 'ensure [their] continuity what-ever conditions may prevail'.[17] She wished also to separate its interests from those of the opera. For all these reasons Lord Waverley applied for the grant of a Royal Charter. When this honour was granted on 15 January 1957, HRH Princess Margaret had already agreed to become President of the Companies in 1956. The title 'Royal' applied to both companies and the ballet school, which became accordingly The Royal Ballet, the Royal Ballet Touring Company and the Royal Ballet School.

One cannot leave, however temporarily, the subject of ballet without mention of the visit to Covent Garden in 1956 of the Bolshoi Ballet Company, led by Galina Ulanova, one of the greatest dancers of all time. Lord Drogheda, who describes the productions as dated in style and unimaginative, says, however, that 'the technical skills displayed, the poetry of movement revealed by the pure classical dancing, the strength and virility of the men of the company, were a revelation to the ballet-going public and acted as a tremendous challenge and stimulus to our own dancers'. This visit also had the welcome effect of making a contribution to the finances of Covent Garden for the year 1956/7.

Otello, sung in Italian, with Ramon Vinay in the leading role, was the first opera conducted by Kubelik when he took over as Musical Director. Although remembered now chiefly for the fact that, because Tito Gobbi was late for rehearsals, Kubelik cancelled his contract and substituted Otakar Kraus as Iago, this was a fine performance. Lord Harewood speaks of 'an incomparable assumption of one of the greatest roles' by Vinay, and Gré Brouwenstijn was a notable Desdemona. A new production of *Aida* was also sung in Italian.

Yet Kubelik believed implicitly in the policy of opera in the vernacular and had little use for stars, whom he said 'come and go and have no idea of real artistic co-operation'.[18] According to Lord Harewood, in his first production of *Otello* he 'caused virtually a change of mind in public and critics about the possibilities of the young company. Admittedly we had Ramon Vinay and Gré Brouwenstijn as guests, but the remainder of the cast was from the ensemble, and the results were very good indeed.'[19]

Yet if, as Lord Harewood says, the performance caused a change of mind in the critics, this was not apparent. Indeed Kubelik's period is often remembered as the occasion of the most bitter of all press attacks on the administration and the standards of Covent Garden. In spite of the success of the 'special' operas, dissatisfaction with the run-of-the-mill performances was still strongly felt, and it came to the surface in 1956 after the publication of a report on the first ten years of the administration – a report which was followed by a press conference and was a prelude to the publication of regular annual reports.

Lord Drogheda, who was on the Board at the time, had supported Professor Lionel Robbins – also on the Board – in urging on Lord Waverley that Covent Garden had a duty to produce an annual account of its activities. He nevertheless speaks of the ten-year report as 'a somewhat inadequate self-laudatory document covering in a slightly smug way the ten years from 1946 until 1956, glossing rather ludicrously over the various failures and mistakes'. Even so, since several of the recent performances had been received with so much pleasure, an adverse reception might have been avoided but for some remarks of the Chairman. Lord Waverley's loyalty to the administration

166

was insufficiently tempered by any just appreciation of the operatic standards for which it was responsible. At the press conference presenting the report, he said: 'If we play our part and do everything to secure economies, and if in the end the Government find it impossible to provide what we think necessary and that is their last word, then we shall shut down'. And, speaking of the public, he said: 'If they want what we provide, they must be prepared to pay for it.'

These remarks proved rash. They were answered first by Martin Cooper in a long article in the *Daily Telegraph*, in which he explained that no opera public anywhere in the world had ever paid for its opera and that the Arts Council grant to Covent Garden 'looks small beside the subsidies granted to established opera-houses in other countries'. Then he went on: 'The second point to remember is this: if, despite the smaller subsidy, seats at Covent Garden cost less than corresponding seats in foreign opera-houses and are still not bought in sufficient numbers, it is possible that the public are not being given what they want. They may even be right.'

Cooper explained that the vast stage at Covent Garden would intimidate even the greatest artists, and then said that in the past ten years singers with little or no operatic experience and 'with the characteristically small, drawing-room type of voice (produced by our climate, our singing teachers, our food, our plumbing, or whatever it may be) [had been asked] to walk in boldly where giants of another age feared to tread'. The critic here touched on two themes given much airing by writers of the time – the small, light quality of English voices and the unsuitability of Covent Garden Theatre as an opera house because of its size. Then, having said that, because the routine performances by our native singers were not good enough, the management

167

had to indulge in lavish or eccentric productions 'in the hope of making up in inessentials the indubitable inferiority of the main product', he went on to suggest that, since Covent Garden was too big and Sadler's Wells too badly placed, and since the two companies were 'solemnly cutting each other's throats each with a Government subsidy too small to be really effective', they would be better amalgamated in some theatre in central London, like the Stoll or the Palace.[20]

Martin Cooper wrote later that he had received many letters supporting his view, but the press response was predictably led by Sir Thomas Beecham. Sir Thomas had a particular interest since he was more or less the inventor of the theme that the voices of British singers, however delightful, were unlike those of other nations and lacking in power and brilliance. 'Really robust tenors and true dramatic sopranos hardly exist among us', he had said, 'and high baritones are as rare as a perfect summer.' Launching into the fray and quoting from himself to prove his right to command attention, he remarked that 'Anyone who has not got ass's ears on his head knows well that we have few singers . . . who can even begin to hold their own against those of the Continent or the United States.' He supported Martin Cooper on the unsuitability of Covent Garden as an opera house, and said it should be rated as 'a public monument' where two seasons of only one month's duration should be given each year.[21] This and much more besides was routine stuff for Sir Thomas, and might have done no more than routine damage had not Kubelik himself chosen to answer him. In a letter to *The Times* the conductor defended both British singers and the Opera House.

I think it is not true that the Briton has a small voice in comparison with the Continental: what is true is that the

168

Continental has no inferiority complex and almost no inhibitions – that is why he projects his roles better. . . . After all it is the projection, the focus, and the resonance of a voice, rather than its size, which really carry acoustically. Nobody can deny that Covent Garden Opera House as it is now has favourable acoustics in every respect. We should all strive for a British national opera, supported by the critics who must ignore the snobs and instead fight for communion between the British public and British composers and singers.

Critics should not, he said, condescendingly dismiss their artists with two or three lines of criticism 'but ought to help them to build a British opera which could compete with the best houses in Europe'. This would never be possible by asking for a *stagione* style – a few singers gathered together with almost no rehearsal for *ad hoc* performances. The finest ensemble must consist of high-class singers, confident in their own ability as soloists. He added that to achieve this would be his work at Covent Garden.[22]

A large number of letters giving every point of view followed this, the longest and most impassioned being once more from Beecham. After recapitulating, not always accurately, his own experience in opera, he said that he had found that the disabilities of British singers could be overcome by appreciation of the strong as well as the weak points of our language, and that this should be the prime task of anyone taking charge of the 'English side of opera'. Then he went on:

But how did the management of our national institution set about this task? In defiance of all common sense they engaged as Musical Director a foreigner, and let him loose upon the unhappy creatures who had been led to expect beneficial results from this monumental stroke of stupidity. . . .

Now we have another foreigner in charge. But does he possess any of the qualifications essential for the creation of a truly national organization. . . . The dignity of our nation is today at stake and we are presenting a sorry spectacle to the outside world.[23]

Kubelik, in the words of Lord Drogheda 'not knowing what Beecham could be like', immediately wrote two letters, one to Lord Waverley and one to *The Times*. The first read as follows:

Through the recent attacks on the policy of the administration of Covent Garden I learned that my status as a foreigner might be regarded as a handicap to creating a British national opera. Feeling that my person could be a serious obstacle to the successful achievement of this noble goal I prefer to resign as musical director as from the beginning of the coming season.

I can assure you that it is my love for the work I have started at Covent Garden which brought me to this decision. I admire British musicians and their friends in administration who are striving for a better future in the opera field in Great Britain. I hope that sooner or later they will unanimously find a way to work together with goodwill towards new operatic horizons which some other nations have already attained.

My sincerest wishes are with them and also my gratitude to all who gave me the privilege of working with them for a short period on the same lines.[24]

Lord Drogheda tells us that he was dispatched with all haste to prevail on Kubelik not to send a similar letter to *The Times,* and an urgent Board meeting was summoned for the following afternoon. When Kubelik arrived Lord Waverley read him a draft of the following letter which he proposed himself to send to *The Times:*

My colleagues and I on the board of the Royal Opera House, Covent Garden, think it right that the public should know that, after reading the strictures contained in the letter from Sir Thomas Beecham, published in *The Times* yesterday, Mr Rafael Kubelik formally tendered his resignation on the ground that it appeared that his status as a foreigner might be regarded as an obstacle to the development of a British national opera.

The board have informed Mr Kubelik that they are unwilling to accept his resignation. They have assured him that he has their entire confidence and that he can rely on their unstinted support in pursuit of the policy he has outlined during his tenure of his present office.[25]

It is said that when Kubelik heard the terms of this letter he cried 'It is finished', and embraced Lord Waverley.

The controversy in the press did not immediately die down. Sir Steuart Wilson took the opportunity to write to the *Daily Telegraph* demanding statements about the powers of the General Administrator, the constitution of the Board of Directors and the system of engaging artists at the Opera House. This demand was backed by a leader in the *Daily Telegraph* on the grounds that the Opera House was 'a national institution of international fame, receiving a Government grant of £270,000."John Christie

171

also wrote stressing the need for British singers to be inspired by foreign artists. Finally the whole unhappy episode was given some grace by Desmond Shawe-Taylor in an article in the *New Statesman*. This began: 'The future of Covent Garden, that hardy annual of British controversy, has blossomed splendidly this summer', but went on to say that the comedy had turned over-night, if not into tragedy at least 'to something unforeseen and most unwelcome'. 'What does seem a little odd', he went on

and more than a little unfortunate, is the choice of this particular moment to propose sweeping votes of no confi-dence. . . . No one, I hope, will accuse me of being a blind partisan of Covent Garden. In its early post-war days I made no secret in these columns of my conviction that the operatic side of its work was in the wrong hands: the singers ill-chosen, the orchestra rough, the stage designs outland-ish, the productions absurd. But since those days there has been an immeasurable improvement; during the four years interregnum (1951–55), when Covent Garden had no Musical Director, the frequent presence of absolutely front-rank conductors, such as the late Erich Kleiber, Clemens Krauss and Issay Dobrowen, and more recently Rudolf Kempe, has transformed the musical scene out of recogni-tion; while the staging of the operas has simultaneously shown a steady advance. . . . That the Italian wing of the repertory lags behind the German is not to be denied; but might we not at least wait a year or so with our denuncia-tions and our radical projects in order to see how things are going to shape under the theatre's new Musical Director.

Shawe-Taylor also argued that Covent Garden was smaller than either La Scala or the Metropolitan, 'and smaller than Drury Lane. . . . What counts . . . is not mere brute volume, but firmness and purity of tone. . . . Think of Elizabeth Schumann . . . think of Joan Cross or Maggie Teyte or Lisa Perli.'[26]

In 1957 one further attempt was made to ensure closer collaboration, even amalgamation, between Covent Garden and Sadler's Wells. This was precipitated by a resolution of the directors of the Sadler's Wells Trust that:

> In view of the fact that the grant of £142,000 offered by the Arts Council falls short by some £25,000 of the minimum considered necessary by the Directors to carry on their work in accordance with the policy which they have hitherto followed, and that to carry on at a reduced level would involve a new policy and ultimately lower standards, the Trust recommend to the Governors that they should make some other arrangements to run opera and ballet at Sadler's Wells Theatre.

In a paper circulated by the Arts Council containing this information, it was stated that none of those concerned with the provision of opera and ballet in London was satisfied with the present position. The two theatres received, year by year, subsidies insufficient to carry out their policies, and both had accumulated serious deficits; the Arts Council, although devoting more than one-half of its total grant-expenditure to the two theatres, was nevertheless apprehensive about the financial security of both, while the Treasury had warned that the situation must not be allowed to drift.

In response to this situation, the Arts Council set up a committee to consider plans to secure 'the fullest integration of Covent

173

Garden and Sadler's Wells'.** A report by Professor Robbins and Mr Lund to the Board of Covent Garden suggested that any savings by amalgamation would be uncertain and not very big, and in October of that year the Arts Council dropped the scheme in favour of a proposed fusion between Sadler's Wells and the Carl Rosa Opera. This merger also fell through, although after the Arts Council had decided to withdraw all its grant from the Carl Rosa, a company called Touring Opera 1958 was formed and administered by Sadler's Wells under the direction of Professor Humphrey Procter-Gregg.††

When Kubelik's contract came to an end in 1958 he refused to renew it. He had, it is believed, been deeply wounded by the bitterness of the press attacks in 1956, and in spite of the glowing tributes he received in his last two years, he could not forget that. During his period at Covent Garden he did much

---

** An amalgamation of operatic resources was an idea much supported by the critics. Andrew Porter, writing in *Music and Musicians,* June 1958, said: 'But surely the time has come to pool resources – the money and the singers. Mr Webster as an administrator, Mr Tucker as artistic director, should be able to devise a grand operatic plan for the country, using Covent Garden, Sadler's Wells and the provinces to best advantage.' And Peter Heyworth, more hostile, said: 'If it can only offer what it now provides then the question must be faced of whether we can afford to keep Covent Garden open, for at present the operatic scene resembles a grand dining-room in a house where the larder is bare, the kitchen ill-equipped and the cook and butler absent'. *(Observer,* 23 March 1958.)

†† Touring Opera 1958 had only two seasons after which its demise was caused by lack of funds. It nevertheless achieved a good standard and gave opportunities to young singers from both Covent Garden and Sadler's Wells.

to bring on young English singers – Amy Shuard, Joan Sutherland, Elsie Morison (whom he subsequently married), Joan Carlyle, Jon Vickers, and Josephine Veasey, while he engaged Marie Collier. He was Musical Director when new productions of two operas were given the fame of which rings through the years, like the fame of *Der Rosenkavalier* in the days of Lotte Lehmann. *The Trojans* by Hector Berlioz and *Don Carlos* by Verdi have in common that both are operas which previously had been thought unsatisfactory for stage productions – indeed *The Trojans* had never been performed except heavily cut, in amateur stagings, or in concert versions. At Covent Garden *The Trojans* was sung in English by the resident company with the addition only of the American mezzo, Blanche Thebom, as Dido. *Don Carlos* (given for the centenary celebrations of the opening of the present theatre) was performed by an international all-star cast, with only one principal, Jon Vickers, from the resident company.

The Berlioz opera, produced by John Gielgud with scenery and costumes by Mariano Andreu and conducted by Kubelik, was received ecstatically by the critics. No former production and nothing written about *The Trojans* had prepared them for the great masterpiece revealed at Covent Garden. 'Today is a red-letter night in the history of British operatic effort', Philip Hope-Wallace wrote, 'and a milestone in musical history.'[27] Martin Cooper remarked that one of music's bad debts, outstanding for a century, had been handsomely paid off by the performance at Covent Garden which was 'worthy in scale, in musical quality and visual magnificence.'[28] And Peter Heyworth wrote' *The Trojans* is indeed a triumph for the whole company and for Rafael Kubelik both as conductor and as musical director'.[29] Andrew Porter said:

It is a sumptuous and splendid and glorious experience and Mr Kubelik and his colleagues at the Royal Opera House win our heart-felt gratitude for the boldness and faith – and skill – which have ensured this triumph. . . . The orchestral playing throughout was flawlessly beautiful. The scenes, the acts and the whole opera were shaped in the conviction – which all who were present must now share – that *The Trojans* is a magnificently constructed entity. Covent Garden had the right tenor for the heroic role of Aeneas: Jon Vickers. He looked magnificent, and sang finely both the stirring and the lyrical music. Amy Shuard was a splendid Cassandra, dark-toned, tragic and noble. Blanche Thebom, the Metropolitan mezzo, gave a strikingly sensitive performance as Dido, for she conveyed both the regal dignity of the young empress and the passionate heart of the woman. Her music covers an enormous, expressive range; she went to the heart of each phrase with unerring artistry.[30]

The premiere of *Don Carlos* in 1958, with a production and designs by Luchino Visconti, conducted by Carlo Maria Giulini and with a cast so resplendent as to equal any of the historic performances, was received with no less delight. Peter Heyworth wrote:

The Covent Garden performance of this great work is something we shall talk of for years to come. Planned as a celebration of the theatre's centenary, it is entirely worthy of it. It is not merely the finest thing that the Royal Opera House has provided since the war, but one of the outstanding operatic productions to be seen in Europe today.[31]

And Desmond Shawe-Taylor said it was hard to imagine a more splendid celebration of the centenary:

> We may feel a twinge of sadness that England should have played so small a part in the result, and that of the five principal singers only one, the Canadian tenor, Jon Vickers, should belong to the resident company. But all such patriotic regrets are soon forgotten in the solemn joy of watching one of Verdi's noblest, most difficult and least familiar creations restored to its rightful place. It is even doubtful whether 'restored' is the appropriate word: one may wonder if, among the many distinguished revivals accorded to this opera in Italy, Germany and the United States, Verdi's intentions can ever have been so clearly discerned and so fully realised as by Signor Visconti, Signor Giulini and the present Covent Garden company.[32]

The 'present' company at Covent Garden, included, besides Jon Vickers as Carlos, Boris Christoff as King Philip, Tito Gobbi as Posa, Gré Brouwenstijn as Elisabetta, and Fedora Barbieri as Eboli – singers who, in the age of the gramophone record, need no introduction to opera lovers. They gave a performance which no one who saw it will ever forget. *Don Carlos* was repeated in the following year, when Geraint Evans emerged as a Posa 'who could worthily succeed Tito Gobbi in one of the great Verdi roles'.[33]

10

Administration
1958–1962
Lord Drogheda

On 5 January 1958 Lord Waverley died. He had lived to see the production of *The Trojans* but not that of *Don Carlos*. Lord Drogheda has remarked that the informal method of David Webster's selection in 1946 would later have been unacceptable. 'His lack of previous experience would have ruled against him, and I think it unlikely that he would have been chosen.'[1] Even more improbable was the choice of Lord Waverley to follow Keynes, since, having appointed as General Administrator a man who had never run an opera house, the Covent Garden Trust, backed by the Arts Council, proceeded to elect a Chairman who had never seen an opera.

Many tales are told of Lord Waverley in office, among the best of which was his rebuke to his wife when she made some criticism of a performance. 'Don't crab them Ava, you must

178

remember that they are doing their best.'[2] More important perhaps are the words with which it is said he would bring to an end any attempt by members of the Board to pursue a discussion or criticism of administrative policy. 'I think', he would say on those occasions, 'this is a matter we can safely leave to Mr Webster.'[3]

Lord Drogheda went to Covent Garden originally as secretary to the Board, a post he took over when his predecessor, Denis Rickett, left to become Treasury Representative and Minister Economic at the British Embassy in Washington, and held until he was elected to the Board in 1954. The obvious successor to Waverley in 1958, he had deputized for him during his final illness. As Chairman he had no difficulty in conforming to the stipulation, subsequently laid down by one of his Board, that the first requirement in anyone elected to it should be that music was a central passion in his life. Drogheda was immensely musical and his wife a fine pianist. He was forty-eight when he succeeded Waverley and he already had considerable administrative experience. In the war, after a short period of military service in France, he had been attached to the War Secretariat, and he later served as one of two private secretaries to Oliver Lyttelton at the new Ministry of Production. He had been one of the principals concerned in the negotiations which preceded the merger of the *Financial News* and the *Financial Times,* and, when he became Chairman at Covent Garden, he was Managing Director of the combined newspapers now called the *Financial Times.* Yet, if a good administrator, he succeeded by methods peculiar to himself, which, he himself has best described when speaking of his relationship with Gordon Newton, editor of the *Financial Times.*

As to Gordon and myself, there is no doubt that at first we were quite good at getting on one another's nerves. In this respect I was the active and Gordon the passive agent. I made myself a great nuisance because if I felt a certain line of development was desirable I kept on pressing for action. . . . Gordon once referred to me as his goad, a charge to which I admit. . . . I was very persistent and fortunately we managed far more often than not to see eye to eye.[4]

This then was the goad which now fell upon Webster, and no one who has read both Lord Drogheda's and Lord Harewood's accounts of the period immediately following can believe that the Chairman and the General Administrator also quickly saw eye to eye. Lord Drogheda had shown his mettle earlier when, as chairman of the opera sub-committee, he had resigned, because, after discussion at a meeting of possible designers for *The Trojans*, Webster had appointed Gielgud's choice, Andreu, without further reference to the sub-committee. 'It may well be quite wrong', Drogheda wrote to Waverley, 'for the Directors even to discuss the question of designers etc. but if so I feel that this is a matter which should be quite clearly laid down so that the sub-committee do not waste their time.'[5]

Lord Waverley did not accept this resignation, but he asked Webster for a note on the duties of the Opera and Ballet sub-committees. Predictably this did not satisfy Lord Drogheda, who wrote:

According to it [Webster's note] the Board's decisions on the artistic side are confined to what he terms the deployment of the two companies and to the approval of their repertoires 'more especially new works'. The

180

Sub-Committees he visualises as a convenient medium for exchange of ideas between the Executive and individual members of the Board, but he does not appear to accept that decisions relating to the appointment of conductors, producers, designers, etc. should not be taken by the Executive without reference to the appropriate Sub-Committee.... In my view, if the Opera Sub-Committee is to fulfil its duties satisfactorily, all major decisions relating to the employment of artists should be discussed by the Sub-Committee before action is taken by the Executive. The minutes of the Opera Sub-Committee . . . are always circulated each month in time for the Board's monthly meeting, so that any proposal can be questioned if any member of the Board so wishes. This cannot be so if decisions are taken by the Executive without reference to the Sub-Committee.

He made suggestions for dealing with questions that had to be resolved rapidly, and then went on:

The last thing I wish to suggest is that either Sub-Committee should undertake the functions of the Executive. My only concern is that they should be in a position to discharge the duties which I believe should be laid upon them by the Board, who bear the ultimate responsibility for success or failure.[6]

In this note Lord Drogheda gave full warning of the tactics he was likely to pursue as Chairman, and his first move on taking over this role was to pack the Board – not merely with people whose central passion was music but who could also be trusted to get on with him. Lord Waverley had had a great affection for him and had previously relied on him for ideas, particularly in making appointments to the Board. In 1958 the members were Sir Isaiah Berlin, Sir William Coldstream, Mr Burnet Pavitt, Lord Robbins, and The Hon James Smith. Lord Drogheda proceeded to add three new names. (The process is by election of the Board but the Chairman's choice is seldom rejected.) The first was Dr Thomas Armstrong, representing the world of academic musical life (following the retirement of Edric Cundell), the second Mark Bonham-Carter, the third Jack Donaldson. Of Mark Bon-ham-Carter, an enthusiast for the ballet, Drogheda remarks: 'There were plenty of others who might with justice claim that their knowledge of ballet greatly exceeded Mark's. I wanted him more particularly because of his very acute mind, his sharp astringent wit and because he was a fighter for what he believed in and a splendid debunker of nonsense.' The third, Jack Donaldson, Drogheda describes as a 'tried and trusted friend of almost thirty years standing with complementary tastes and reactions to mine, with whom in 1932 I had started the Quartet Society in London'. He says too 'I knew that he would be a staunch supporter of the cause of Covent Garden' and adds that, when Donaldson became Minister of the Arts in 1976, 'it was indeed a turn up for the book'.[7]

A Board, then, composed of amateurs, one might even say 'snobs'. Yet the advantage, too often overlooked, in appointing amateurs to public Boards is that objectivity of judgement is more likely to be achieved by people whose personal ambitions lie elsewhere. The Board Lord Drogheda appointed followed him through thick and sometimes very thin, not only from personal friendship, but because of his earnest desire to achieve excellence at Covent Garden.

Some understanding of the position which had been reached in 1958 is necessary in order to appreciate the measure of Lord Drogheda's services to opera. To everyone but the most doctrinaire believers in the virtues of singing in English it had by now become obvious that it was not succeeding as a policy for what was traditionally an international opera house. The performances so lavishly praised by the critics in the previous year or so were all of what were called 'special' productions, most of which were sung in the original language, while the run-of-the-mill repertory performances showed little improvement on those of the forties. Thus Harold Rosenthal, after writing of some of the triumphs of Kubelik's reign, said: 'On the other hand there were many evenings best forgotten: the dreary repetitions of *Bohème, Rigoletto, The Magic Flute* and *Carmen*.'[8]

However, the most important reason for the failure of the policy so confidently embarked upon in 1946 was the unwillingness of foreign artists to learn the traditional roles in English, an unwillingness now shared by some of the best of our own singers, since they, too, had to learn the roles afresh it they were to advance on the international stage. Now that most of the cities of the world could be reached in a matter of hours, the policy of singing in the vernacular would soon be abandoned in many of the leading opera houses of Europe as well as in England and America. A determination to adhere to it could lead only to a total lack of that stimulus which John Christie had rightly protested could be achieved only through contact with artists of genius. Finally, although Sadler's Wells had succeeded at much lower prices in establishing a public for opera sung by English singers in English, the Covent Garden public, particularly in the higher-priced seats, showed an obstinate disinclination to fill the house for these performances. Of the 'dreary repetitions' of which Rosenthal speaks in 1957 *La Bohème* averaged 54 per cent of capacity in paid attendances (with a low of 22 per cent), *Rigoletto* 46 per cent (with a low of 31 per cent), *The Magic Flute* 54 per cent (with a low of 33 per cent), *Carmen* 74 per cent (with a low of 45 per cent). Other figures for this time include *Turandot* 66 per cent (with a low of 37 per cent), *Tales of Hoffmann* 53 per cent (with a low of 46 per cent). These are in contrast to *Madam Butterfly* with Los Angeles, Evans and Kempe which averaged 97 per cent (with a low of 93 per cent), *The Trojans* 87 per cent (with a low of 73 per cent), and two performances of *Norma* with Callas which averaged 93 per cent.

These, or reasons approximately these, led the new Chairman and his Board to the conviction that the main plank of the 1946 policy ought to be discarded, an opinion given great impetus by what were, and at the time of writing, still are, known as the Donaldson figures. In his autobiography Ix>rd Harewood says that after *Don Carlos* the cry was for more and more international singers, and goes on: 'David asked me to "cost" the forthcoming season as if we were engaging everyone from outside, as he believed this might convince the Board that the cost of the change of policy would be too great.'[9]

Lord Harewood does not tell us whether he carried out this commission or what, if he did, was the result. Nor does he seem aware that the instruction to him coincided very nearly with a request from a member of the Board for information of the same kind. In consequence of this request, Douglas Lund, the head accountant, prepared a set of figures showing the difference in the average loss on performances of opera and ballet known as 'special' and given at higher prices but with higher costs, and on the ordinary performances, chiefly sung by members of the resident company. These figures, have been issued regularly ever since. In 1960 it was a surprise to everyone that, with very few exceptions., the loss on 'special' performances was considerably less than on the ordinary ones. For instance, the average loss on ordinary performances of *Cavalleria rusticana* and *Pagliacci* was £1,559, whereas special performances of *The Trojans* lost on average only £945; even more marked, ordinary performances of *Elektra* averaged a loss of £2,883, while special performances of *Otello* averaged a loss of only £825.* This pattern was repeated in the figures for ballet, the loss on higher-priced performances with Margot Fonteyn (paid a special fee) being often only about 25 per cent of the ordinary performances without her.

At a meeting of the opera sub-committee on 30 April 1958 Mr Webster argued that matters of principle were involved and put the case for 'repertory' opera. The policy of 1946 was 'to train a *native company* that would base its work on a repertory of foreign opera *in translation* in the hope that if it succeeded in establishing a genuine national style of operatic representation it

---

* When these figures were presented to the Board, Sir Oliver Franks pointed out two dangers in the method. The cost of new productions was charged against the Opera House and therefore shared equally among all operas performed during the year; secondly, no allowance was made for the number of times a production might be repeated. Thus *The Trojans* was unlikely to be performed more than fifty times whereas the cost of *Carmen* might be written off over two hundred. The Board therefore concluded that, although this might be the most satisfactory method of spreading capital cost, the resulting figures ought not to be used to determine whether an opera should be dropped from the repertory. It was proposed that in future the cost of each new production should be included as a footnote to the figures.

would attract native composers and librettists to write for it'. This implied: (1) Some sort of commitment to British artists, and—not entirely unconnected with that – (2) a policy of putting on foreign operas in English.

After discussing these points the sub-committee agreed that it should be the object of policy to reach and maintain the highest possible artistic standards in all performances; and to provide works and performances which would bring the public into the theatre. To the extent that these policies were inconsistent with existing policies and commitments the sub-committee had to consider and recommend to the Board how far these existing policies could be departed from.

In February 1959 the sub-committee put forward a paper called 'Policy for Opera'. The first aim should be to fill the house, and paid admissions of 70 to 75 per cent of capacity should be the target except for prestige operas. The policy of 'Opera in English' should not be discontinued, but there should be no objection to performances in a foreign language if, in the opinion of the administration, these could be given more successfully: 'In other words, where there is a conflict between quality of performance and performance in English, the latter may be sacrificed.'[10] Nevertheless, the greatest possible opportunities should be given for the development of British artists, providing there was no lowering of standards. Prestige operas, especially new British works, should be produced on their artistic merits.

David Webster had been correct in thinking that questions of principle agreed with the Arts Council were involved here, but in a record of a meeting with its Chairman, Sir Kenneth Clark, he is quoted as follows:

Sir Kenneth . . . [said] that . . . an abrupt change from one policy to another would make it difficult for the Council. . . . His impression was that the percentage [of opera in English] was now very small, and he regretted that the Board had not been able to bring the change more gradually. . . . If however Covent Garden did not wish the Arts Council to interfere with its policy, it must not expect the Council to take sides in any controversy which that policy might arouse.[11]

The new policies did arouse some criticism (notably voiced in an article by the music critic of *The Times* and in a letter following that by Harold Rosenthal), but in terms of what they were intended to achieve they were immediately successful. 'As the opera in English policy was departed from', Lord Drogheda wrote later, 'so the quality of performances tended steadily to improve, and with it the attitude of the music critics, who in the earlier days had castigated the Royal Opera House with terrible consistency.'[12]

The gradual change in policy, not merely from opera in English to opera in the original language, but also to what is called *stagione* – that is productions (usually with stars) given a number of performances over a short space of time after special rehearsals, rather than occurring throughout the repertory during the season – was not a cause of conflict between the new Chairman and the General Administrator. Because Webster had supported the policy of singing in English, his position was difficult at the Arts Council, but he had a nose for success and had for too long endured the inflictions of failure to resist the change.

There were, however, other things. Lord Drogheda, by his own confession, a natural goad, had shared the general inability of members of the Board under Waverley to influence the administration. Both Haltrécht and Harewood have made the point that Webster's dilatoriness was to some extent a policy, and the latter quotes him as saying: 'You should never have to *take* a decision. The right course should be obvious. If it isn't you may be committing yourself the wrong way' – a doctrine which will not bear a moment's consideration when it is applied to the routine decisions necessary in any business and certainly not to the extraordinarily complicated work of planning the schedules of an opera house. At Covent Garden under Webster it led too often to a failure to engage the best singers; to artists, particularly conductors, being seriously overworked; and, because there are few singers at any one time suitable for a particular role, to what Harold Rosenthal has described as 'the occupational disease of the House' – a lack of understudies. This last in turn led to some rather ludicrous polyglot performances when foreigners had to be sent for as last-minute substitutes. Philip Hope-Wallace described one of these:

> Libero de Luca, a Swiss, sang in Italian and the rest of the company in English – or such at least was the intention. Mme Grandi sang in either language as best suited: thus after trouncing the American baritone villain in English, she resorted to Italian to explain things to the tenor lover, and incidentally sang even better in that language.[13]

All these things contributed to low returns at the box office.

Lord Drogheda's method was to look into everything. He was determined to achieve first-class standards at Covent Garden and he was remorseless in his attention to detail. He carried a pad and pencil everywhere, making notes as he journeyed through the day, not merely for his own consumption but to prompt enquiries addressed to others.

In about six months in 1959 and i960 he addressed Webster on the following subjects: the exact arrangements for the 'Bedford' box (next to the stage and reserved for Covent Garden Properties Ltd); the loan of Marie Collier to Sadler's Wells; designs for *Fidelio;* and for the ballet *Two Pigeons'*, a plea that he, Webster, would go back stage after performances; the whole question of presenting first nights at weekends; the suitability of Claire Watson for Sieglinde; a draught which caused movement in the cyclorama; questions affecting the British Council; his desire to dissociate Covent Garden from a protest being made by the West End managers; and finally appointments made to the press office. On 26 July 1961 he began a letter as follows:

I do not want to be stuffy on your return from holiday but I do think it is a pity that you should have decided to revert to the custom of not consulting one at all before appointing a designer for a new production. . . . I do beg you, not for the first time, to see that one is consulted beforehand on all future occasions and I should be grateful if you would give me an undertaking in this sense.[14]

This last request brings up the whole question of the duties of the Chairman of a Board of a grant-aided institution. Lord Harewood thinks that in the matter of designs and the casting of operas Lord Drogheda considerably exceeded his. In *The Tongs and the Bones* he quotes the memorandum written by Drogheda at the time he offered his resignation from the Chair of the opera sub-committee. (See p. 180.) 'All major decisions relating to the employment of artists should be discussed by the sub-committee before action is taken by the Executive.' And he then goes on:

I could never have subscribed to such a view, which seems to me to a great extent to beg an important question. Is an Intendant fully executive, or is he mainly the mouthpiece of a Board or a committee, to which he must refer decisions? Should he visit Rome to see Giulini and Visconti and then refer their choice of designer and singer to a committee? The mind boggles.

Lord Harewood says that he had never been put in such a position 'nor could I ever have accepted it. . . . The chief executive of such organizations is to my mind appointed to carry out the Board's *policy*, and he in his turn accepts it as an implied condition of the job that major failure will lose him that job, and failure on a lesser scale will endanger it.' He goes on to say that the system of Board and intendant is sophisticated, rather like democracy itself, and demands acceptance of unwritten provisions, understanding, considerable give-and-take and, above all, trust between a Board and its chief executive.

Garrett at heart to my mind rejected such an arrangement, which he felt left the Board impotent, and he believed that he had cause not to trust Webster. Webster however was a senior and experienced executive used to running his own show and taking responsibility for his actions. There was clash of personality here and, but for the advent of Georg Solti as Music Director, who brooked no questioning of the artist's absolute authority and in whom Garrett believed, the outcome of the clash could have been unpleasant.[15]

The question of the proper relationship between the Board and the administration of public institutions is a matter which constantly exercises the minds of those concerned with it and is not really solved by the 'trust me or sack me' attitude, allowing no compromise, which some directors take up and which Lord Harewood seems to go near. The other side of the case was put by Lord Drogheda in answer to a letter in which Webster asked: 'Surely you don't intend that I should consult the Sub-Cornmittee for everyone that is asked to submit sketches?'[16] In his reply, Drogheda said:

> My short answer . . . is 'certainly not'. But, at the same time, I think that in the case of most designers, and certainly in the case of designers who are relatively unknown in this country, sketches should be seen by the Sub-Committee (or by selected members . . .) before an artist is actually commissioned. . . .
>
> There may be one or two occasions where an artist is so distinguished that it is impossible to get him to submit sketches beforehand. These occasions should be extremely rare. When they occur, then I think the designs should be seen by the Sub-Committee (or selected members) before the work of execution is put actually in hand.
>
> The Board are put in a difficult position if none of their number has seen the proposed designs for costly productions before heavy expenditure is incurred.[17]

In practice the relationship between administration and Board differs according to the personalities of those involved and in the case of the Chairman and General Administrator at Covent Garden, Lord Harewood probably exaggerates the extent of the friction. In the first place Drogheda took over the chairmanship in January 1958 and Solti's appointment did not begin until the autumn of 1961. The relationship therefore survived for nearly three years without his intervention.

There seems to have been more than one reason for this. In the first place Webster was not likely to resign and particularly not when the change in policy could be seen to be bringing success so near. Secondly, whatever he said to his staff in moments of frustration, the hostility between the two men never grew to unmanageable proportions. Georg Solti was to say many years later that there was a certain amount of love in the love-hate relationship 'because David could never resist Garrett's looks.' (Drogheda is of exceptionally distinguished appearance.) Whether or not this is so, in the extensive correspondence between them there is often a kind of stylized offensiveness on Drogheda's part and a robustness in Webster's rejection of it which could not have been possible without some degree of understanding and cordiality between them. Finally, with the mixture of dilatoriness and secretiveness which made up his temperament, Webster succeeded in many ways to continue doing as he pleased. He was known to certain members of the Board as the AP or Arch Procrastinator, to others as the AD or Artful Dodger.

Then there was Walter Legge, potentially a source of great trouble. His election to the Board came about in the following way. Soon after Donaldson joined, the Chairman asked him to see Legge because he felt that he was hostile to Covent Garden and 'discouraged artists whom we wanted to appear from doing so'.[18] Legge, who it may be remembered, was married to Elisabeth Schwarzkopf, had much influence with musicians because of his position in charge of the classical section of the Columbia Gramophone Company, and Donaldson, who had known him since the days of the Beethoven Sonata Society (see

192

p. 75), therefore asked him to luncheon. At this meeting he learned that Legge's dearest wish was to run an opera house and, although there was at no time any suggestion quite of this sort, when Donaldson reported back, it was, after some discussion, decided to invite him on the Board. This invitation was accepted and Legge became a member in the summer of 1958.

He was an extremely dangerous man. Widely experienced and with impeccable taste in music, he possessed a certain coarse charm and wit, but was nevertheless arrogant, unreliable and with a contempt for other people easily aroused. He had many of the characteristics of Sir Thomas Beecham under whom he had served in 1939. Nevertheless, he was a power in the musical world, widely known by opera singers, and the creator and administrator of the Philharmonia Orchestra. Donaldson and several of the other directors, none of whom knew him well, considered the possibility of appointing him Artistic Director, but the Chairman rejected the suggestion on the ground that he 'was nervous of the possible repercussions on an organization which was improving all the time . . . and frightened of the shock effects of his appearance as a very senior member of the staff.'[19] He was appointed to the Opera Sub-Committee – despite David Webster's grave opposition.

In all conventional senses his appointment was a failure. His attendances were bad and he resigned after five years. Nevertheless, during the short period he was there, his unquestionable knowledge was invaluable and he was tolerated because of the part he played in the battle with what one of the directors in a moment of exasperation called 'Webster's vested interest in mediocrity'. 'W.L.'s presence', someone else said, 'is the greatest single factor which at present keeps the Administration up to the mark and his resignation would

193

genuinely lower the quality of opera produced.'

His second service was both less obvious and less certain. His violent, often unsubstantiated, criticisms of the administration may have put the Chairman on their side. When Webster and Harewood were attacked untruthfully and unfairly, Drogheda's allegiance was to them. In this way, what might so easily have become a reason for the unpleasant clash Harewood had foreseen may actually have had an ameliorating effect.

But Webster must have been partly won over by the new Chairman's evident concern for all those who worked at the Opera House. He began immediately to press for pension schemes, in the first place for Ninette de Valois and Webster himself, later for artists and members of the staff.[†] He was always approachable and always concerned to help. Small notes were made on the pad he carried about – reminders to help get a job for somebody's son, or in the cause of some artist in distress, and these on the following morning were converted into action. He was also responsible for inaugurating the annual opera gala which like that of the already existing

---

[†] At Covent Garden as at other government-aided or funded institutions, there was much difficulty in getting adequate pensions for the staff, and even greater difficulty in the case of artists, who are self-employed. During the sixties and seventies it became nationally accepted that pensions are a necessary part of employees' benefits and the State Earnings Related Scheme came into effect on 1 April 1978. In 1986 all employees of the ROH, other than artists, became eligible to join the house-run pension schemes which provide retirement benefits that compare favourably with those outside. Equity artists contribute to a national pension scheme which is supplementary to the State Earnings Related Scheme and musicians benefit from somewhat similar arrangements. Those who do not contribute to these schemes are covered by the basic State Earnings Related Scheme.

ballet galas, was in aid of the Benevolent Fund.

One of Lord Drogheda's first acts on becoming Chairman was to change the arrangements for what is known as the Royal Box (second from the stage on the right of the auditorium as seen by the audience). Previously this box had been available for members of the Royal Family and was used for Government entertaining, but otherwise was exclusively the prerogative of the Chairman. On the evenings when he was not there it was empty. Lord Drogheda immediately made it available to all the Board members on a first-come, first-served basis, with the proviso only that the Chairman should have priority on first nights. Soon this privilege was so much appreciated by the directors that only bids for the box made immediately the programme was announced were likely to be successful. In the early days there was no great rush to go to the routine repertory performances and Webster's secretary often telephoned round directors to get someone to fill it.

The year 1958 was one of great financial stress as were most years after the generous early days of Dalton and Cripps. In the first of the annual reports (1957/8) there is a table showing the income and expenditure accounts for the years 1951—6 inclusive. Excepting 1946 and the years immediately following, opera in London has never received the financial help needed to achieve the best results. Nevertheless, in each year it has finally been saved from disaster. The crisis of 1957 was because the Treasury warned the Arts Council not to expect any increase in its grant for the next three years, which in its turn meant that the Opera House could not expect to receive from the Arts Council more than the £362,000 which had been granted for 1958/9.

In a letter to the Arts Council the Chairman of the Board

stated that the estimates had already been cut 'even to the point of imprudence', while seat prices had been raised and maintenance work deferred. Most of the additional expenditure estimated for the years to come was for increased salaries and wages, but the effect of taking over Sadler's Wells Theatre Ballet had been to increase outgoings by more than receipts. (In the annual report for 1957/8, it is pointed out that, had Covent Garden not been prepared to assume responsibility for it, this company 'built up for many years with fine traditions and talented artists might well have been lost'.) Receipts could not be swollen by an American tour of The Royal Ballet because of a commitment it was hoped to fulfil in Moscow.

> We have recognised the need to bring back the tour profits [of The Royal Ballet] into our general fund during the present financial difficulties; but we feel that it is wrong to be doing this. The Royal Ballet's profits on overseas tours should in our view be set aside from our general receipts and used for the development of ballet. Such things as the development of the Second Company's repertoire with new productions, a pension fund for the dancers . . . and the support of the Royal Ballet School are items of expenditure which could justifiably be met from these special receipts, if we were in a position to set them aside.

Most serious of all however was the overdraft, which because of the accumulated shortfall of previous years had reached a figure of £140,000 for which the payment of interest was considerable. Lord Drogheda said that it seemed to him that 'the time has come for the Arts Council to consider, with the Treasury, the long term future of Covent Garden.'[20]

The annual report for 1958/9 announced that the major event of the year was unquestionably the announcement of the new financial relations with the Arts Council and Treasury. Assistance was provided for the reduction of the overdraft, which by the end of the year had reached the figure of £183,248, by payments of £20,000 a year for five years, 'at the end of which if no further indebtedness has been incurred, our relations with the bank should have become normal'. The report continued:

Secondly, as regards annual expenditure, for a period of three years we are guaranteed 43 per cent of 'allowable' costs. This does not mean that, whatever we choose to spend, we can call on the Arts Council and the Treasury for 43 per cent of the total: our estimates will continue to be scrutinised and at the end of the year our actual expenditure will be examined to see if it falls within allowable categories. It should be added that, since the Arts Council may not subsidize foreign tours, provision has been made in the detail of the arrangements whereby this item in our expenditure is cut out when the subsidy is being calculated, although allowance is made for the expenditure which would have been incurred if the company concerned had remained in the United Kingdom.

In relation to the budget estimates of 1959/60, it was stated, 'the lump sum subsidy which results from the application of the 43 per cent formula does appear to save the situation'.

However, there was an upper limit to the Arts Council subvention of £500,000. In the annual report of 1961/2 it is recorded that during the year under review the maximum sum was not fully called upon but the Opera House was left 'appreciably short of the full entitlement had there been no such limit'. The objection to the system geared to expenditure was that it would obviously always be necessary to impose an upper limit to the amount of subsidy in any one year. Therefore at the end of the trial period a formula based on a percentage of the receipts during the preceding year took its place. After negotiation it was agreed that the grant should be 17s 6d for every pound of 'reckonable receipts'. This agreement was subject to review after twelve months but the annual report of 1962/3 recorded the satisfactory fact of a surplus of £70,117 'due to the attractive power of the performances throughout the year which resulted in the house takings being some £47,032 ahead of our budget estimates'.

This Report nevertheless warned, as it turned out with foresight, that it was not to be expected that the current year would yield a comparable surplus; and also said that owing to the need to close the house for a period in the summer to complete the rewiring of the theatre and replace certain electrical equipment to meet the requirements of the Lord Chamberlain, receipts for that period would be lost; while, because the majority of those employed at Covent Garden were engaged on a year-round basis, costs would hardly be reduced.

The early sixties saw the foundation of the Friends of Covent Garden. Notes prepared for the Board record that the original intention was to have two bodies, Sir Leon Bagrit to be Chairman of both. The first would be called the Society of the Royal Opera House, and would consist of an exclusive set of people 'who will have no other privilege on the face of it than the glory of giving money to the Opera House for the promotion of opera and ballet'.[21] Not only individuals would be asked to join but also corporate bodies and companies. This Society was formed and lasted until 1973 when it was wound up and gave way to the Royal Opera House Trust. This again has the sole function of raising money, although members were to have the privilege of belonging to the second society known as the Friends of Covent Garden, launched in 1962 with the primary objects of generating interest in opera and ballet and providing a well-informed audience. The magazine *About the House* (much quoted here) edited by Kensington Davison, who was also appointed organizing Secretary of the Friends, immediately achieved and has maintained exceptionally high standards of quality and interest.

The third tier of lights in the auditorium are a memorial to Lord Drogheda's period. In designing the theatre Edward Barry had planned a series of decorative figures on the three-tier fronts depicting the Three Ages of Woman, the figures to be illuminated by the lights of the auditorium. For some reason not on record, when the theatre was built the top row, representing Woman as Child, was not installed and in 1958 was still absent. Lord Drogheda raised a private subscription to meet the cost (£2,670) of making thirty-five replica wall brackets, wiring and installing them. One of the first persons to subscribe to his fund was Queen Elizabeth the Queen Mother, after which everything was easy.

11

Musical Direction 1958–1971
Georg Solti; an International
Opera House

When Kubelik resigned it was hoped that Rudolf Kempe might be persuaded to take his place. Kempe was much loved in London, having conducted not only the two cycles of the *Ring* in 1957 but also a memorable *Elektra* in which the German singer Gerda Lammers, previously unknown in London, scored an extraordinary success after taking over the tide role at a moment's notice. However, Kempe was unwilling to accept the appointment, although he was prepared to conduct regularly. In the 1957/8 annual report it was explained that it had so far proved impossible to appoint a successor to Kubelik:

It is not always recognised that in the modern age, with its rapid means of transport and its greatly varying burdens of taxation, it is not necessarily easy to induce persons of international standing to forego the amenities and the great rewards of independence and mobility for the anxieties and the greater financial sacrifices of attachment to one particular centre. It has been with mixed feelings that we have had to listen to injunctions to engage persons who had already rejected decisively the offers we had made.

The statement went on to profess the administration's belief in the desirability of making such an appointment but to point out 'that one thing worse than leaving the appointment unfilled would be to make an appointment which proved unsuitable or unworthy'.

In fact, the period which followed was one of many triumphs for Covent Garden, the greatest of which was the new production of the Donizetti opera *Lucia di Lammermoor.* The preparations for this production were notable for a terrible error on the part of the opera sub-committee, which gave much joy to the administration and which its members have never been allowed to forget. Presented with the suggestion that Joan Sutherland should be allowed to sing the title role in the new production of *Lucia di Lammermoor,* they were reluctant to agree. Although possessed of a voice of such superb quality that no one could fail to recognize it, she was inexperienced and, at that time, without much stage presence. Since it was proposed that the opera should be sung in English, the sub-committee feared a repetition of the many sound but unexciting performances of the past. Their opposition, although understandably derided in the aftermath of her sensational triumph, nevertheless contributed to it, because they agreed to the casting only if Tullio Serafin could be persuaded to conduct; a stipulation which caused the opera to be sung in Italian and, more important, resulted in Joan Sutherland going to study with the maestro in Italy for some weeks before rehearsals began.

In a production by Franco Zeffirelli with his own designs and with a cast almost entirely from the resident company, the first night of *Lucia di Lammermoor* with Joan Sutherland gained a place among the memorable evenings at the opera house, while the Australian soprano's name joined the list of eminent singers famous in this coloratura role. At the end of the first act she received a standing ovation, and next morning the critics endorsed all the enthusiastic and emotional response of the first-night audience.

Martin Cooper in the *Daily Telegraph* noted that it was bold to reintroduce this opera without a famous singer in the role in which so many of the great prima donnas of the past had made their names, but said that Joan Sutherland's singing more than justified the choice and had won her a deserved ovation 'such as very few British singers have enjoyed in recent years'. He also said that Zeffirelli's set had a 'baronial magnificence and also a note of elegance perhaps more Italian than Scottish but admirably suited to Donizetti's conception of Sir Walter Scott's story'[1]. *The Times* critic spoke of a dramatic as well as vocal triumph for Miss Sutherland, and in the most interesting of the critical articles, Andrew Porter wrote:

Briefly: Franco Zeffirelli's production of *Lucia di Lammermoor* for Covent Garden takes its place beside the great Scala revivals of *ottocento* opera which have been so striking a feature of post-war musical life; and with her performance of the tide role the young Australian Joan Sutherland becomes one of the world's leading prima donnas. . . .

The great soprano that her admirers have always felt she would be was now conclusively revealed (and since the war only Mme Callas has won an ovation at Covent Garden to equal last night's, after the Mad Scene). A new beauty shone in her face; her gestures, her bearing were unfailingly expressive. . . .

From the start, in the recitative to the Fountain aria, Miss Sutherland showed that Lucia was of stronger mettle than, say, Ophelia: she had the stuff of violent tragedy in her. Her singing was exquisite: particularly notable were the sustained notes followed by an octave drop. Her decorations were tastefully and justly conceived, and beautifully executed. Arpeggios were delicate and lovely. Trills were confident. But beyond this, there was *meaning* in everything she did. A singer who can make florid decorative bursts in sixths with the flute heart-rending in effect has understood the secret of Donizetti's music.[2]

Thus Sutherland, to be christened in Italy 'La Stupenda' was, like Vickers, launched on a long international career, in this case with support not from international singers but from the resident company.

Other notable performances of this period included a marvellous *La traviata* with Callas, conducted by Rescigno, *Fidelio* with Klemperer conducting and Sena Jurinac in the title role, as well as the prestige opera *The Carmelites* by Francis Poulenc, conducted by Kubelik followed by Matheson.

Historically more important than any of these was the revival of *Der Rosenkavalier* with Georg Solti conducting, Elisabeth Schwarzkopf as the Marschallin and Jurinac in the name part. In the long run, the presence of the Hungarian-born conductor was to become of first importance to this production in the well-tried old sets, but, at the time, the treatment of Schwarzkopf by the London critics on her return to Covent Garden after eight years gave rise to the greatest concern. No critic was entirely satisfied with her performance, Martin Cooper, Desmond Shawe-Taylor and Philip Hope-Wallace all finding her too much the *grande soubrette*, too little the great lady. Peter Heyworth in the *Observer* gave serious offence. Having said that Mme Schwarzkopf might have seemed the best equipped of all present-day singers to 'don the illustrious mantle of Lotte Lehmann' since 'she is a prodigiously accomplished singer with the ability to draw a remarkable variety of colour and expression from her voice', and having praised her opening scenes with Oktavian, he went on:

> But the heart is revealed in flirtation as well as in consuming passion, and by the time of the baron's abrupt entry Mme Schwarzkopf had presented a character of awful archness and artificiality, flashing huge black eyelashes and a toothpaste smile in a manner that might do for Adele in *Die Fledermaus* but is sadly far removed from the human warmth of Oktavian's Marie Therese. Thereafter the day was lost. . . .[3]

When the great singer read these words, she said that the job of the critic was to comment on her acting and singing and not on her eyelashes, and she also said she would never sing in opera at Covent Garden again—a vow she kept for the rest of her career.

This brought up the whole question of the severity and arrogance of the London music critics as compared with the rest of the world. In this account it is inevitable that the great successes are often singled out for detailed analysis, and the resulting effect may be to suggest that London critics were generally generous in their praise. The opposite is probably nearer the truth. On 23 February 1960 the Board at Covent Garden is recorded as stating that it agreed that the present state of English music criticism was a national misfortune, but that there was nothing that the Board could do about it.

Lord Drogheda was well known for his brushes not merely with the critics but also with newspaper proprietors during his reign at Covent Garden. However, he says he did not ever question a critical opinion as such, but:

> I hated it when criticism became carping, and I sometimes took strong exception to needlessly vehement language, or to words written with a lack of humility and an assurance of infallibility. . . . I was also aware of the possible effect upon foreign artists whose services we required and who were very fearful of the London critics: and if I ever said to a singer, 'But think of that marvellous applause!' I would be told 'I can't take that away with me. All I can take are my notices.'[4]

And whether justifiably or not, international artists' fear of the London critics is a matter of record; nor was Mme Schwarzkopf the last singer to refuse to return to Covent Garden because of the treatment he or she had received from them.

Georg Solti on his first appearance in opera in London was also given a mixed reception, the consensus of opinion being that, although full of dramatic élan, his reading lacked the delicacy of detail that Kleiber, for instance, had found in the score. The Board at Covent Garden had no such doubts. Solti had a wide experience of the opera houses of Europe and in 1937 had worked with Toscanini at Salzburg. A concert pianist by the age of twelve, he had turned to conducting by the time he was fifteen, and he worked as répétiteur and conductor at the Budapest State Opera. His career was interrupted by the war, which he spent in Switzerland, but afterwards he devoted most of his life to opera, becoming Musical Director at the opera houses of Munich and (later) Frankfurt.

When it seemed possible that he might consider coming to Covent Garden, no chances were taken with the Artful Dodger who, Lord Drogheda felt, 'was far from wholehearted in his desire to find a successor to Kubelík', and, when he met Solti, was 'hesitant although impressed'.[5] Drogheda therefore arranged to meet Solti himself at the house of a friend, and he had more than one talk with him there. Solti himself was at first hesitant, because at the time he did not want to go on working in opera. But he was persuaded by Bruno Walter, who said that it was his duty to go on: 'You are between generations. You know exactly the old generation and can pass over to the next one. If you stop, there will be an enormous gap and nobody will know what German opera tradition meant at the beginning of the century.'[6]

However, this was not the end of the matter. After he returned to Frankfurt, Solti asked Lord Drogheda to go to see him there. 'He was suffering agonies of doubt because he felt that David did not seriously wish him to come to London, and I persuaded him that however true that might once have been, it certainly was no longer the case.'[7]

Sir Georg Solti—honoured for his services to British music— is certain of a leading place in the annals of Covent Garden. During the ten years he spent there (1961-71) he succeeded in raising the status of the opera house to one of the greatest in the world. He achieved this by his outstanding musical gifts, and also because of his long experience in European theatres and his world-wide renown. During his regime the best foreign artists—singers, designers and conductors – were anxious to come to Covent Garden; and, of even greater consequence, he succeeded where so many had failed and opened the doors of international opera houses to British singers. At the end of his first year, he said:

> There is an enormous amount of brilliant talent, both in this country and in the Commonwealth, and I feel that it must be given a chance to develop. However, we must also bring internationally famous singers to this House, since the public has a right to hear them, and from them our own singers can learn much.[8]

This was the method advocated for so long by John Christie and others. Because of the recent deliberate change of policy at Covent Garden, but also because of his energy, faculty for recognizing talent and again because of his world-wide contacts, Solti was able to find and bring on young singers and then send them abroad. As his term at Covent Garden came to an end, he said:

> I had the fantastic luck to meet a very talented generation of English singers—fantastic luck, but with that luck I think I used my luck, giving them the chance. So we are here today with a very strange thing. Wherever you go in America or on the Continent the first choice is an English singer, even at Bayreuth; and that, of course, is a marvellous thing, but it is entirely new. I don't say it is entirely due

to me, I just had wonderful luck and used my luck to give them a chance.[9]

As a natural consequence of his work at Covent Garden, Solti opened the way for all British opera singers.

He had no difficulty in acknowledging the merits of the orchestra he took over – 'one of the best in the world' – and 'of our equally expert chorus'; but he turned his attention immediately to the needs of the repertory, which in the absence of a Musical Director had tended to become unbalanced. What is one to think', one critic asked, 'of an artistic policy . . . that in a whole season provided not a single performance of a work by Mozart, and offered more performances of *Car* and *Pag* alone than of the whole output of Wagner?'[10] And Lord Drogheda has told us that one of Solti's first acts was to insist that the absence of works by Mozart other than *The Magic Flute* must immediately be put right.

Finally, as a conductor Solti was unsurpassed and, according to several authorities, among those who had conducted regularly at Covent Garden only Kleiber could be compared to him. He had no fear of rivalry from the finest conductors, and during his regime the best of both British and foreign were regularly heard in the house.*

---

* English conductors included Atherton, Balkwill, Downes, Goodall, Pritchard, Mackerras, James and Alexander Gibson, Sillem, Lockhart, Matheson, Loughran, del Mar, Sargent. Foreigners were Abbado, Erede, Dorati, Kempe, Varviso, Wallberg, Schippers, Horenstein, Kertesz, Klemperer, Gardelli, Kubelik, Krombholc, Wich, Giulini, Krips, Melik Pashayev, Leitner, Silvestri, Rossi, Cillano, de Fabritiis, Prétre, Cillario, Schmidt Isserstedt.

He failed, according to his own estimate, in only one thing – he could not achieve an English style of production, 'a common scenic language in the house'. Talking to Bernard Levin at the end of his term at Covent Garden, he said:

> I established that every piece should be conducted by a decent conductor . . . but although I invited first-class designers from everywhere many for one reason or another didn't come. On the production side I also tried very hard to get producers from the wonderful theatre. In my first year I tried to get Peter Hall and Peter Brook but I failed . . . I also tried other theatrical producers but I never managed to find a common language. Every production looked different.[11]

Solti appeared once at Covent Garden between his appointment and actually taking it up, and on that occasion he made the felicitous choice of Benjamin Britten's *Midsummer Night's Dream* in a new and much-praised production by Sir John Gielgud with sets by John Piper. He is quoted as saying that this was the most important opera written in the last twenty-five years, and it was heard now on a large stage with a big orchestra for the first time. The critics were agreed that new beauties were revealed. Andre Turp, a young Canadian tenor who had recently joined the Covent Garden Company, and Geraint Evans were both much praised, as indeed were the rest of the cast, while of the opera itself one critic said: 'Two English geniuses have met.' Nevertheless, on this occasion it was the new Musical Director's evening. Andrew Porter wrote:

> His direction of this opera is masterly. There is magic

in the sound from those first warm sighs which portray the midsummer forest— It is not just that Solti has heard inwardly and then elicited the kinds of sounds that are needed. It is not just that his reading is infused with lyricism – but also that he has understood the different kinds of lyricism – fairy, mortal, and rustic – which make up the opera.[12]

And the *Times* critic said:

Mr Solti draws, with the utmost sensibility, all the magic from Britten's score; where the composer presented the music for what it is worth, the admiring and analytical curiosity of another conductor strengthens the less effective passages and enhances all the rest.[13]

When he took up his appointment, things were less easy. Solti was asked some years after what were his first impressions of Covent Garden and, after some thought, he replied: 'I thought there was no one there who knew anything at all about how to run an opera house.' And to anyone with his experience of the long and disciplined traditions of the German houses, this may well have seemed true. He did not easily impose his own ideas of discipline and hard work either on the orchestra or on the singers, and he found great difficulty in accepting the limitations of the old and underfunded opera house. At his first press conference in 1962, describing his first year, he said:

The main difficulty has been the lack of rehearsal space. The only large area is the stage itself, and this must be made available not only to the Opera Company but also to The Royal Ballet. There is a small rehearsal room opposite the Stage Door but this is almost valueless. When, therefore, the stage itself is not free we have to hire halls if and when they are available. Fortunately we have now at last managed to obtain a cinema which should be ready for rehearsals in November. This is a tremendous step forward. . . .[†]

Secondly, we have only one orchestra for the two companies. This inevitably results in the need to introduce what I may describe as 'easy' operas, i.e. those in the repertory, to allow the orchestra time to cope with new or difficult opera and ballet scores which they often have to play. The possibility of solving this by having a second orchestra is unfortunately out of the question for financial reasons. . . .

Thirdly, there have from time to time been comments on the actual production of repertory operas. We have a very able House Producer [Ande Anderson] but he is severely limited in the time available for rehearsals, since star singers are seldom able or willing to give sufficient time to rehearse, and in most cases the maximum period is something less than ten days. This, of course, is a problem not confined to London, applying equally to Vienna and New York and other great houses.[14]

[†] This was the Troxy Cinema in Commercial Road which was shared with an organization called the London Opera Centre, an advanced opera school which came into being following the recommendations of the Bridges Report to the Arts Council, and, after a stormy start, continued for fifteen years, when it was replaced by an organization called the National Opera Studio.

Solti's first years were unhappy in other ways. For some unexplained reason, a small and unimportant but noisy claque formed and booed him from the amphitheatre. He had no initial great successes, and one near disaster with a production of *La forza del destino* in which there were some absurd sets and a soprano of his own choice who sang consistently flat. Finally, he had to get used to the British music critics.

True to his word, he began the Mozart operas with new productions of *Don Giovanni* in 1962 and *Le nozze di Figaro* in 1963. The first had new sets by Zeffirelli and a marvellous Don in Cesare Siepi, while the cast included Sena Jurinac, Richard Lewis, David Ward, Geraint Evans and Mirella Freni. The very elaborate sets gave much pleasure to the critic of the *Observer* – 'one of the most ravishingly beautiful succession of sets that I have ever seen'[15] – but were said by others to be too elaborate and to result in long stage waits. Zeffirelli's staging was criticized as often lacking focus and tension, while Solti himself was treated to a mixture of praise and some rather obscure and condescending complaints. The critic of *The Times* said:

> The orchestra played as well as they always do for Mr Solti, yet the result was in some way strangely inhuman, alternating between extremes of tension and languor. The performance as a whole certainly had grandeur, yet Mozart's infinitely diverse humanity remained only partly realized; a film of romanticism blurred the conception.[16]

Le nozze di Figaro the following year fared little better. With a cast including Ilva Ligabue, Tito Gobbi, Teresa Berganza,

Mirella Freni and Geraint Evans, it is remembered with exceptional pleasure by members of the audience. However, the article by the critic of *The Times* carried the headline 'Mr Solti skates over the score', while David Cairns in the *Financial Times,* although praising the production and singers, concluded: 'Solti conducts brilliantly. It is characteristically flowing, fast, fiery, with marvellously lucid wood-wind, and the rhythmic role of the trumpets played down. I am bound to say that I prefer Mozart both more rhythmically articulated and more expansive. . . .'[17]

Solti's contract was for three years, and Lord Drogheda tells us that in 1962 there was great danger that he would not renew it. Learning also that David Webster did not intend to bring the matter up until the following year, he wrote to him:

> I am personally very clear that we should be heavily condemned if we did not secure an extension of Solti's contract for at least a year or preferably two. . . . What really matters is that he is quite outstandingly good and if he is allowed to be lost to us we shall stand to be heavily criticised. . . . Of course, there may be a few bloody noses from time to time but I would rather that than everything being slightly or more than slightly below par.[18]

Thus exhorted, Webster, who could be both warm and reassuring when he wished, persuaded Solti to extend his contract, although the latter did so only on conditions. He said that the orchestra must be enlarged, and to do this it was necessary to overcome the orchestra director's prejudices against women. He said it must be given opportunities to

213

appear on the concert platform. Thirdly, he said that more must be done to present him to the outside world, since at present he felt he was working anonymously. In the end, 'relendessly urged and encouraged' by Lord Drogheda, he signed the contract.

Solti is acknowledged to be the leading Strauss conductor of his generation, and one of his most memorable productions was of *Arabella* in 1965 with L isa della Casa and Dietrich Fischer-Dieskau, and Joan Carlyle as Zdenka. This has been compared to the famous production of *Der Rosenkavalier* with lotte Lehmann. 'All and every means are justified in getting to the new production of *Arabella* at Covent Garden,' a critic on the *Times Educational Supplement* wrote. 'A critic's job here is simply incitement. It is something quite exceptional, a glimpse of paradise in a world which is usually standing proof of man's fallen condition.' [19]

The new *Ring* under Solti was given in instalments—*Die Walküre* in 1961, to which was added *Siegfried* in 1962 and *Das Rheingold* and *Götterdämmerung* in 1964. All were directed by Hans Hotter, 'the outstanding Wotan of our time', but the scenic designer, Herbert Kern, was replaced after the first *Walküre* for the whole cycle by Günther Schneider-Siemssen, who was responsible for the raked platform surrounded by a gigantic ring.

In these performances Birgit Nilsson's Brünnhilde was much praised as the most authentically Wagnerian experience and Hans Hotter sang Wotan in the first *Walküre*, but the outstanding fact was that the roles were largely sung by singers of the Covent Garden Company. David Ward, coached by Hotter, sang Wotan in the second cycle, Amy Shuard followed Nilsson as Brünnhilde, and Josephine Veasey scored a remarkable success as Waltraute and more particularly as Fricka.[‡]

From the start, Solti's rendering of the score was praised unreservedly. 'Mr Solti gave such a magnificent account of the score,' the *Times* critic wrote after *Walküre*, 'orchestrally the finest since the war. . . .'[20] Philip Hope-Wallace spoke of a 'superb performance . . . his first production as Musical Director and a labour of love not lost on the wildly enthusiastic audience',[21] and Edmund Tracey of the 'sheer, physical excitement of the performance'.[22]

The reception of the later operas in the cycle was no less enthusiastic, even those who preferred a more lyrical rendering admitting that the orchestral playing was very fine. After *Götterdämmerung* had completed the cycle, Desmond Shawe-Taylor wrote:

> However fine the cast, this is a work which needs first a masterly conductor; and on Wednesday it had one. Mr Solti's energy and attack were again in evidence; but they did not lead him on this occasion into any neglect of the finer points of the larger structures. The performance was classical in feeling: nobly proportioned, restrained, in all but some trifling orchestral mishaps, uncommonly smooth. . . . I doubt if a better *Götterdämmerung* is to be seen or heard anywhere in the world.[23]

And summing up, in a tribute to the conductor at the end of his

---

[‡] With the exception of Siegfried (Windgassen), Siegmund (Kozub) and Hagen (Frick), every part in one or other cycle was sung by a member of the Company.

term at Covent Garden, the same writer said:

> He belongs to a rather different tradition from that typified
> by the lyrical restraint of Kempe or the contemplative
> breadth of Goodall.§ Nothing if not red-blooded he offers a
> reading of the score that is vivid, full-textured, powerful.
> There have been moments when his lively temperament
> has led him into excessive emphasis. . . . But during his
> decade at Covent Garden his style in conducting all compos-
> ers, not only Wagner, has perceptibly mellowed and
> matured, his *Götterdämmerung*, more especially, now offers a
> masterly demonstration of his ability to see those long acts
> as musical unities. The clarity of detail is admirable but not
> obtrusive; the vast score is unfolded with a rare combina-
> tion of fire and sensibility, compulsive power and refined
> judgement.[24]

In 1963 the first performance outside Russia of Shostakovich's
Katerina Ismailovna was given at Covent Garden. Conducted by
Edward Downes and using his translation, it was a *succès d'estime*
but a failure at the box office. No account of these years would
be complete without mention of the Zeffirelli *Tosca* with Callas
and Gobbi, conducted by Prétre, a performance about which it
was said that it would 'influence all that we henceforth think and
write about the work, and leave its mark on all successors'. The

---

§ The musical critics were at this time much under the spell of Reginald
  Goodall's rendering of the *Ring*. This conductor had been on the staff at
  Covent Garden since 1946 but, to the great enjoyment of everyone except
  the administration of Covent Garden, it was left to Stephen Arlen at
  Sadler's Wells to show his outstanding quality as a Wagnerian.

only criticism made at the time was of the behaviour of the audience, the critic of *The Times* choosing to take it to task for 'the noisy, vulgar, artificial, vacuous philistinism' of its reception of this great performance.[25] Andrew Porter wrote:

> The tragedy as it was played last night had the inevitability of classical tragedy. It was not *verismo*, but supra-naturalistic. One responded not in the narrative way one does to melo-drama, but rather as one might to *Medea* or *Phaedra*, knowing the whole story before – though not for that reason being any less involved in the dramatic situations.[26]

And a critic writing more than twenty years later, having just seen the second act of this performance for the first time on television, obviously experienced the same response:

> Above all, we could see the unfailing continuity of Callas and Gobbi's work –the unwavering concentration, the total commitment that suggests the reality of dramatic truth rather than mere performance. Neither artist seemed at all pleased with themselves as performers, neither drew attention to themselves. Both had acted and polished up their interpretation over many years. But every performance, as was utterly clear here, has to involve discovering the work new and afresh.[27]

Most exciting of all was the performance in 1968 of *Così fan tutte*—with the exception of three performances by the Vienna State Opera in 1947, the first ever heard in this house. Produced by John Copley with designs by Henry Bardon, this was highly praised for its careful preparation and sound

217

singing. 'It looks charming and sounds ravishing'. Philip Hope-Wallace wrote.

> The other night I heard people saying that of all the operas they liked *Così* the best—a strange shift, if you think that not even Beecham could popularise it and that over 30 years of Glyndebourne revivals still left it out of the 'popular' bracket. It probably boils down to a new taste for satire.[28]

Then, writing of Solti's performance of *Otello* in 1964, the *Times* critic began his article as follows:

> Many years hence when nannies, or the then equivalent, have chilled the marrow of their charges with tales of the dreadful opera performances that used to be seen at Covent Garden, there will be grandparents, we hope, to interrupt with the oft-told legend of a Verdi's *Otello* . . . in which by some miracle every element in the performance was ideally calculated, every voice and every actor, the playing of a superb orchestra, the direction of an inspired and understanding conductor, and a production which almost by accident proved worthy of a great play.[29]

In a tremendously praised production of Schoenberg's *Moses und Aaron* (the third in the world, after Zurich in 1957 and Berlin in 1959) Solti succeeded in his ambition to get Peter Hall into the house. Once more the *Times* critic was ecstatic:

> Granted that Schoenberg's *Moses and Aaron* is one of the outstanding operas of this century and deserved to be

produced at Covent Garden there was one obvious course for the Royal Opera House; to present it not merely more cogently than either of the previous productions, in Zurich and Berlin, but so impressively that nobody, however unsympathetic to Schoenberg's music, could possibly fail to be bowled over by the experience. This the Royal Opera House has managed to achieve. Last night's British premiere of the work was in particular a triumph for Mr Georg Solti who has been working patiently towards this aim ever since he became musical director at Covent Garden; and it is a triumph for Mr Peter Hall whose production of the crowd scenes alone sets new standards in the staging of opera. The roars of applause at the end were of a volume and enthusiasm that one expects for a concourse of great prima donnas but not for a dodecaphonic opera about the nature of God.[30]

Andrew Porter in the *Financial Times* spoke of 'a performance so assured, so powerful, that it is surely the greatest achievement in Covent Garden's history',[31] while all critics spoke of Solti's mastery of the immensely complex score.

By 1966, and with a new production of *The Magic Flute* (sung in English, produced by Peter Hall, with sets by John Bury and unusually imaginative lighting), Solti was also recognized as a great Mozart conductor: 'A highly enjoyable *Magic Flute* . . . certainly the best Covent Garden have put on these 19 years'.[32] 'Mr Solti conducts the wonderful score with perfect tact and understanding'.[33]

In his last year as Musical Director, he conducted a new production of *Eugene Onegin* which introduced Ileana Cotrubas to the house. John Warrack wrote: 'Georg Solti's conducting of it is unexpectedly delicate: he can let the dances go with a swing, but he ensures that the words of the guests are heard over them, and he accompanies the singers watchfully and affectionately.'[34] And Desmond Shawe-Taylor:

> Everything fell into place: the vocal and instrumental texture assumed the lightness and clarity and flowing movement that, under Solti's watchful beat, persisted throughout the evening. It is an absurd view that would see this conductor as a sort of Straussian and Wagnerian heavyweight, incapable of the finer shades. His reading was fresh and airy, blessedly free from those swooning tempi and exaggerated *rallentandi* that are not unknown even in Russia.[35]

In 1967 Georg Solti married Valerie Pitts, by whom he had two daughters. In 1971 he was honoured by the Queen with a KBE; in 1972 he took British citizenship. Replying to speeches at a farewell luncheon, he said: 'You keep telling me what I have done for England. Look what England has done for me.'

12

Ballet 1960–1970
Frederick Ashton

The glory of opera in the sixties was at least equalled by
that of the ballet. The results of de Valois' long-term
undertakings—the schools and the steady preparation of young
dancers – coincided with such a swell of talent that, as in opera,
standards were set against which all performances would be
judged for many years. From the vantage point of twenty years
later, there seems no doubt that audiences of those days
witnessed one of those recurrent phases when everything
contributes to miraculous creativity in some particular sphere
or spheres of art.

Early in the decade Ashton, 'swept by a longing for the country
of the late eighteenth and early nineteenth century',[1] began
work on a new version of Dauberval's *La Filie mal gardée,* one of
his greatest inspirations and a ballet which has been in the repertory ever since. Unlike some of his outstanding earlier works, at

its first performance in January 1960 it was immediately welcomed by the critics as well as by the public. With designs by Osbert Lancaster and choreography requiring great virtuosity, danced by Nadia Nerina and David Blair, with comedy roles for Alexander Grant and Stanley Holden (who, in the tradition of English female impersonators, danced a clog dance), this ballet showed Ashton at his most observant, wittiest and most profound. 'The more trivial the subject, the deeper and more beautiful is Ashton's poetic view of it.'[2]

Ashton's method was to mount his ballets on the dancers at rehearsal, taking ideas from their movements and exploiting their personal characteristics and style. Nerina was a strong dancer with a quite exceptional technique, yet, as one critic put it, the success of the ballet was subsidiary to the fact that Ashton had done for her what he had earlier done for Fonteyn.

Nerina has been known as the pre-eminent technician in the company, an astonishing virtuoso but one lacking apparently in the higher artistry. Mr Ashton's choreography has, in effect, added the artistry—or rather shown Nerina herself how very considerable technical skill may be altered from a thing in itself to a servant of lyrical dance.[3]

Then, in 1961, he created *The Two Pigeons*, a two-act ballet, somewhat in the same vein as *La Filie mal gardée*. This time he mounted the ballet on two young dancers of The Royal Ballet touring section – Lynn Seymour and Christopher Gable, who danced it at Covent Garden in February of that year.

The great event of 1961 was the first visit of The Royal Ballet to Russia, a visit arranged to coincide with that of the Kirov to London. The company danced both in Leningrad and at the Bolshoi in Moscow. After the opening in Leningrad with a performance of Ashton's *Ondine,* danced by Fonteyn and Somes, the repertory given included *The Sleeping Beauty, La Filie mal gardée* and a number of short ballets including *Les Patineurs, The Rake's Progress, The Lady and the Fool* and *The Firebird* – performed for the first time in Russia and afterwards introduced into the Bolshoi repertory. Predictably, Fonteyn scored a triumph, although Nerina, who had danced before in Russia and was known and admired, was also much applauded in *La Filie mal gardée,* a ballet which was the greatest success of the tour.

> The English ballet company surprised us, not by the standard of their performance, though that was very high, nor by revelations of new artistic experiences, though some of these were indeed very interesting, but by the impression made by what I call their nobility of style.[4]

And:

> The English dancers' technique lacks bravura, but enchants by its lightness and expressiveness. . . . The flowering of ballet during the last decades has been influenced by the Russian school of dancing. Even so . . . grafted on from within, ballet in Britain has acquired the finest traits which characterise English literature and art.[5]

In the long term, more important was the visit of the Kirov Ballet to Europe, since it was during this visit to the West that Rudolf Nureyev defected. He appeared for the first time at a gala at Drury Lane in November 1961 and created a sensation.

Two thousand people signed a petition asking that he should be invited to dance with The Royal Ballet and, more important, now that they had seen him, both Ninette de Valois and Margot Fonteyn agreed with this view. In addition, there had occurred the necessary coincidence that Michael Somes, Fonteyn's partner over the years, had at this time decided to retire.

Somes, about whom it was said that 'he was like a rock round which waters eddy and swirl', had gone to the Sadler's Wells Ballet School when he was seventeen and Fonteyn fifteen. He had emerged an accomplished *danseur noble* at a time when English male dancers were rare, but historically his importance is as a worthy partner for Fonteyn. Ashton had used these two dancers in the gradual development of his own style, and all over the world they were regarded as the greatest pair of the age. When Somes retired, he devoted himself to the development and promotion of young dancers, notably Antoinette Sibley.

Once Fonteyn had seen Nureyev dance, she was confident she wanted him to succeed Somes, and de Valois, who, in spite of her insistence on the idea of 'the company' and dislike of stars, never hesitated to compromise her principles when confronted with a situation she thought more important, agreed. To quote the historian of The Royal Ballet: 'de Valois insisted on the importance of injecting this heady new strain into its [the company's] now sturdy constitution, and she never deviated in her support of Nureyev's continued presence'.[6] Nureyev was given the compromise title of 'Permanent Guest Artist'. Thus began one of the legendary partnerships in ballet history.

However, as is well known, Nureyev was not merely a partner for anyone, even Fonteyn. He had the greatest stage presence since Helpmann, and was probably the most talented dancer seen in London since Nijinsky, to whom he was often compared. In descriptions of him one often comes across the word 'fawn' and, like Helpmann, his face was certainly part of his fortune. But he was temperamentally reckless, even dangerous, and he had an authority so immediate that no one could have mistaken him the moment he appeared on the stage.

When de Valois first saw Nureyev dance, she decided at once that for his debut he should dance Albrecht in *Giselle*. His success in this role was immediate – 'Complete Conquest for Nureyev', and 'Comet at Covent Garden' were two of the headlines – yet no greater than the recognition that Fonteyn, at the age of forty-two, had, in her new partner, found a source of inspiration and an extension of her art. Caryl Brahms wrote: 'Nureyev's dancing has been not only a joy and a top talking point for audiences but it has acted as an incentive and a tonic to Fonteyn, who has never danced the white act more finely than at their first performance.' And the same writer asked 'Is Nureyev the finest dancer in the world today? I would say that he is one of the finest and certainly the most exciting.'[7]

Nureyev was praised not only for his dancing, but for his acting.

> Nureyev's acting, small-scale and idiomatic . . . contrasts violently with much of the heavy-handed sign language going on around him. With most of the cast gesturing fit to bust, Nureyev's simple naturalistic acting seems at times almost over-casual. His dancing has the cat-like spring and bite . . . coupled with all the mellifluous flow and beautifully musical phrasing one could wish for. . . . I had not reckoned on his stylishness and precision.[8]

225

Alexander Bland wrote:

> To innate romanticism Nureyev adds a variety of gifts. Technically he is endowed with a neat figure, natural turn-out, exceptional elevation, impeccable turns and beats . . . and a suppleness laced with a fiery dash of Slav temperament which permits him more grace than most men could get away with.
>
> When he makes one of his great loping runs round the stage like a cheetah caught behind bars, he seems to be made of more elastic material than normal humanity.

And he went on:

> He appears unaware of the audience. Caught up in the greater reality of the drama, he does not actively project emotion; he enables us to look in on it (this is Ulanova's style).[9]

Nureyev appeared regularly at Covent Garden for the next fifteen years in partnership with Margot Fonteyn and in all major roles. He had a remarkable memory for the Russian classics and great gifts as a coach. His partnership with Fonteyn, which enraptured audiences all over the world, was given a permanent art form by Sir Frederick Ashton's *Marguerite and Armand,* the ballet based on Dumas' *La Dame aux camélias.**

---

* This was never danced by anyone other than this pair, and became a kind of signature work. 'With his usual perception Ashton saw that Nureyev had found the key to unlock Fonteyn's final reserve as an artist, and he gave their partnership its perfect vehicle.'

Yet Fonteyn and Nureyev was not the only outstanding part-nership of the sixties. The 1962 series of *Giselle,* in which Nureyev was first seen with Fonteyn, was also danced by Svetlana Beriosova – 'an occasion to be written in letters of gold, for complete characterizations of Giselle are rare, and always ravish-ing'—with Donald MacLeary, who danced 'admirably, fluently, fully'; by Anya Linden – 'quite astonishingly beyond her previ-ous interpretations of this type of role . . . every movement she made, every gesture and nuance were excellently placed and firmly accented' – partnered by David Blair, 'dancing with heart-warming ease and vigour'; and by Nadia Nerina with the Danish Erik Bruhn, 'individually splendid, the two dancers each comple-ment the other, and their duets have a lyrical strength and unity astonishing in so new a partnership'. In Brighton the title role was danced by Antoinette Sibley, only recently from the Ballet School, of whom it was said that 'Giselle is going to be one of her finest interpretations'. Also appearing in these performances in subsidiary roles were Merle Park, Deanne Bergsma (as the Queen of the Willis), Monica Mason and Georgina Parkinson.

The same surge of talent was apparent among choreogra-phers, chief among them Kenneth MacMillan. Early in 1961, *The Invitation,* which he had created for Lynn Seymour and Christopher Gable, was brought into Covent Garden from the Touring Company. This ballet, of which the theme is the destruction of innocence, tells of a boy and a girl seduced by an older pair. Immediately recognized as a work of major impor-tance, it gave Lynn Seymour, who excelled as an actress as well as a dancer, her first great opportunity. Clement Crisp wrote in the *Financial Times:* 'In the central role of the girl, Lynn Seymour gives a performance of such beauty and authority that it must rank as one of the outstanding dance interpretations of the decade; it is a further indication of the extent and richness of her talent.'[10]

Then, in 1962, MacMillan followed with a new version of Stravinsky's *The Rite of Spring*, a ballet which in 1913 had provoked a riot at its first performance in Paris. This ballet, with sets designed by Nolan, was very successful and enhanced MacMillan's reputation and also that of Monica Mason, who danced the sacrificial maiden.

MacMillan has coped, without cheating, with the tangle of Stravinsky's percussive rhythms, observing them fairly and giving them their appropriate visual values in accordance with their place in the music's texture; and the dancers have sufficiently concealed the fact that they must have been counting the beat for all they were worth.[11]

In New York in 1963, Dame Ninette de Valois, at the age of sixty-five, announced her retirement as Director of The Royal Ballet. Alexander Bland wrote:

She had based her early successes on established stars but had developed a steady opposition to the 'star system'. She had mostly limited the ranks of her dancers (though not her designers or composers) to native talent – and then, in her last two years she had abruptly reversed direction by opening up her Company to foreign Guest Artists.[†] Above all, through every twist and turn of circumstance and

---

[†] Recent guest artists included Erik Bruhn, Yvette Chauviré and Sonia Arova, who danced *Swan Lake* with Nureyev.

personal vacillation, she kept her eye steadily on her target—the establishment of a dance organisation as tough and lasting as the British Monarchy.

Bland then quotes de Valois' words, written in an article of 1932. 'It is the belief of the present Director, and this is the point to be driven home, that if the Ballet does not survive many a Director it will have failed utterly in the eyes of the first dancer to hold that post.'[12]

However, in the light of all ballet history, it is apparent that de Valois' beliefs were quite unrealistic. From time to time companies have risen through the genius of one impresario, but they have nearly always broken up or sunk to a level of well-presented but uninspired performances when he has died or retired. In ballet, more than in any of the other performing arts, inspiration is necessary to achieve more than technical brilliance.

Under Ashton, de Valois' immediate successor, The Royal Ballet would lose nothing in musicality, technical excellence or in the uprush of young talent. On the contrary, the Ashton decade was one of the most splendid of all. He had no taste for administration, however, and he appointed three assistant directors—John Field, who was to continue to run the Touring Company, John Hart and Michael Somes to work at Covent Garden. Dame Ninette remained as Supervisor of the Ballet Schools and was constantly available for advice.

Ashton proved generous to other choreographers, and his first years were notable for revivals of de Valois' *The Rake's Progress*, Andrée Howard's *La Fête étrange*, Helpmann's *Hamlet*, and three works by Balanchine – *Ballet imperial*, *Serenade*, and a *pas de deux* to music composed by Tchaikovsky for *Swan Lake*. In the autumn of 1963 he presented Nureyev's reconstruction of the fourth act of

La Bayadere. This ballet, which was to become a permanent part of the repertory, was danced on its first night by Fonteyn and Nureyev and three soloists, Park, Seymour and Mason, of whom Alexander Bland says: "they brought off their fiendishly difficult variations with perfect aplomb'.[13] In *La Bayadere* the star turn, nevertheless, is the opening *défilé* of the corps de ballet. 'Under Ashton's direction the Royal corps was to become the finest in the world, and no ballet has displayed them more magnificently than *Bayadere?'*[14]

In 1964 in *The Dream*, a ballet which was originally part of the celebration for the 400th anniversary of the birth of Shakespeare, Ashton showed his extraordinary understanding of dancers by bringing together the young and comparatively unknown Anthony Dowell and Antoinette Sibley. *The Dream*, an important contribution which in 1986 still has an honoured place in the repertory, was not immediately recognized by the critics. Why do indifferently what Shakespeare has already done so well?' Clive Barnes asked, while others complained of the amputation of Mendelssohn's music. However, Barnes praised one feature of this ballet: 'Here for the first time Ashton seems to have recognised the new parity of accomplishment now achieved by the male dancers in the company, and, apart from the entirely female corps de ballet of twinkling fairies, the men are allowed to dominate the ballet.'[15] Nor could the exceptional quality of the two principal dancers be missed. 'Many others have danced these roles,' David Vaughan would write some years after, 'but no one has managed to emulate Sibley's swiftness and her impersonation of a half-wild creature, nor the silken fluidity of Dow-ell's phrasing.'[16] The partnership of Sibley and Dowell would soon become second only to that of Fonteyn and Nureyev.

In Ashton's second season he invited Nijinska to come over to mount a revival *of Les Biches,* and he himself created a small masterpiece in *Monotones, a pas de trois* danced by Vyvian Lorrayne, Anthony Dowell and Robert Mead.

However, the sensation of the 1965 season was Kenneth MacMillan's first full-length ballet, a new version of *Romeo and Juliet* with sets designed by Nicholas Georgiadis, which compared favourably with the Bolshoi's masterpiece. All critics agreed that this was a triumphant success, a work which would remain in the repertory for many years to come. One of its strengths was that it included many excellent roles and drew on a large company of dancers. 'Yes, we were all wrong' was the heading of one review, and the critic said: 'MacMillan has created a magnificent work in its own right which need fear no comparisons.' The ballet was also regarded as a triumph for its designer, Georgiadis.

The excitement attending the first season of this notable work was much increased because it was danced in quick succession by four different pairs of dancers. The ballet had been rehearsed with Lynn Seymour and Christopher Gable in the title roles, but it was first danced at a gala by Fonteyn and Nureyev. (Lynn Seymour has described how, in the usual manner of Covent Garden when treachery is afoot, she was not told that she would not appear at the first performance but was left to find this out.) However, Seymour danced it with Gable following the gala, quickly followed by Antoinette Sibley with Dowell and then by Merle Park and Donald MacLeary.

Of these pairs, the forty-six-year-old Fonteyn danced the four-teen-year-old girl with her accustomed magic; 'a beautiful Juliet, clear, precise and perfectly formed in every movement'; 'consciously cast perhaps in the heroic mould of Ulanova yet with an ecstatic radiance of her own'. Yet for many critics, the performances of Seymour and Gable excelled. Oleg Kerensky wrote:

> It isn't often that the second cast give a new ballet greater depth and significance than the first one, especially when the first one was Margot Fonteyn and Rudolf Nureyev. But that is what happened. . . . Seymour gave Juliet a youthful tenderness and a dramatic poignancy which combined to make it a great interpretation. It also made Seymour a great ballerina.[17]

And Andrew Porter, after saying that choreographers more than any other creative artists have their human uses, went on: 'In that sense *Romeo and Juliet* is Seymour's ballet as surely as *Ondine* is Fonteyn's or *La Filie mal gardée* Nerina's.' Later, he wondered whether it was too much to ask MacMillan to recompose some passages of his ballet in different versions, since there were 'passages conceived so completely in terms of Seymour's physique, and her particular way of weighting a phrase or moulding a gesture, that anyone who is not her must find it very difficult not to strike a false note.'[18]

Park and MacLeary in their first season made less mark, although Park's Juliet was thought intelligent, while her dancing was 'neat, excellently placed, and her characterisation was charming'.[19]

In the following week, however, Richard Buckle said that, while 'Nureyev and Fonteyn were incomparable for the luminosity of their personalities', and Lynn Seymour 'the most acceptable as the heroine–victim while Gable matched her in charm and modernity', it could nevertheless 'reasonably be held that Antoinette Sibley and Anthony Dowell danced MacMillan's

Romeo and Juliet better than either of the couples that preceded them.'[20] David Blair was an outstanding success as Mercurio at the first performance, while Desmond Doyle danced Tybalt, and Benvolio was shared between Dowell (first performance) and Graham Usher.

The year 1966, in the words of Alexander Bland, was a 'bumper year in a bumper decade'. Beginning with a further Nijinska ballet, *Les Noces*, it included the addition of a second *pas de trois* to *Monotones* and MacMillan's *Song of the Earth* danced to Mahler's Song by the Stuttgart ballerina Marcia Haydée, for whom he had originally created the role. There was yet more to come for Ashton was in a mood of marvellous creativity. In 1967 he produced *Jazz Calendar*, an amusing ballet on the theme of Monday's Child, and in 1968 the far more important *Enigma Variations*.

Enigma Variations, to Elgar's celebrated music, and with beautifully appropriate sets by Julia Trevelyan Oman, features 'My Friends Pictured Within', to whom the composer dedicated the score. The critic of *The Times* devoted two reviews to the ballet, in one of which he explained that it was not just about Elgar's friends, 'but the quality of friendship itself': 'There have been plenty of ballets about love, but friendship as a subject is rare, and Ashton finds rare and moving expression for it.' Mr Percival also said: What a pleasure it is after so many ballets about fairy tale characters and melodramatic situations, to see credible, adult characters like these on the stage of the Opera House. This is what makes the ballet to me, and many others, irresistible.'[21]

And Nicholas Dromgoole said:

Yet just as Elgar was expressing, in a sense, the quality of his own life, as the sum of his relationships with those around him whom he loved, so Ashton manages in dance not merely to illustrate but to illuminate the whole theme of the variations. The music has become a part of something else, and in simple but intensely moving imagery Ashton makes a golden poem.[22]

All critics praised the dancers – Derek Rencher as Elgar and Svetlana Beriosova as his wife; Anthony Dowell, Georgina Parkinson, Brian Shaw, Alexander Grant, Desmond Doyle and Antoinette Sibley as the friends.

The Royal Ballet visited America in both 1967 and 1968, a four-week visit being undertaken in the second of these years because of a cancellation by the Bolshoi.

In the meantime the Touring Company had succeeded in creating an enthusiastic public for the ballet in the provinces. The company developed its own dancers—among others Doreen Wells, Shirley Grahame, Brenda Last and Alfreda Thorogood, Christopher Gable, David Wall, Paul Clark and Stephen Jefferies, but they were also often joined by principals from Covent Garden. Their repertory included *The Sleeping Beauty*, *Swan Lake* and *Coppélia*, but, as has already been seen, several of the most successful new ballets were created for them, notably MacMillan's *The Invitation* and Ashton's *The Two Pigeons*.

A successful development of the mid-sixties was the formation of the group known as Ballet for All. A series of lecture courses on the history and aesthetics of ballet had been initiated by the Extra-Mural Department of Oxford University, followed by similar courses at Cambridge and London. Directed and often delivered by Peter Brinson, these were notable for a theatrical style and for bringing many leading figures from the ballet world to the lecture platform. Occasional lecture-demonstrations using students from the Ballet School to dramatize the subject were also given in schools and at festivals and university extension classes near London.

This collaboration between the universities and the staff of the Royal Ballet School soon attracted the attention of the administration of the Royal Opera House, which persuaded the Calouste Gulbenkian Foundation to give a grant of £9,850 spread over three years to develop the lecture demonstrations on a professional basis. A small group of dancers was formed under the direction of Peter Brinson to tour community centres, festivals, small theatres and schools throughout the country. This group, given the name Ballet for All, had a specifically educational function, but was presented in an entertaining way. It was so successful in reaching theatres and halls too small for a ballet company or full orchestra (in the year 1968/9 performances averaged six a week and the figure for attendance over the year reached 94,000) that it was developed to include actors, given a certain amount of scenery and some support from dancers of The Royal Ballet Touring Company, and had ballet dramas specially composed for it. It received support from the Arts Council, and in 1969 reached a large audience through seven educational programmes shown on television. Many artists of the Covent Garden Company appeared with this group, which continued until 1982 when it gave way to more purely educational activities.

All good things come to an end, and the Ashton period came to an untimely one. As early as 1967, Ashton had begun to say that he wished to retire at the end of the 1969/70 season. He has that passive artistic temperament which, entirely aware of its own genius and completely confident in the exercise of it, neverthe-less demands outside incentives, and perhaps reassurance. During the whole of his career he has seldom produced new work except when commissioned to do so, and recently, in bring-ing him on to the stage to take a call, Anthony Dowell assumed the knees-bent position of someone taking part in a tug-of-war and, in a symbolic gesture, hauled him on to the stage. No one who knew him well believed that when he spoke of resignation he expected to be taken seriously. No explanation has ever been given as to why Webster, who knew him extremely well, chose to do so. Since the publication of Edward Thorpe's book on Kenneth MacMillan, we know that in Berlin in 1967 he had offered the succession to MacMillan 'three years hence when Sir Frederick Ashton is due to retire'.[23] Here is Lord Drogheda's account of how the news reached Ashton himself:

It was therefore agreed that David should speak to him [Ashton], so as to establish the position clearly. Unfortunately he baulked at doing this, and delayed for several months; and then when he finally did so it was in a brusque and insensitive manner, telling him in effect 'your time is up.' This took Fred completely by surprise. . . . Matters were made somewhat worse because David chose to make the actual public announcement while The Royal Ballet was appearing on tour in New York. Not surprisingly Fred was deeply offended, and told people that he had been fired.[24]

Another thing which has never been explained is why no member of the Board, most of whom knew Ashton well, ever spoke personally to him on this subject. Lord Drogheda has told us that he reproached himself that he did not do so, 'but David

236

was General Administrator and if I had usurped his function he would have had a legitimate grievance'[25] – an excuse which sits oddly on this particular Chairman. There is some evidence that the Board was persuaded that the administrative side needed strengthening and that John Field, the administrator of the Touring Company, who had been offered the Directorship of the Festival Ballet and without some quick decision might be lost, was the only man who could do this. Certainly, there was a complete reorganization of the ballet companies immediately after Ashton left. Whatever the reasons for this ungrateful and unreasoning act, as well as greatly wounding the man most responsible for the creativity of The Royal Ballet, it caused much bad blood and great difficulty for the next Director, Kenneth MacMillan.

13

Administration 1963–1970
A Minister for the Arts

The decade of the sixties, perhaps the most successful in the whole history of the Opera House, was, as most of the years of the future would be, a time of preoccupation with finance. The period 1962/3 was an exception to the rule. Because house takings were some £47,000 ahead of budget estimates and the subsidy calculated on each pound of reckonable receipts, there emerged a surplus of £70,117, making it possible to pay off the overdraft which for so long had threatened the existence of the entire enterprise. The years 1963/4 were unusual because the theatre was shut for two months for necessary alterations (including an improvement to the cheaper seats), and the annual report of 1965/6 records the fact that the Opera House was once more heavily in debt. The formula of subsidization according to a percentage of reckonable receipts was necessarily subject to an upper limit, and consequently had proved unsatisfactory.

However, in 1964 there was a change of government and the first Minister for the Arts took office. There is a belief among many of those concerned with the arts that the Labour Party in office is more appreciative of their importance and more generous in support of them than the Conservative Party.* Be that as it may, the advent of Jennie Lee as Minister for the Arts, and of Lord Goodman as Chairman of the Arts Council, inaugurated an era of support for the arts unknown since Dalton and Cripps were looking for customers. For Covent Garden it meant a respite, if only temporary, from the eternal difficulty of finding sufficient funds to maintain the standards of an international opera house.

Early in 1966 it was announced that the arts would receive an extra £2 million a year from the Government, an increase of nearly 50 per cent on the previous year's figure of about £4 million. Since this was both the biggest jump ever known in Treasury support for the arts and, although in itself tiny, the biggest percentage increase in any government department's estimates, it was, in Jennie Lee's own words, evidence 'that the Government cares passionately about the quality of life'. At Covent Garden, the formula of subsidization according to a rigid percentage of receipts was abandoned, and it was agreed that in future the subsidy would be determined on a year-to-year basis according to the total financial situation as it developed. At the same time, provision was made for repayment

---

* One of the Conservative Party's own supporters recently made the point that state intervention touches on one of the main ideals of Conservative philosophy, the belief in the pre-eminence of individual freedom and in the concept that the State's participation in ordinary affairs should be restricted rather than enlarged.

of past debt by a series of yearly payments.

In spite of this generous settlement the respite from the anxiety about finance was short lived. In the Annual Report of 1967/8 there is an explanation of the effect of rising costs. In that year, as it happened, both sides of the account were some £400,000 higher than in 1966/7, but the increase on the income side was from factors that would not necessarily be repeated. Nearly £200,000 was from higher receipts from touring, mainly from The Royal Ballet's tour of North America in 1967, and this could not be undertaken every year. £130,000 was due to a rise in seat prices of about 10 per cent in each of the two previous years, again something which could not be continually repeated. Demand normally recovered to some extent after the first impact of a price rise, but there was great danger that too frequent an increase in prices could be carried to the point of diminishing returns. The last £100,000 on the income side was due to an increase in the grant from the Arts Council.

On the expenditure side, the increase was spread throughout the account and consisted almost entirely of increases in costs of labour and materials, 'which being no more than a reflection of the general rise in costs and prices were beyond our control'. The outstanding figures were an increase on salaries and wages of more than £30,000, and an increase on new productions of over £50,000. The second figure (due again to rise in salaries and materials) is the subject of an interesting explanation in the report.

Savings could be made by reducing the number of new productions, but these would not be proportionate to the reduction, because the workshops had to be maintained at a level to include repairs and general maintenance. In any case, the administration believed that to cut the number of productions would be a misguided and dangerous policy, only to be contemplated as a temporary expedient in circumstances of extreme difficulty.

New productions are the life-blood of a repertory company. They provide a focus for the efforts of all the forces engaged in the theatre; not merely the performingartists, but the production, lighting, design and workshop staff as well. It is by a steady succession of new productions that the standards, traditions and morale of a company are built and maintained; it is in them that the style of a company is expressed. They also maintain the vitality and variety of the repertory; if the repertory gets stale, not only the morale of the company but also the interest of the public – and thus receipts at the box office – are diminished. Moreover, if we are to continue to attract conductors and singers of international standing, and at the same time fulfil our obligations to put on new works by contemporary British composers, we must be able to maintain an adequate flow of new productions. We believe that a minimum of eight new productions a year on average is necessary for all these purposes.

These eight productions were equally divided between opera and ballet, whereas the average for most European opera houses was eight to ten for opera alone. The report explained that there was a great difference between various productions – *Aida* could never be cheap, whereas many ballet productions were comparatively so—£4,000 for an average one-act ballet, £78,000 for *Aida*. Nevertheless, the cost of new productions of full-length classical ballets could be as much as an opera production.

Having said that there is no direct or inevitable relationship between the cost of a new production and its distinction, the report goes on to say that standards at Covent Garden are those of an international opera house, and it was by these standards it aspired to be judged.

The administrative arrangements of the Opera House had been the subject of an inspection by an outside firm of business consultants, who 'here and there' made suggestions which might in the long run produce greater efficiency and economy, but who found that the extent of practicable economies was exceedingly small. Various steps to reduce costs had, nevertheless, been taken by the administration on its own account. The Annual Report ends with the robust statement:' We are here to try to give value for the resources entrusted to us; whatever may be the expedients forced upon us by a situation of peculiar, and we sincerely trust, temporary difficulty, we are not here to produce opera and ballet on the cheap'.

That the situation was neither peculiar to those years, nor temporary, will become apparent but, while Jennie Lee was at the Ministry of Arts and Arnold Goodman at the Arts Council, it was at last taken care of each year.[†] In his introduction to the Annual Report of 1968/9, following the change in Government, Lord Drogheda had this to say:

> She [Jennie Lee] recognised the need for the highest stan-
> dards at Covent Garden, and she ensured that the necessary
> finance was forthcoming. I thank her for her unfailing
> support. She set a splendid example to her successor, Lord

[†] The amount of the Arts Council grant for each year and the results of inflation will be found in Appendix D (p. 349–50).

Eccles, whose devotion to the Arts is well known and to whom we therefore look with the highest hopes for the future. . . .

One of the major events in the operatic world of the late sixties was the movement of the Sadler's Wells Opera Company from the theatre in Islington to the Coliseum. Stephen Arlen, who had succeeded Norman Tucker in 1966, was a man of enormous drive and energy. He was determined to improve upon what one commentator described as the 'Islington strait-jacket'; and, indeed, Sadler's Wells was far off the theatrical beaten track, small and inconveniently short of backstage facilities. The move was made in 1968, the company renamed the English National Opera, and the question of language for opera in London finally settled, since the capital now had an international opera house at Covent Garden and a national company singing in English at the Coliseum. For the Sadler's Wells Company the move proved immediately successful, the audience figures rocketing in the first year, although in the very large theatre total performances just failed to reach the target of an average 60 per cent of capacity. (The Coliseum seats 2,350, against the Royal Opera House which seats 2,113.) Nevertheless, at the cheaper prices there proved to be a West End audience for the more unusual operas such as *Gloriana*, *The Violins of St Jacques* and *Orféo*. In the same year, the Queen honoured the Opera Company at Covent Garden by approving that it should henceforth be known as the Royal Opera Company.

For the rest, the end of the decade was also the end of an era. As we have seen, Dame Ninette de Valois retired in 1963 and Sir Frederick Ashton in 1970. Sir David Webster was actually the next to go, retiring in 1970, but the negotiations for a successor to Sir Georg Solti began in 1967, when it became clear that he would not renew his contract in 1971, and Webster was present throughout these.

While there was general agreement that a British conductor should in any case be preferred, it was also thought very unlikely that an international conductor of the stature of Solti – for example Giulini or Kempe – could any longer be persuaded to tie himself down in this way. The most obvious candidate for the post was Colin Davis, and a decision had to be made very early because of other bids for the services of this conductor. At a meeting of the Board of Directors in December 1967, Sir David Webster was empowered to offer Davis a contract for appointment as Musical Director following the termination of Mr Solti's contract.

At this time aged forty, Davis had established himself as a conductor of exceptional gifts, particularly as an interpreter of Berlioz, Mozart, Britten, Stravinsky and Tippett. He was chief conductor of the BBC Symphony Orchestra and had been Musical Director at Sadler's Wells from 1961 to 1965, while he had conducted opera at both Glynde bourne and Covent Garden. At the Royal Opera House he had been responsible for a revival of *Le nozze di Figoro,* and performances, described as 'thrilling', of *Tippett's Midsummer Marriage.* He was in all the circumstances the obvious choice.

Soon after his appointment as Musical Director designate, Davis was introduced to Peter Hall. The meeting took place at dinner in Lord Drogheda's house where, speaking of his wife and himself, he afterwards wrote, 'after a short time we felt quite *de trop,* such was their mutual response.' And he added: Within days, Colin was more or less saying to me that unless he had Peter to work alongside of him he did not think he could undertake the position of musical director at all.'[1] This arrangement, obviously desirable in a theatre which had so far failed to create a style in production, meant creating the new post of Artistic Director, and with David Webster, 'unenthusiastic but unresisting', Lord Drogheda brought this about. In March 1969 Peter Hall signed a contract which would have created a 'duumvirate' at Covent Garden. However, this agreement was due to end in tears, although, before Solti's retirement in 1971, Peter Hall was responsible not only for that conductor's last two productions, *Eugene Onegin* and *Tristan und Isolde*, but also, with Colin Davis, for the premiere of Michael Tippett's *The Knot Garden*.[‡]

However, in July 1971, immediately before he should have taken up his engagement, Hall wrote Drogheda a letter which the latter quoted in full in his memoirs. He began by saying that he had to admit to a great mistake and, having recognized it, the only course open to him was to apologize personally and publicly. He had, he said, signed a contract to give Covent Garden twenty-six weeks exclusive work in every year, but had found that this was muddled thinking. To do the job properly he would have to devote all his time to it, and twenty-six weeks was a compromise which would not work.

> I must also recognise that temperamentally I am not suited to the needs of a Repertory Opera House. I have always worked very personally with the people I am directing and found my solutions through their individuality. . . . The

---

[‡] *Eugene Onegin* had designs by Julia Trevelyan Oman, *Tristan und Isolde* by John Bury and *The Knot Garden* by Timothy O'Brien.

method is not possible where revivals have to be speedily mounted and moves and business given out quickly, no matter who is executing them. I hate doing this. . . .

My heart has gone out of the future since I realised that I had put myself in this impossible position. . . . I realise that I am creating difficulties for you, the Board, and for John; [§] and particularly for Colin. He gave me half his new kingdom gladly, and it is a poor way to answer his generosity. . . .

But I have to ask you to release me from my contract. I feel that I would compound my mistakes by continuing.

Drogheda says:

To Colin it was a harsh and bitter blow, for he had banked on their collaboration together, and all his plans seemed to him to lie in ruins. Nor was the blow softened when some months later it was announced that Peter had been appointed to succeed Laurence Olivier as director of the National Theatre.[2]

To the Board of Directors it was also a blow, but for them there were compensations. Peter Hall is artistically completely self-confident and brooks no interference. Even in his short association with Covent Garden, two matters had arisen on which he had shown himself unwilling to compromise. First had been the new production of *Figaro*. Both Hall and Davis

---

[§] John Tooley succeeded David Webster as general administrator in 1970. See p. 250.

took the commonly held view that it is important to render comedies in the vernacular. (The opposite view is that comedy in opera is apt to be of a fairly crude and unsophisticated kind and is really funny only when the unity of words and music make it so. Thus, there is no way of translating 'Sua Madre' in *Le nozze di Figaro* or 'Buona Sera' in *Il barbiere di Siviglia* which does not lose most of the delightful effect of the originals.) Hall and Davis pressed the view that to open their first season *Figaro* must be sung in English, in spite of the fact that artists had already been engaged to sing it in Italian. To quote Lord Drogheda on the subject: 'Letters were exchanged and rather tense meetings took place, the issue moving away from language to the question who had the ultimate power of decision.'[3] The Board was divided in its opinions, some taking the view that, while 'only big questions of principle . . . should be the subject of Board rulings', the Artistic Directors could not claim full autonomy 'when there is involved our position in relation to Sadler's Wells, our position in relation to the engagement of foreign artists and the training of our own company in such a way that they are available for employment in foreign parts'; while others thought that, although policy should firmly remain original-language, having argued at length the Board should on this occasion 'accept English as a definite exception to our policy, if, after all our discussion, this is what Colin and Peter still favour'.[4]

However, there were contracts with foreign artists which could not be repudiated and, since these artists refused to sing in English, the matter was dropped; not, however, before the Board had accepted that in the final analysis 'those charged with the artistic responsibility must have the final say.'[5]

Another thing that mitigated the directors' distress at losing

Peter Hall was that, in effect, Ken Russell went with him. Russell had recently produced a film biography of the composer Richard Strauss which had been shown by the BBC and which those directors who had seen it (and, it is fair to say, many other people) thought a vicious distortion of the truth and 'cheap, crude and vulgar'. Hall insisted that he could manage Ken Russell if he came to Covent Garden, but it was a source of relief when this matter was also abruptly closed.

But if the Board could be partially consoled for the loss of Peter Hall, this could not be said of Colin Davis, whose loyalty and trust had been so rudely shattered. Nor did it help his relations with the Board. Whereas Peter Hall, who had been the spokesman, is a person of immense ease and charm in all his relationships, Davis chose to regard the members of the Board as foreigners from an establishment world with which he neither had, nor desired to have, many contacts. For some time he was inclined at meetings to rather self-indulgent expressions of his feelings of contempt and distaste for his associates. 'One must always be prepared to make wide allowances for the artistic temperament,' one of the directors, Lionel Rob-bins, wrote, 'but I am aware that some members of the Board are not pleased with such manifestations as we have been exposed to from time to time.'[6] However, time is a great healer for this kind of thing, and Davis was to spend fifteen years in friendly contact with the Board of Directors.

In 1970 Sir David Webster retired and in 1971 he died. Both occasions were marked by strong expressions of gratitude and admiration for his services and, on the part of staff and singers, of the great affection they had felt for him. Most of these, although undoubtedly heartfelt, were of a conventional kind, and the most vivid account of this extraordinary man was given, not in an obituary notice, but in a long article by Peter Heyworth printed in the *Observer* on 15 October 1967, called 'How did the garden grow?' Heyworth refers to the outburst of fury that greeted Peter Brook's production of *Salome* with sets by Salvador Dali. Then he goes on:

It was at moments such as this (and there were plenty of them in those desperate post-war years when Covent Garden was struggling to establish itself) that David Webster showed his mettle. A portly, rubicund Scot, unfailingly dressed in a dapper, double-breasted suit with an expanse of white cuff, Webster has all the toughness and resource that one might expect of a successful businessman who had also played a large part in building Liverpool's Philharmonic Hall.

Officially Webster's job was administration and financial control, but his real qualities lay in a remarkable ability to ride storms that would have long since swept a lesser man overboard. Bland, resolute, flexible, he has through sheer staying-power over the years become the anchor of the whole operation.

Even when that grave pro-consul Lord Waverley was succeeded as Chairman of the Board by Lord Drogheda, whose lofty manner hides a fanatical concern with every detail of his opera house, and the fiery, self-willed Solti became musical director, Webster, pink and unruffled as ever, remained the mainspring at Covent Garden. The Board and the musical director may plan and project, but decisions have a way of reaching finality across the large and spectacularly uncluttered desk of the General Administrator. Essentially the achievements, which are

249

many, and the shortcomings of Covent Garden since the war are his.[7]

The Board had no difficulty in choosing Webster's successor. For the last two years of his working life, the General Administrator was suffering from the illness which killed him, and the administration of the opera house had been successfully undertaken by his assistant, John Tooley. Although it is sometimes thought that it is a mistake to perpetuate the old regime by appointing someone from within the administration to the senior post, the Board was unanimous that in this case Tooley should succeed. He is obviously a man of great ability, and, if without Webster's sheer presence, he is far more musical, and had already shown himself capable of the enormously complex and difficult task of running an opera house. There were one or two others who might have been considered, but none had any knowledge of the equally important world of the ballet. John Tooley was well known to the Ballet Company, who would have been dismayed if anyone else had been appointed; he had a unique experience of the touring arrangements, and had also dealt with all labour negotiations. He had represented Covent Garden on the working party concerning the redevelopment of the market area. (See p. 283.)

The actual appointment was held up because the Minister for the Arts, Jennie Lee, and the Chairman of the Arts Council, Arnold Goodman, believed that the post of General Administrator of a large state-aided institution should be advertised. Members of the Board took the view that, since in the end the appointment would go to John Tooley, they would merely be wasting the time of anyone answering the advertisement. A compromise was reached by which a few suitable people were asked to apply for the job but, since the whole of the musical world understood what was happening, few actually did so. Nevertheless, it was established that on all future occasions the post should be advertised. John Tooley was to reign at Covent Garden for nearly twenty years, and his name will recur constantly in these pages.

Of the company of the sixties, the last to resign was Lord Drogheda, who continued in office until 1974. In 1969 he apparently began to consider retirement since in that year he invited Lord Harewood to return to the Board of Directors with a view to succeeding him as Chairman. Lord Drogheda had no power of appointment, but he had discussed this proposal with many of his colleagues and secured agreement. In recording Lord Hare-wood's return, several of the press accounts appear to have been well informed on the point, and one or two suggested that after eleven strenuous years in a job beset with financial difficulties, Lord Drogheda might even go before his time. But the death of Stephen Arlen in 1972 aged fifty-nine, was to alter the course of opera in London for the next decade, since Lord Harewood was invited to succeed him as General Administrator of the Coliseum. Lord Drogheda remained for the first years of the new musical director, and for most of Kenneth MacMillan's period as Director of the Royal Ballet.

He lost none of his ardency of purpose in his last years, nor any of the proclivity for unabashed intervention in any matter concerning the Opera House. Even the work of the music critics seemed to him a matter on which he could properly comment. As managing director of the *Financial Times*, he allowed complete freedom of expression to his own critic, for many years Andrew Porter, but he conducted an enormous and argumentative correspondence with him on the subject of

251

his published reviews. Lord Hartwell, the proprietor of the *Daily* and *Sunday Telegraphs,* lived near Lord Drogheda in Westminster, and claims that he regularly received letters of complaint about his critics, which Lord Drogheda delivered before breakfast in his dressing-gown.

Since the accounts of music critics have been made much use of here, it may be as well to emphasize that those quoted have largely been named and have been chosen for specific qualities (see p. 110). In general, the London critics are regarded as more severe and more arrogant than their counterparts in other operatic centres and, as has already been said, some leading singers have refused to appear here because of the damage they feel may be done to their reputations. At a meeting of the opera subcommittee at Covent Garden in the early sixties, Mr Solti said that Cesare Siepi could not be engaged for the new production of *Don Giovanni* because he had been upset by some of the notices he had received when he had sung in London before. These had criticized certain aspects of his performance without giving sufficient recognition to its undoubted and great virtues. The sub-committee noted that there were signs that some of the critics were themselves dissatisfied with the lack of good manners shown by the writings of many of their younger colleagues, though it remained to be seen whether this led to any improvement.

Nor are critical reviews necessarily consistent. At one time, the Director of the Festival Hall, Ernest Bean, made a practice of printing in the programmes of his concerts a section called 'Point Counterpoint' which gave the views of several critics on a previous performance – using them to show that musicians were praised by one critic and criticized by another for exactly the same quality.

However, that is a digression. To return to the last years of Lord Drogheda's period. In 1972 he founded the American Friends of Covent Garden, and persuaded Mrs Walter Annenberg, the wife of the American ambassador, to become chairman. Another of the legacies he left, by which he clearly set much store, was the Royal Opera House Trust. He persuaded Lord Kissin, who joined the Board in 1973, to become responsible for replacing the Society of the Royal Opera House (see p. 199) with a new fund-raising body, which became known as the Royal Opera House Trust, and was to perform important functions in the years ahead.

A splendid gala—attended by the Queen and Prince Philip, the Queen Mother and Princess Margaret—was held in 1974 to mark Lord Drogheda's retirement, and many articles and letters were written on the subject. Here are extracts from a letter written to him by Sir Isaiah Berlin which he quoted himself in his memoirs:

> You ask me what I think all right about Covent Garden? You know perfectly well that the business of Committees such as ours is to goad the enterprise on to greater and greater heights. No doubt praise where praise is due is right, and it is ungenerous and wicked to refuse it; but the danger of complacency is far greater than that of excessive self-criticism. . . . The older Covent Garden from which you as much as, and indeed, more than anyone else rescued us, was guilty of precisely that. What is right about Covent Garden is that (a) there are now very few really bad performances, (b) that we achieve heights, from time to time, that no other Opera House, on the whole, can out-climb. . . . We have absolutely nothing to be ashamed of, indeed the

reputation of Covent Garden has shot up, as well you know, since those difficult and ill-attended, rightly attacked, early patriotic days. I think the brio has slightly gone out of our general condition, partly I think because of our success . . . a strongly critical voice or two—Walter Legge did us no end of good—helps. . . .

On the credit side also is the fact that the British company and the singers we have trained have risen far beyond the hopes of realists, even fifteen years ago. If you think where we were musically at any time in the twentieth century, so far as singers were concerned, and compare that with the fact that there is today a highly respected resident company at whom foreign Opera Houses cast eyes—when the history of these years comes to be written, not even the most biased critic will be able to attribute this mainly to the early post-war period, but to the subsequent dozen years.

On the debit side we must place the fact that we don't search for singers with sufficient zeal: we don't find out about marvellous new young singers in Italy or Peru or Sweden as early as we might—Glyndebourne in that respect, sometimes does better, I do not know how, but they do—

The real point is that Covent Garden has become an absolutely central part of London and indeed British culture—It is as intrinsic and traditional and national as the BBC and that would not have happened without—as you very well know and do not need me to tell you although I do so with the greatest of pleasure—your administration. Long may you flourish.[8]

254

14

1971–1976
A New Regime – Colin Davis and
Kenneth MacMillan

In 1970 there was a change of government, the Conservative Party winning the general election and Jennie Lee, described by Lord Goodman as 'our beloved first Minister of the Arts', was 'whisked away'. Two years later Lord Goodman himself retired, giving way to Patrick Gibson. 'I can offer my successor,' he said on that occasion, 'a tattered banner and a dented sword, but he can accept them with pride, and will, from what I know of him, use them with a resolution that will, alas, be needed if he is to preserve the Arts Council along the paths which we regard as desirable if not crucial'. Lord Goodman's banner had presumably become tattered in resisting the philistines, and his sword dented in the fight to get money for the arts.

The change of government appeared to bode no obvious difference in the policy for the arts. Edward Heath, the new

Prime Minister, was known to be a deeply committed and prac-
tising musician, while the new Minister for the Arts, Lord Eccles,
was a most cultivated man, a retired politician brought back
especially for the job. Mr Gibson, who succeeded as Chairman
of the Arts Council, was Chairman of the Pearson Company
which owned, among others, the Pearson-Longman publishing
company and Penguin Books. A former trustee of Glyndebourne,
when he took over the Arts Council in the spring of 1972, he was
on the executive committee of the National Trust, and at the
beginning of a long career of public service devoted to the arts.

In his first year the promise of Lord Eccles' appointment was
fulfilled by the announcement that the Arts Council grant for
1971/2 would be increased by £2.6 million to £11.9 million, an
increase which the Minister pointed out was bigger than the
combined increases of the last four years of the Labour
Government. Yet the long inflationary period lay ahead, and the
days when a Chancellor of the Exchequer made personal undertakings to the Chairman of Covent Garden were long past.

At Covent Garden the first of the new generation to take over
was Kenneth MacMillan. In 1966 he had gone to Berlin as
Director of the German Opera Ballet, and Lynn Seymour, who
inspired him as Fonteyn inspired Ashton, went with him.
MacMillan had found it a wrench to leave The Royal Ballet, but
Ashton, on being asked his advice, had said he should take
advantage of the opportunity to run a company. At the end of
1970 Ashton resigned, and MacMillan returned to take his place.

Several factors contributed to a rough start. In the first place,
ever since Webster had spoken to him in Berlin in 1967,
MacMillan had understood that, as with both his predecessors,
his appointment would be as Administrative and Artistic Director.
Nevertheless, when asked by John Tooley whether he would

accept John Field (then Administrative and Artistic Director of the Touring Company) as co-director to lessen the burden of administration, he had been glad to do so on the understanding that decisions on artistic policy would be entirely his. However, Field had been allowed to believe that he would share both positions, and, although MacMillan had his way, the relationship between the two men did not survive this misunderstanding. Field resigned at the end of the year.

Field's appointment, which had meant that John Hart, Ashton's assistant, would leave, had been thought necessary because of a complete reorganization of the two Royal Ballet Companies which took place at this time. For financial reasons and because of some overlap in the work of the two companies, it had been decided to disband the Touring Company and replace it with a group of twenty-two soloists without a corps de ballet, which would perform a repertoire of popular one-act ballets, supplemented by the works of young choreographers of a more experimental kind. This reorganization meant that some of the dancers of the Touring Company had to go but that others joined The Royal Ballet at Covent Garden, so that MacMillan had the task of finding work for too many soloists, not all of the highest quality, and of somehow unifying the differing styles of the two corps de ballet, trained by different ballet masters.

Kenneth MacMillan's biographer tells us that this reorganization had been determined upon long before he took over at Covent Garden, and there is some evidence to support this statement. This might account for the passivity of the Board of Directors in relation to the retirement of Frederick Ashton. The evidence is slight, but suggests that Webster had convinced the directors that there was need for this reorganization and also that John Field was the only man who could successfully carry it out. If Ashton were persuaded to remain, it would be for a year or two only, during which time Field, who had received an offer from the London Festival Ballet, would be lost. This would go some way to explain a curious *non sequitur* in Lord Drogheda's account of the circumstances of Ashton's retirement. He is describing and deploring the events leading up to it when, apropos of nothing, he interjects the sentence: '*Ironically*, the partnership of Kenneth MacMillan and John Field lasted barely six months, temperamental incompatibility resulting in the departure of John Field in the early months of 1971.'[1]* Be that as it may, the manner of Ashton's retirement also made difficulties for MacMillan in America. He made the mistake of not appearing on the first night of the opening in New York in 1970, and, on his arrival two weeks later, fans at the stage door called for Ashton.

Finally, there was the press. MacMillan had been used to being treated as a brilliant young choreographer and the natural successor to Ashton. Having reached the height of eminence, he had now become a target. In his first season he had a great and deserved success after having, by sheer persistence, persuaded Jerome Robbins to produce *Dances at a Gathering* (danced at the first performance by a cast which included Rudolf Nureyev, Anthony Dowell, David Wall, Michael Coleman, Lynn Seymour, Antoinette Sibley and Monica Mason).

However, his own ballet, *Anastasia*, produced in 1971, received much hostile criticism. As performed at Covent Garden, this was a reworked three-act version of a ballet he had created in Berlin

---

* (Author's italics.) Field left in December 1970.

on the subject of Anna Anderson, who believed herself to be Anastasia, the youngest daughter of the last Tsar. 'It seemed to me,' John Percival wrote in *The Times*, 'that what we saw last night was a short dramatic work preceded by a disproportionate prologue comprising two acts of sheer padding.' He complained, as other critics did, about the use of Tchaikovsky's first and third symphonies: 'MacMillan has said that a friend suggested these. With many such friends he would not need enemies. The music is pretty enough and danceable too; but it is too long for his purpose, with innumerable repeats, leading to inordinately repetitious choreography.' This critic also advanced the view that the ballet was a mixture of Ashton's *Enigma Variations* and the Bolshoi's *Spartacus,* 'both very insipidly copied'. And he ended his criticism: 'As the only new ballet created at Covent Garden all season . . . it is a sad disappointment; and as MacMillan's first creation there since becoming director, it hardly augurs well for the future.'[2]

Anastasia was liked and admired by the dancers and by the public, and it stayed in the repertory for a decade; but with the exception of Andrew Porter in the *Financial Times,* who called it 'one of those rare and precious works of art in which a major creator consolidates all that he has done before and on this firm foundation goes on to build something new, larger and stranger than anything he has made before',[3] it was received badly by the critics.

MacMillan's next three-act ballet, *Manon,* produced, with designs by Georgiadis, in the spring of 1974, had three major roles (danced on the first night by Antoinette Sibley, Anthony Dowell and David Wall) was again successful with the public but received a mixed reception from the critics. Once more Andrew Porter pronounced it a success and 'a feast of wonderful choreography', and several critics praised it on its second appearance when it had been shortened and otherwise adjusted, but again *The Times* critic condemned it in the most wounding terms:

> Inside the three sprawling acts of Kenneth MacMillan's new ballet there seems to be a presentable one-act work struggling to be born. At three hours duration with two intervals, the production is far longer than either its dramatic content or its dance interest will justify. Increasingly it becomes evident that MacMillan the choreographer is in serious need of an artistic director to help him make the most of his ideas. Trying to fulfil both functions, his own work suffers.

He also complained that there was too much dancing:

> By padding out the action with innumerable divertissements MacMillan has relinquished the prospect of making a serious impact. Even when individual dances are attractive . . . the procession of one dramatically irrelevant solo or ensemble after another has a trivial effect.[4]

Manon has been regularly revived and grew into a box-office success, but the hostility and unfriendliness of some of the criticism produced a deep depression in MacMillan 'so much so that it threatened to overwhelm his ability to function, both as Director of the company and as a private person'.[5]

There is some agreement that MacMillan's creativity suffered at this time, and on the debit side was an unsuccessful production of *The Sleeping Beauty*, particularly disappointing because it had been sponsored by the American Friends of Covent Garden. Yet the standard of dancing remained consistently high. Ann Jenner made her debut as Aurora in this production, and Clement Crisp spoke of Merle Park as 'sailing through the ballet with all the ease and unaffected enjoyment of a bird singing'.

> Miss Park's account of the role is remarkable in its fluency and sheer brilliance of technical resource; the most vertiginous moments are taken with a sunny assurance that makes them seem both natural and even undemanding, and it is this quality of total physical control of the choreography that gives the reading its special merit.[6]

In addition, in spite of the difficulties caused by the amalgamation of the two companies, Clive Barnes wrote of the *corps de ballet* on the American tour of 1972: 'This has become the greatest ballet ensemble in the world. . . . These girls and boys dance exquisitely and with a unique mixture of precision and passion.'[7]

There was an *embarras de richesse* in solo dancers. According to MacMillan's biographer, he had to find work for eleven soloists.[†] Fonteyn, now over fifty, still danced in performances with Nureyev; since higher prices were charged for these, they made

---

[†] In a different context Edward Thorpe names the following dancers of the time: Deanne Bergsma, Svetlana Beriosova, Vergie Derman, Monica Mason, Merle Park, Georgina Parkinson, Jennifer Penney, Lynn Seymour, Antoinette Sibley, Michael Coleman, Anthony Dowell and Donald MacLeary, and younger dancers such as Lesley Collier, Laura Connor, Ann Jenner, Marguerite Porter, Rosalyn Whitten, David Ashmole, Wayne Eagling, Julian Hosking, Stephen Jefferies and Wayne Sleep. The name of David Wall should also be added.

a significant contribution to the finances of the house.

In the early seventies, the repertoire was enriched by four works by Jerome Robbins – *Dances at a Gathering, In the Night, L'Après-midi d'un Faune* and *The Concert* – and a triple bill by Balanchine—*Prodigal Son, The Four Temperaments* and *Agon*. There were new works by Cranko and Tetley, and MacMillan's own *Elite Syncopations,* an amusing and successful ballet to ragtime music by Scott Joplin. This had roles for many of the leading dancers and was rapturously received by the public.

MacMillan did everything he could to persuade Ashton (still chief choreographer) to create a new work but he, too, was depressed and, since he had always moulded his ballets on the dancers in class or at rehearsal, he suffered from a lack of stimulus. It was to be seven years before he produced a major new work.

In 1970, Natalia Makarova defected to the West. Her association with Covent Garden began in 1972 when she danced *Swan Lake, Giselle, The Sleeping Beauty* and *Les Sylphides*. She was anxious to extend her range and appear in contemporary works, and she has danced in many MacMillan ballets, as also in Ashton's *Cinderella* and in *A Month in the Country.* Described as 'a gorgeous dancer . . . whose blend of steely exactitude and rich, eloquent fluency is unmatchable',[8] Makarova proved again and again that she could adapt magnificently to British and American choreography. In the late seventies she appeared so often with The Royal Ballet that she seemed almost a regular member.

In 1974 Mikhail Baryshnikov also defected to the West, dancing with the National Ballet of Canada before joining American Ballet Theatre. He made his debut at Covent Garden in 1975, dancing Romeo and Prince Siegfried in *Swan Lake*. These roles illustrated his dazzling virtuosity and classical purity, while, when he later danced Colas in *La Filie mal gardée,* he showed dramatic gifts which included a natural talent for comedy.

MacMillan was naturally disposed to the work of the New Group, as the Touring Company was called at this time. This opened in Nottingham with two outstanding ballets, Balanchine's *Apollo* and Ashton's *Symphonic Variations,* and with *Field Figures,* a new work of an avant-garde nature by the American Glen Tetley. A few weeks later, Beriosova and MacLeary joined the company to dance a new MacMillan ballet, *Checkpoint.*

However the modern ballets were not accepted by provincial audiences, who expected the classics, and the Company was increased to thirty-four dancers and the repertoire changed to include such old favourites as *The Rake's Progress, Les Patineurs, Façade* and *Pineapple Poll.* The new group toured overseas as well as in the provinces, and, when it came to London, danced at Sadler's Wells.

The new Music Director,‡ Colin Davis, began with a highly successful performance of the new production of *Le nozze di Figaro,* which had been the subject of so much controversy. 'This *Figaro,'* Peter Heyworth wrote, 'is one of the most lively, warm, humane and blissfully unaffected performances of the opera I have ever seen. . . . It is an event not to be missed.'⁹ John Copley, the resident producer who had had the unenviable task of taking over where Peter Hall had left off, received great praise, as did the conductor:

---

‡ Colin Davis preferred the title Music Director to that of Musical Director, previously used.

We were all looking forward to a fresh, exciting, valid new view of this inexhaustible human and social drama. Grant Mr Copley credit: he has given us just that.

The approach must have come if only collaboratively from Colin Davis, who, we know, believes in the strongly contentious and passionate aspects of Mozart's score, and who deploys them here with knowing insight especially into rhythm, pace and balance, though if the spectator shuts his eyes and listens solely to the music . . . it can be heard how lovingly Mr Davis is nursing the miracle in his charge.[10]

However, the first night of this *Figaro* will be remembered above all for the arrival, before an unprepared and relatively unexpectant audience, of a new soprano of international class – the young Kiri te Kanawa. Speaking of her first audition, Colin Davis said: 'I couldn't believe my ears. I've taken thousands of auditions but it was such a fantastically beautiful voice that I said "Let's hear her again and see if we're not dreaming".' And he added: 'I just had to be sure that the voice was consistent. It seemed much too good to be true.'[11] When, in December 1971 Kiri te Kanawa, sitting at a dressing table and singing from cold, began the beautiful and fiendishly difficult aria Torgi amor', she took the audience as much by surprise as she had Colin Davis. In the words of Desmond Shawe-Taylor, she poured out 'a stream of pure radiant ample tone which remained ringing and assured, even on those bridge notes between the middle and head registers where all but the most accomplished sopranos are apt to falter', and he added that Kiri te Kanawa had come 'to the threshold of international fame'.[12]

After *Le nozze di Figaro* things went less well for the new regime. It was followed by an unsuccessful *Nabucco* and a very disappointing *Don Giovanni*. At both these the new Music Director was booed (as Solti had been before him), adopting in response the novel and not very successful expedient of putting his tongue out. However, in April 1974 he established himself once and for all in the Opera House and in the annals of operatic history with a production of *La clemenza di Tito*. 'Colin Davis', wrote William Mann in *The Times,* 'a dedicated Mozartian, will have justified his post as music director at the Royal Opera House with this reinstatement of a great and half-neglected Mozart opera, even if he never does another hand's turn in Floral Street.'[13] Although the parts were sung 'with intensity and passion' by Janet Baker, 'brilliantly' by Yvonne Minton, and 'deliciously' by Anne Howells and Teresa Cahill, the evening was accounted 'first Mozart's, then Mr Davis's', while Anthony Besch was praised for 'making the action move quickly as Mozart intended'.

At eight performances of this opera there was an average paying audience of 95 per cent of capacity. Some idea of the popularity of opera at this time can be illustrated by the following figures for paid attendance: *Aida,* 98 per cent; *La Bohème* (a new production), *Carmen, Don Giovanni* (the Copley Lazaridis production) and *Falstaff,* all 97 per cent; *Fidelio, Death in Venice* and *La forza del destino,* 94 per cent; *Boris Godunov* 92 per cent; and *Elektra* and *Eugene Onegin* 91 per cent.

In 1973 Sir Claus Moser was unanimously elected by the Board of Covent Garden to succeed Lord Drogheda as Chairman, and at the end of the following season he took over. Sir Claus was born in Berlin in 1922, but came with his family to England in the thirties. He has been described as 'combining a mathematician's logical mind with a lifelong passion for music' and was, at the time of his appointment, Director of the Central Statistical Office and head of the Government Statistical Service.

Yet his talent as a pianist was such that as a young man he had even considered making this his professional career. He had been a member of the Board of Covent Garden since [965 and he was prepared to give much time to the affairs of the Opera House. On assuming the Chair he gave up membership of all other boards except the BBC's Music Advisory Council and the Board of Governors of the Royal Academy of Music. He took over at a time when none of the opportunities for striking improvements so eagerly taken by his predecessor was available to him. However, one of his most notable successes came early in his reign, when in 1975 he persuaded HRH the Prince of Wales to become patron of The Royal Opera.

The new Chairman was faced with one of the most inflationary periods in British history, and the whole of the foreword to his first Annual Report is devoted to the subject of finance. The year had closed with a deficit of £209,000 and only by using up the whole of an Arts Council guarantee intended to tide over the three years to March 1976 had it been possible to get close to balancing the books for the first of those three years. 'The plain fact is that our finances have been thrown out, first by the imposition of vat and now, quite basically, by the steep increase in the rate of inflation.' Total expenditure in 1973/4 had been 24 per cent higher than the previous year, while the Arts Council grant was up by only 17 per cent.

The report explained that support from public funds was down to 50 per cent of expenditure, 'which makes our financial situation one of the seven wonders of the balletic and operatic world'. 'One German Intendant called it sensational5, the report goes on. 'None of the great opera houses of Europe expects to cover more than a third of its costs from the box office. For some the figure is only a fifth.5 Seat prices had once more been raised by

266

10 per cent in the past season, but because of the imposition of vat the opera house budget had benefited by less than a tenth. An opera house, more than any other theatrical undertaking, is vulnerable to cost inflation. More than 75 per cent of total expenditure consists of wages, salaries and artists5 fees, and in the case of an international house, it is also subject to exchange rates.

Earlier reports had made it plain that nothing more could be achieved through attendance figures. The average attendance for ballet had reached 94 per cent – probably as high as would ever be attained – while that for opera was well over 90 per cent if the figures for modern works were excluded. (While in the season 1972/3 operas such as *Aida, Fidelio* and *Lucia di Lammermoor* had reached figures of 97 or 98 per cent, *The Knot Garden* had averaged 51 per cent at six performances, *Taverner* 49 per cent at five, *Owen Wingrave* and *Wozzeck* just above 70 per cent.)

> In the end, if we are to be able to maintain standards . . . to extend activities as we should like, and to provide performers and staff with the rewards and facilities they deserve, without at the same time pricing ourselves out of the market – and certainly out of reach of those whose enjoyment of opera and ballet our support from public funds is intended to make possible – we are going to have to increase the proportion of our expenditure met from public funds to much nearer the European levels of 60–70 per cent or so – indeed to something like the corresponding figure for the English National Opera Company (which stood at 61 per cent for 1972/3).

In future, the Opera House would be kept going by the Arts Council, but only just. The Council usually accepted the basis of the Opera House estimates, but often had insufficient money to meet them, and this was true irrespective of which political party was in power. The difficulties thus imposed were much increased by the fact that, while the plans of an opera house must be made three or four years ahead, the amount of the grant was announced only two months before the beginning of each financial year.

The Board and administration responded to these circumstances in two different ways. In the first place every effort was made to raise money from industry. Lord Kissin, the Chairman of the Royal Opera House Trust, began by appointing an influential body of trustees and inviting industrial firms to become corporate members and to sponsor productions or contribute to a general fund. In an interview given in 1975 he said that, whereas he had aimed to find at least £50,000 for one new production in the first year, he had in fact succeeded in raising the money for three—a new production of *Das Rheingold* had been backed by Commercial Union, *Die Walküre* by the Baring Foundation, and *The Masked Ball* by Imperial Tobacco and the National Westminster Bank. Such is the prestige of the Opera House that, at the time of writing, the Royal Opera House Trust regularly raises about £2 million a year towards the cost of new productions, and in contributions towards the general fund.

Secondly, every effort was made to widen the facilities for the general public and to create opportunities for young people to see opera and ballet. In 1972 changes were made in the pricing of the seats, which had the effect of increasing the number at lower prices (in that year available at £2) to 60 per cent of the total capacity of the house, while the price of the more expensive seats was increased.

One of the most important innovations, dear to the hearts of the Chairman, John Tooley and Colin Davis, was the introduction of promenade performances, made possible by the support of Midland Bank. Stalls were taken out of the theatre, an informal atmosphere created and admission prices kept low. The first prom, a performance of *Boris Godunov,* produced by Ande Anderson, the Resident Producer, was given in July 1971 in association with the BBC, but in the second year the Covent Garden Proms were separated from the BBC and three performances of opera and ballet given, after which they became a regular annual event.

Probably the most colourful of the expedients to attract new audiences was the use of the Big Top. There are very few provincial theatres which have stages big enough to take ballet or opera performances, and the administration hit upon the idea of presenting the ballet in a large tent originally designed for Cinerama. The Royal Ballet appeared for the first time in the tent in Plymouth in a season which ran from 23 July to 3 August 1974. This attracted capacity audiences and was sold out before opening night. In the following year The Royal Ballet was forced to cancel a season at the Coliseum Theatre because of a strike among stage hands, and the tent was erected in Battersea Park. Here, the Ballet Company danced for four weeks to full houses, while a survey established that almost half the audience were seeing ballet for the first time. Since that time, the tent in Battersea Park has become a regular feature of the summer season, and it continues to be seen in some provincial cities. These tent seasons were made possible with the assistance once again of Midland Bank, and were held in Battersea Park with the co-operation of the GLC.

In the early seventies, television transmissions of opera and ballet, so important in reaching a wide audience, had been made impossible by disagreement between the BBC and Actors'

Equity.[§] In the season 1974/5 there were television performances of *La Bohème* on Southern Television, *Un bollo in maschera* on the BBC, and MacMillan's *Elite Syncopations* at the Big Top, also on the BBC.

Since the early sixties, performances had been given in co-operation with Sir Robert Mayer's Youth and Music, when seats were allocated to young people between fourteen and twenty-five years at reduced prices, and in the season 1973/4 a total of 4,685 members of Youth and Music saw between them ten performances at the Royal Opera House—seven operas and three ballets.

In 1964 it had been decided that the compromises involved in adapting Royal Opera House productions of opera to small provincial theatres were unacceptable (apart from the Hippodrome, Bristol there was no theatre outside London with a stage comparable to Covent Garden), and touring of the main company had ceased. It had been hoped that certain regional theatres, particularly in Manchester, might be improved but in 1975 John Tooley had to report that no positive progress had been made. Opera for All and Ballet for All continued to visit small towns and villages, the former touring in 1973/4 from the beginning of October to the middle of May, the longest tour in its twenty-five-year history, while the latter continued to increase its audiences.[¶]

[§] The first transmission of a complete opera from a theatre had been of *La traviata* from Covent Garden in 1967.

[¶] Opera for All was a small group founded by the Arts Council in 1949 to take opera to small towns and villages. Many well-known singers had their first opportunities with the group which was replaced by 'Opera 80'.

15

1976–1979
Extension to the Opera House:
Phase I

Of all problems in the presentation of opera, production and design seem the most intractable. It may be remembered that Solti remarked that he had failed in his intention to improve design. There have been a few brilliantly talented designer-producers – Visconti, Zeffirelli – but as a rule the two things are separate functions. Because it is necessary that those involved should be able to work closely together, it very often happens that the producer decides for himself the style of production, and therefore the designer he thinks appropriate. Nor is it unusual for a conductor undertaking a new production to choose the producer, although musical talent does not in any way guarantee visual taste. In a highly critical paper on design, written by one of the directors of Covent Garden, it is remarked that the best results could not be attained so long as Covent Garden was wedded to what he called 'delegated taste'.

Colin Davis seemed to be aware of these problems when he took over at the opera house, since he attempted to 'share his kingdom' first with Peter Hall and later with Götz Friedrich. Lord Drogheda has told us that when Davis first met Götz Friedrich 'he began once more to fall under a spell', and decided that he would like him to take the part intended for Peter Hall. 'He believed, he said, that the artistic supervision was not what it should be, and he wanted someone with whom to share the responsibility.'[1]

In fact this collaboration did not develop as intended, because of Friedrich's heavy commitments to other opera houses, but for some years he was given the tide of Principal Producer and he was immediately engaged for some productions, notably that of *Der Freischütz, Idomeneo* and a new production of the *Ring.* Opinion is sharply divided on Friedrich's work, although few would deny his imaginative talents. 'Friedrich's productions', one critic remarked, 'usually contain something to stimulate, delight and enrage any spectator who isn't merely passive.' Bernard Levin wrote rapturously at the conclusion of the *Ring* cycle in 1976 and Peter Heyworth described it as 'the most illuminating production of the *Ring* I have seen . . . a tremendous achievement. . . . Without any finger-wagging, Friedrich uncovers a wealth of metaphysical, political and psychological allusions, yet leaves the listener free to make of them what he will.' William Mann also praised the production, although with some reservations. Others, including Philip Hope-Wallace and Ernest Bradbury of the *Yorkshire Post,* preferred at least some parts of the production at the Coliseum, while Bradbury said Friedrich's production was 'just about the silliest' *Ring,* although he added that he had not seen 'this year's French debacle' at Bayreuth.[2] Philip Hope-Wallace, summing up, said this:

> Götz Friedrich is certainly a purposeful producer: one feels that everyone involved knows exactly what he is due to deliver in dramatic terms. I believe it may yet become clearer that this laudable aim is being achieved. It is certainly not 'a ridiculous mouse' that these mountains in labour have produced but is it quite impressive enough for the time (or money, if one dare say)?[3]

Yet if there were differences of opinion about Götz Friedrich, there was much praise for Colin Davis. At Covent Garden booing for a new Music Director seems required, but, once settled into this role, Colin Davis was generously acknowledged a master. Writing of his *Ring* two years later William Mann said: 'For those of us who have been in Bayreuth it was a joy last night to hear the orchestral music of *Das Rheingold* played with such sterling resonance and cogent style . . . so appreciatively, with a care that did not exclude boldness.'[4] And Max Loppert, in the *Financial Times,* wrote: 'Flow, follow-through, a control of the music through transitions, over long spans of time, and towards bravely achieved climaxes: these are now notable features of Mr Davis's conducting.'[5]

The greatest triumph of the mid-seventies was the exchange with La Scala of Milan. After the success of The Royal Opera in Berlin and Munich in 1970, John Tooley had held discussions with the British Council with a view to following up the impact then made. An allocation of funds from a special grant set aside by the Government for cultural purposes made the simultaneous exchange possible. Three operas were performed

273

at La Scala: *Benvenuto Cellini*, *Peter Grimes* and *La clemenza di Tito*. This visit, received with cries of 'Bravo Inglese', was a triumph for the company and for its Music Director.[*]

In London the repertory introduced by the new Music Director was admirably adventurous. The new productions included *Uelisir d'amore* in 1975, *Ariadne auf Naxos*, *La fanciulla del West*, *Der Freischütz*, and *The Icebreak* in 1976/7, *Lohengrin*, *Die Fledermaus*, *Idomeneo* and *Luisa Miller* in 1977/8 and *Die Zauberflöte*, *Parsifal*, *Werther*, *The Rake's Progress* and *L'Africaine* (in a production borrowed from Florence) in 1978/9. Of these, *L'elisir d'amore*, *Werther* (sung originally at Covent Garden by Jean de Reszke), *Der Freischütz*, *Luisa Miller*, and *L'Africaine* were all operas which had not been done for a long time; *L'Africaine* not for ninety years, and *Luisa Miller*, apart from a production at Sadler's Wells in 1954, not since 1874. *The Rake's Progress* was given for the first time at Covent Garden and *The Icebreak* was a world premiere of a new opera by Michael Tippett.

L'elisir d'amore, Donizetti's most lovable comic opera, conducted by John Pritchard, with designs by Beni Montresor and sung by Sir Geraint Evans, José Carreras and Yasuko Hayashi was predictably a great success.

Ariadne auf Naxos was less successful. There was general agreement that the house was too big for this opera and the producer, John Copley, and his designer, Philip Prowse, were criticized, William Mann remarking that 'Mr Prowse's sea looked like corrugated iron, his cave like a pile of chocolate pepperrnint creams left too long by the fireside.'[6] Harold Rosenthal thought

---

[*] The Scala Company at Covent Garden performed *La cenerentola*, *Simon Boccanegra*, and gave a concert performance of the Verdi *Requiem*.

none of the voices sounded large enough for the house, and everyone mourned the loss of Rudolf Kempe, to whom the first performance was dedicated.

The first night of *Die Fledermaus*, on New Year's Eve 1977, was a special occasion. Sponsored by Girozentrale, Vienna and the Royal Opera House Trust, this was relayed live round the world by BBC Television and seen, it was estimated, by twenty million viewers. The problems of singing in the original language, yet making the lengthy and indispensable dialogue comprehensible to the audience at Covent Garden, were dealt with by the multilingual method of turning Dr Falke into an English friend of the Eisensteins, and allowing him to speak in English to Rosalinde, who also acquires English nationality. Alfred, the tenor, spoke operatic Italian and after that everyone dropped into English when they pleased. This was not approved by the more purist of the critics, but it delighted the audience and often produced most amusing effects. Peter Heyworth said that Kiri te Kanawa sang 'sumptuously as Rosalinde', but had yet to develop the air of sophistication required. Her rather downright manner amused many in the audience. Hermann Prey was outstanding as Eisenstein, and Mr Heyworth said that if anything could justify the decision to cast a baritone in what was normally a tenor role, it was Hermann Prey's performance. Best of all, perhaps, was Josef Meinrad, 'a blissful Frosch'.[7] Altogether a splendid New Year's Eve for Sir Claus Moser, whose dream it had been to see a performance of *Die Fledermaus* at the opera house on this night.

Der Freischütz, conducted by Colin Davis (a known admirer of Weber), and in a production by Götz Friedrich with design by Günther Schneider-Siemssen, was said by one critic to be 'Yet another glimpse of *Mother Courage*, but rather resembling

275

Les Sylphides after a tornado'.[8] It was nevertheless welcomed. David Cairns said that the great achievement was to 'have made a serious drama out of a work which had become a byword for operatic absurdity',[9] and William Mann praised the production.

When *The Icebreak*, the latest of four operas by Michael Tippett, was given its world premiere at Covent Garden, Peter Heyworth declared it to be 'every bit as idiosyncratic as its predecessors, as wayward in its dramatic movement, as radiant in its imaginative richness',[10] while Desmond Shawe-Taylor, having said that there were, no doubt, those in the audience who found the work disconcerting or puzzling, went on: 'But the sustained warmth of the reception seemed to reflect . . . a strong emotion aroused by the work itself, not indeed in every detail, but in its general impact.' And he said that, although he had and retained reservations about Tippett insisting on writing all his own librettos, he found *The Icebreak* the best of the series. The performance did immense credit to the Royal Opera House, to its orchestra and to Colin Davis to whom the score was dedicated.[11] *The Icebreak* was given five performances and revived in 1983.

The same year *Idomeneo* was given its first performance at Covent Garden. Who better', asked William Mann, 'to preside over its Bow Street baptism than Colin Davis who has championed it vociferously, and with deeds as well as words, since his early conducting days.' And he went on:

Last night the enthusiasm of his reading was tempered only by respect for the classic nobility of the score, and concern for an apt balance between voices on stage and instruments in the orchestra. The glories of the music, tenderness, grandeur, solemnity, pity, terror, emerged as

276

vivid as ever. The overture swept uninterrupted into Ilia's first recitative, and thereafter we were given the strongest demonstration of the opera's dramatic coherence, its extraordinary vitality, and a totally human compassion that bursts the conventions of Italian *opera seria* in which Mozart had been trained to mastery. . . .

He thought the opera was beautifully played and sung, and praised particularly Yvonne Kenny and the chorus, but said that he would remember most 'the impassioned singing of Janet Baker as Idamante, and the poignant yet heroic Idomeneo of Stuart Burrows, the finest performance I have heard from that justly admired tenor.'[12]

There was some criticism of the production and designs by Friedrich and Stefanos Lazaridis, Rosenthal complaining of 'Mr Friedrich's habit of overloading the stage with unnecessary and often incomprehensible business' and of Lazaridis's 'cumbersome platforms and staircases'.[13] But Ronald Crichton in the *Financial Times* found Friedrich's direction fascinating 'for his grip on the drama and for his illuminating and visually effective use of the singers – both soloists and chorus'.[14]

Three months later *Luisa Miller*, conducted by Lorin Maazel, and staged by Filippo Sanjust, was performed for the first time at Covent Garden since Patti sang it in 1874. The enthusiasm which greeted the first performance sung by Luciano Pavarotti (who subsequently gave way to José Carreras) and Katia Ricciarelli made it surprising that the work had not been performed for so long. The critics, as well as the audience, were this time full of praise, the greatest accolades going to Ricciarelli of whom David Cairns said that she sang 'with both scrupulous control and purity of tone and passionate commitment', acting touchingly and phrasing vitally, 'a glorious, complete performance.'[15]

L'Africaine had not been seen at Covent Garden for ninety years and was given now in a production borrowed from Florence with Peter Maag conducting and Grace Bumbry and Placido Domingo in the leading roles. Ronald Crichton in the *Financial Times* summed up the general opinion:

> How nice it would be to say that the evening had been fully rewarding on musical or dramatic grounds! But that was hardly so. The story . . . is little more than a prolonged excuse for song and spectacle. The music is constantly intriguing for what Meyerbeer gave to others – the Verdi of *Don Carlos and Aida* high among them. . . . He was an exceedingly gifted musician, clever as a million monkeys, a good deal more than merely meretricious.

And he added that a few pages of either of the Verdi operas would 'blow the whole structure sky high, and yet – without *L'Africaine* they would not by any means be what they are.'[16]

Both Glyndebourne and Sadler's Wells Opera had given performances of *The Rake's Progress*. Its first performance at Covent Garden was received with mixed feelings, and, although Colin Davis's handling of it was once more praised, there were differing views about Elijah Moshinsky's production, as also about the opera itself. However Philip Hope-Wallace wrote that it was one of the best things 'they have managed in this indifferent season'.[17] He spoke of the season of 1979, which had included new productions of *Die Zauberflöte*, *Parsifal* and *Werther*. The *Parsifal*, in a production by Terry Hands with designs by Farrah, caused Peter Heyworth to congratulate the thwarted

Wagnerians who had been unable to get seats. Rodney Milnes said that it was a mistake on rather a grand scale: 'The prospect of revival, for instance, is one too horrible even for the Garden management . . . to contemplate.'[18]

Peter Heyworth also described it as a 'lack-lustre season' and he gave a long and interesting analysis of why this should have been so. He said that for more than one reason he had hesitated before 'thrusting my poisoned pen between Sir John Tooley's ribs'. Crucial among these was the fact that Covent Garden now ranked as the pauper among the world's opera houses. 'Rightly expected to preserve a place in Division One, it has not been provided with the means of doing so.' In 1978/9 Covent Garden's subsidy was little more than half that of the Munich opera house and considerably less than half what the Paris Opera received. As a result it was 'outgunned' by its rivals in bidding for artists.

> That Covent Garden contrives to keep its head above water is due primarily to the fact that it recoups a substantially higher proportion of its outgoings at the box office than does any comparable theatre. It also expends great ingenuity in raising money from outside sources and in striking deals for joint ventures.

Later in this article Heyworth said that an artistic profile was what Covent Garden needed above all else and at present conspicuously lacked. The season [1978/9] smacked of 'intelligent, administrative arrangements rather than of any pressing sense of artistic commitment.' But, he asked, 'Where is that to come from?' Of the twenty new productions and revivals listed for the following season the company's Musical Director, Colin

Davis was to conduct no more than two.

> That seems a very meagre contribution from the man in charge, even if he is bearing the brunt of the coming Far Eastern tour. The case of Gótz Friedrich is still stranger. Although he is listed as 'principal producer' he does not return to the Royal Opera House until he stages *Lulu* in 1980/81. . . .
>
> As a result, everything falls on the shoulders of Sir John Tooley.[†] I do not doubt his ability and devotion. But is it reasonable to expect a man who is charged with the prodigious administrative burden of keeping an under-subsidised international house afloat to show the artistic initiative that Covent Garden so badly needs?[19]

In 1976 the New Group or Touring Company was given a permanent headquarters at Sadler's Wells Theatre. It had offices and wardrobe accommodation there as well as two rehearsal studios, three when performing at Covent Garden or Sadler's Wells. This group, no longer primarily experimental, nevertheless still gives opportunities to young choreographers. Consisting at first of forty-five dancers (later sixty) led by Margaret Barbieri, Vyvian Lorrayne, Marion Tait, Alain Dubreuil, Desmond Kelly, Carl Myers and David Ashmole, it was also sometimes joined by dancers from Covent Garden. Primarily a touring company, it had regular seasons at Sadler's Wells and also performed at Covent Garden.

Throughout the whole of his period as Director of the ballet

[†] John Tooley was knighted in 1979.

MacMillan had continued to press Frederick Ashton to create a new ballet. *A Month in the Country,* first performed in 1976, has been compared to the late masterpieces of Verdi. James Kennedy wrote:

> There is no other choreographer who could have done it who could have achieved this sustained quality of dance . . . while, at the same time [giving] a true sensitive appreciation of the play. . . . The Turgenev essence . . . is there. The choreography is beautiful, expressive, various – charming solos, *pas de deux* and ensembles for the cast of eight; and hardly a moment is lost in mime story-telling – the story is, almost all of it, put across in the dancing.

He praised Anthony Dowell as the tutor for 'a most adroit blend of dance virtuosity with a modest stage presence' and Denise Nunn, picked out by Ashton from the *corps de ballet* for a 'well nigh impeccable Vera – innocent, spirited and a very expressive dancer too'.[20]

Oleg Kerensky, reporting for the *Herald Tribune,* said 'Sir Frederick Ashton's new ballet . . . is an overwhelming and unequivocal success', and that Julia Trevelyan Oman had provided 'a ravishing and a very realistic Russian country house', while Lynn Seymour 'might have been born to dance Natalia Petrovna, by turns charming, gracious, jealous and flirtatious'.[21]

In May 1977 Kenneth MacMillan had to sit through several consecutive performances of his own ballet *Romeo and Juliet.* This experience, we are told, precipitated a decision that had been crystallizing in his mind for a long time. He felt that

281

his administrative duties were not merely too onerous but damaging to his creative power and that he was failing to give of his best in either of his two roles. The Board was sympathetic to his difficulty and accepted his resignation at the end of the 1977 season.

Historically the most important event of the seventies was the successful appeal for funds for Phase 1 of the extension to the opera house, and, in 1979, the beginning of work upon it. The Royal Opera House had been built over 120 years before and the only important alteration since had been the demolishing of the north-west wing in 1933, with a resulting loss of space at the rear of the stage. Conditions behind, unseen from the uniquely beautiful auditorium, were described as lamentable, appalling or inconvenient, according to whether the dressing rooms and general convenience of the performers and staff was described, or the working of the theatre. Years of insufficient funds had meant shortage of rehearsal space (each opera production was still rehearsed at the London Opera Centre in Commercial Road, an hour's journey away, while the ballet rehearsed at Barons Court).

Even more important, the dressing rooms, washing facilities and lavatories were really disgraceful while a canteen used by 1,000 people seated only 130. One cannot help wondering how great international stars were persuaded into the house.

When the Covent Garden vegetable and fruit market was moved to Nine Elms, the opportunity arose for the development of the site in a manner architecturally worthy of one of the most central and important districts of London. For the Opera House it was a chance to make essential improvements. The Department of Education and Science had set up a committee in 1969 to consider the situation which would arise when the market was moved, and in 1974 the Government bought a site next to the Royal Opera House so that the theatre might be developed and modernized.

An Appeal Committee, of which Lord Drogheda and Sir Claus Moser were joint chairmen, and Lord Sieff, vice-chairman as also Sir Joseph Lock-wood to whose efforts much of the success of the appeal was due was formed immediately. The prestige of the Opera House and of the chairmen and vice-chairmen ensured that the members of this committee were personally influential and between them in touch with individuals or firms likely to be persuaded to contribute. In 1977 Mr A.P. Spooner was appointed director of the Development Appeal with the task of organizing and co-ordinating a campaign to raise approximately £10 million.

The campaign was launched officially at a banquet at the Guildhall in the presence of HRH The Prince of Wales, the Lord Mayor of London and 700 guests, by which time £3 million had already been raised. On the same day the Government announced its intention of making a special grant of £1 million to the Development Fund during the following fiscal year. Later in the year the GLC contributed a further £1 million which had been promised on the basis of £1 for every £4 raised from other sources.

The success of the appeal owed much to the Royal Family and much to the appalling nature of the arrangements for staff and artists in the opera house (seventy men of the chorus shared twelve wash basins and four showers). Most people who could be persuaded to visit the opera house were convinced by what they saw and many of them contributed. Early in 1979 the Prince of Wales spent three full days at Covent Garden making a film of backstage conditions, and in May of that year he showed this at St James's Palace to a specially invited audience which included HRH The Princess Margaret. This film, which had been made through the generosity of EMI films, was widely distributed in the cinemas throughout the country.

On 1 May a one-hour documentary on working conditions backstage in the theatre was shown on BBC 1 to an audience of over four million, and on 20 May Richard Baker made an appeal on BBC Television which brought in £13,000. In the first half of 1979 donations received or promised from private sources averaged £100,000 a month.

In October of the same year Princess Margaret visited five cities in the United States (Chicago, Houston, Los Angeles, San Francisco and Cleveland) on behalf of the Development Appeal. In a seventeen-day tour Her Royal Highness carried out thirty-six engagements, showing the Prince Charles film to nearly 700 guests at five private dinners, and meeting representatives of the media. Half a million dollars was raised. A Royal gala auction in London, attended by the Prince of Wales and Princess Margaret realized over £100,000, while a Royal Ballet gala at the Metropolitan Opera House, New York, organized by Mrs Walter Annenberg as honorary chairman of the American Friends of Covent Garden, raised a sum exceeding £250,000.

The architects for the first phase of the development were the GMW Partnership and their achievement can today be seen at Covent Garden. At the time work was started on the building the appeal fund was still somewhat short of the financial target, and, due to the effects of inflation, the appeal for the first phase had to be raised from £7.8 million to £9 million. On 4 June 1980 the Minister for the Arts announced a further grant of £1 million, and later in the month the Prime Minister gave a reception at 10

Downing Street in aid of the appeal fund.

The Prince of Wales and Princess Margaret continued to support the appeal (Princess Margaret attended a performance by The Royal Ballet of *Romeo and Juliet* in the courtyard of the Doge's Palace in Venice, followed by a gala ball in the Palazzo Pisani-Moretta, on the Grand Canal), and by May 1982 £9,342,000 had been raised. A concert given by Vladimir Horowitz at the Royal Festival Hall (the first time for thirty years the great pianist had appeared in Europe), and a donation of £100,000 brought the appeal total to just over £9.5 million. The Prince of Wales, who had laid the foundation stone of the new building, opened it officially on 19 July 1982.

All the most immediate and essential needs were met. The extension contains an opera rehearsal studio, two rehearsal studios for the Ballet Company, a chorus rehearsal room with tiered seats, modern dressing rooms with proper washing arrangements and lavatories, improved space for wardrobe maintenance and storage, offices near the stage for the conductor and the orchestra, the opera producers and the opera company manager, and a new stage-door. There is a plaque in the foyer, which pays tribute to those who made substantial contributions to the fund.

16

Ballet 1979–1984
'What shall we do without a genius?'

When Norman Morrice took over, The Royal Ballet could no longer claim to be the finest ballet company in the world outside Russia. There were many reasons for this but the two most obvious were probably connected. Ninette de Valois, like everyone else who has founded a distinguished ballet company, had administrative ability combined with outstanding artistic qualities. Speaking of the difficulties of administering the large and complex organization of the Royal Ballet at Covent Garden and the Touring Company and the ballet schools, a member of the ballet sub-committee asked when Dame Ninette retired: What shall we do without a genius?' And in spite of what de Valois herself thought, we know that few companies have for long survived the departure of the first Director. Indeed, in the effort to carry through to the second generation the combination of creativity and high technical standards that make a great company, The Royal Ballet was attempting something which had defeated most of its predecessors in ballet history. In this context it may be thought to have succeeded beyond expectation.

The second circumstance, which is probably connected, is that throughout the history of art there have been sudden irruptions of creativity in different spheres – the Italian composers of the early nineteenth century, the French painters and English novelists of the nineteenth – as well as a cyclical excellence which produces what might be termed fallow periods after some marvellous fecundity. No one knows whether talent lies dormant, awaiting a unique combination of circumstances to release it. What is certain is that nothing less than ideal conditions will do so, while history suggests that in ballet much depends on the artistic and administrative strength of the director.

In 1946 the de Valois Company and the Ballet School offered unrivalled opportunities to dancers, teachers, choreographers, and as it happened to designers. Dancers came to London from all the countries of the Commonwealth – the number of outstanding dancers from what was then Rhodesia, Canada and Australia in the great period actually exceeded those born in Britain. Today almost every advanced country in the world has its own ballet company and schools, and, as if to make certain of the consequent losses, foreign pupils at the Royal Ballet School have difficulty in acquiring a work permit at the end of their training.*

Whether because the dispersal of precious resources is unpropitious or the creative moment has passed, few of their successors

---

* Today work permits are given to three pupils a year.

have the authoritative excellence of the last generation of dancers. Again, with so small a classical repertory ballet cannot survive – as opera might – without constant replenishment. There are many promising young choreographers today but none whose name rings through the world as did those of Ashton and Balanchine.

The appointment of Norman Morrice to succeed MacMillan was unexpected. Not only had he had no previous connection with The Royal Ballet, but he was comparatively inexperienced both in the administration of such a large and complex organization, and, by Royal Ballet standards, as a dancer. At the age of eighteen or nineteen he had what he described as 'a brain storm', threw up his studies in science and began to take dancing lessons in secret. He won a scholarship to the Rambert School and spent twenty years with that company, first making scenery and doing the lighting, then as a dancer—choreographer and finally as its Director. As Director he turned a medium-sized company dancing a classical repertory into a small modern dance troupe.

Morrice, by all accounts a man of distinguished intellectual ability and an analytical mind, believed when he came to The Royal Ballet that the first and most important thing was to bring on young dancers who had been held back by the exceptional talent among their seniors. He also wished to have more consecutive performances—at least two blocks of four weeks a year, one at Covent Garden and one on tour in order to give dancers more performances. 'The company is too big for the number of performances we give, but not for the productions we are expected to give.' Dancers work into a role over four or five performances and are unable to develop if they are given only one or two.

In order to improve this situation Morrice decided to have no guest artists for his first season, ruling out the dancers most popular with the public – Nureyev, who for so long had been almost part of the company and who resented his exclusion, Baryshnikov and Makarova. Theoretically attractive, this policy would not instantly recommend itself to anyone who had studied the history of David Webster's attempts to build up an opera company without the stimulus to singers of performing with the best international stars. In this case it was unluckily timed to coincide with the retirement through injury and remarriage of Antoinette Sibley, and the departure of Anthony Dowell to spend a year with American Ballet Theatre, a loss at one blow of a remarkable pair and of two individually shining stars. Lynn Seymour, a ballerina of international standard and unsurpassed in dramatic roles, also left to become Artistic Director of the Bavarian Ballet.

At the time of Norman Morrice's appointment, Linda Christmas wrote an article in the *Guardian* entitled 'How is the tarnished fame of The Royal Ballet shining up again under the new Director?', which was outspoken but chiefly interesting for the correspondence it drew. In this she said that, after seven years under Kenneth MacMillan, the company seemed tired, 'with a shortage of new works, a failure to create new stars, and a haemorrhage of existing talent'. More importantly, she quoted from Clive Barnes, the dance critic of the *New York Post:*

> The Royal has no major dancers at the moment and has therefore dropped in stature and is no longer wanted in New York. I do not understand why they do not go and buy up talent from the Royal Danish Ballet or the Paris Opera. Since Britain is part of the Common Market there would be no difficulty with work permits. When the New York

City Ballet hit a bad patch they did just that, but then I think they have been a bit wiser in looking towards the future.[1]

Kenneth MacMillan wrote immediately, denying the allegations made by Linda Christmas and saying that it was not true that the Royal Ballet was no longer wanted. The company had been invited this season but the management elected to go in 1981. The following week Clive Barnes wrote as follows:

Since Ms Christmas quotes me . . . as saying that The Royal Ballet is 'no longer wanted in New York', and Mr MacMillan refutes this, perhaps some amplification is called for.

The use of the word 'wanted' was indeed hastily idiomatic on my part. What I meant to imply – and I have impeccable sources on both sides of the Adantic – is that at present the company is not viable in New York. Mr MacMillan is in error when he says the company was invited to New York. Certain soundings were made, but no invitation was issued. Even the possibility of the company appearing at Radio City Music Hall was explored, but rejected very wisely by Covent Garden.

In a later paragraph, Mr Barnes said:

I think everyone agrees that all organisations have their ups and downs, and many dance observers feel that the company Mr MacMillan handed over to his successor Norman Morrice was markedly weaker than the company Sir Frederick Ashton handed over to him.[2]

As it happened, the first event under Morrice's direction owed more to the previous regime than to his own. *Mayerling,* one of Kenneth MacMillan's most successful and often performed ballets, was given its first performance in February 1978. Mary Clarke, writing in the *Guardian,* said that the ballet demonstrated how right MacMillan was to give up the Directorship of The Royal Ballet and devote himself to his true vocation, and even John Percival praised the ballet. MacMillan and Gillian Freeman, who wrote the scenario, had used the well-known story, but told it unromantically and as it probably happened, through family disagreements, disease and madness. Describing the ballet, John Percival said that the first encounter with Mary Vetsera is nothing but 'provocation on her side, cold lust on his, and when they meet again it is for the suicide pact'.

> The choreographic idiom for those duets shows MacMillan at his best. He has always been addicted to innovative, sometimes hazardous lifts and manoeuvres. This time, even the most far-fetched inventions are well worth the fetching. Daring swings, right round throws and catches . . . vertiginous falls to the ground all vividly express the increasingly hysterical mood.

Percival says of David Wall's performance as Rudolf that even if *Mayerling* had nothing else to commend it (far from the case) he would 'unhesitatingly recommend you to see it'.[3]

Lynn Seymour as Mary and Merle Park as Countess Larisch had roles of equal importance and there were in addition roles for Georgina Parkinson as Elizabeth, Michael Somes as Franz Josef, Wendy Ellis as Stephanie and as Rudolfs sister-in-law, a newcomer, Genesia Rosato, 'who showed promise of fine things

291

to come'. 'The ballet stands as a fascinating and innovative development', Clement Crisp wrote, 'with MacMillan, Wall and the entire cast meriting every praise.' And he added 'So, too, does IBM International, whose generosity made the ballet possible: industrial sponsorship of the arts in these hard times is of inestimable public benefit.'[4]

There was in fact no shortage of promising younger dancers. In the autumn of 1977, writing of Lesley Collier in a new production of *Sleeping Beauty*, Clement Crisp said that she danced with that 'bravura that is so happily hers: sensitive, radiantly assured and youthful, this was a reading in which the delicacy with which she treats small incidents was matched with a commanding ease in the grandest demands of the role.'[5] And at a later performance the *Times* critic praised Stephen Jefferies:

> He makes the simple offering of a hand in a formal *pas de deux* so expressive that no elaboration is needed. This is a classical performer in the best theatrical tradition; how exciting it would be one day to see him opposite Makarova, who also has the gift of making conventional dances look new-minted to tell a story.[6]

In 1980 Collier and Jefferies were much praised again in a revival of Anthony Tudor's *Dark Elegies,* and so too were Rosalyn Whitten looking 'gloriously sombre as she moved smoothly through difficulties', and Marguerite Porter 'fragile, sensitive and vulnerable'. Wayne Eagling, Rosalyn Whitten, Stephen Beagley and Ashley Page appeared in Glen Tedey's *Dances of Albion,* and once more the critic of *The Times* was full of praise.

Finally, for Jennifer Penney, in MacMillan's *Gloria* – 'one of his finest non-narrative works' – Clement Crisp said there could not be praise enough: 'Her beautiful line, her always easy technical command, are here infused with a radiant simplicity and inevitability. In dancing absolutely pure she conveys exactly the extent of the sorrow at irreparable loss that speaks from Vera Brittain's poem.'[7]

The most memorable event of 1980 was the gala given to mark Queen Elizabeth, the Queen Mother's eightieth birthday. *Mam'zelle Angot* was danced by Stephen Jefferies and Jennifer Penney with Rosalyn Whitten as Mam'zelle. Natalia Makarova danced Natalia Petrovna in *A Month in the Country*, giving it 'a Russian quality that deepened the intensity', while her partnership with Anthony Dowell in the role of the tutor was said to take on 'a magical note that gives it an extra dimension'. The programme also included a new ballet, *Rhapsody*, by Frederick Ashton – his first complete ballet for four years. Set to Rachmaninov's 'Rhapsody on a Theme of Paganini', it was danced by Baryshnikov with Lesley Collier and a *corps* of six men and six girls, of whom it was said that they were 'no mere frieze'. 'The girls all danced with notable elegance, and the boys were particularly hard worked, with choreography very nearly as demanding as that for Baryshnikov.'[8]

So in London there was still much to praise. In 1981 The Royal Ballet went to New York. Antoinette Sibley, making a comeback went with them, and, reunited with Anthony Dowell for the first time in seven years, danced a new Ashton ballet, *Varii Capricci*. Merle Park led the company, dancing with Wayne Eagling; Monica Mason, Lesley Collier, Jennifer Penney and Marguerite Porter danced leading roles, as did Michael Coleman and Stephen Jefferies; while Wendy Ellis, Fiona Chadwick, Anthony Dowson and Stephen Beagley appeared in the supporting roles. The repertory included Robert Helpmann's *Hamlet*,

Swan Lake, The Sleeping Beauty, and Kenneth MacMillan's new ballet *Isadora.*

Unexpectedly, Clive Barnes was full of praise: 'A ballet legend returned to life . . .', he wrote, when Antoinette Sibley and Anthony Dowell were reunited for the first time for seven years.' Antoinette Sibley was, he thought, together with Makarova, 'the most important ballerina of her generation' and now . . . she is proving precisely why she has been so disastrously missed'. Dowell 'gave a nobly impassioned performance'.[9] Eagling, in a later performance, 'danced splendidly', as also did the 'charismatically dramatic' Stephen Jefferies. Stephen Beagley, 'partnering the exquisite Lesley Collier, was fine and stalwart' if not exciting. Michael Coleman 'had a happy charm and danced with vigorous brio'. Best of all, 'the company produced a whole slew of young dancers' for the supporting roles and 'virtually without exception they seemed excellent'. And in a later notice, Barnes wrote that The Royal Ballet's *Swan Lake* was 'as smooth as silk . . . a company where the youth is positively effervescent.'[10]

Anna Kisselgoff on the *New York Times* also was full of praise, saying that 'after the first two performances when the company relaxed, it showed itself "the great company it still is".'

A programme of triple bills including Ashton's *Symphonic Variations,* was a success. Barnes wrote that the Ashton ballet 'sustains itself as one of the three key works of the twentieth century'.[11] The other two ballets were Fokine's *Les Sylphides* and Balanchine's *Serenade.* But almost all the New York critics disliked Kenneth MacMillan's *Isadora.* In America not to be Ashton was still in itself a crime and MacMillan compounded this unavoidable misfortune, not merely by choosing for his theme a heroine who was American, but one who had previously been the subject

294

of an Ashton ballet. Clive Barnes said that although the ballet 'fails almost totally, it is the kind of grand failure one would prefer to have than a cheap success';[12] but Anna Kisselgoff said that the ballet was 'really a padded-out series of simulated-sex duets between the Isadora figure and her lovers'. And she said that as an admirer of MacMillan she had felt a twinge of distress at the literalness of his ballets.[13] Other critics found it tedious, vulgar or tawdry.

The most serious criticisms of the season came from Arlene Croce, the critic of the *New Yorker*. After a long analysis of the art of ballet in which she said 'at peak expression, the conscious elements of style are absorbed by the unconscious, which has an almost moral force of persuasion in performance', she went on:

> If a company has the grand style, has this collective moral elegance, chances are you don't think about technique, so unconscious and unwilled is it. Watching The Royal Ballet do the great classical ballets it brought to New York this season, my eye was repeatedly drawn to the dancers' technique, because it was always just beginning to disappear into style. . . . The technique simply wasn't doing what the dancers needed it for. Like dancers everywhere, they tried to make up for it with extroverted performing; the result was that they were both vivacious and dim.[14]

On his return to London Mark Bonham-Carter, a member of the ballet sub-committee, who had accompanied the company to New York, said that 'they were fortunate just to get away with it'. He said that too many leading dancers were unable to come to terms with their roles in a purely technical way, and that these weaknesses must be the consequence of bad or inadequate teaching at the Royal Ballet School. Mr Morrice suggested that British dancers had qualities of style and breeding which enabled them to perform the totality of a production better than most American dancers. But he too admitted that in terms of sheer technique our dancers trailed a long way behind American dancers, who had drawn ahead since the late 1960s.

It was suggested that when the Director of the schools retired, Merle Park would be the obvious successor. 'She would never be satisfied with any organization for which she was responsible not reaching the highest standards.' A report proposed that until some of the younger dancers had developed, guest dancers should be brought in, 'both in order to get performances of the quality we need and to provide the younger dancers with performers and performances on which to model themselves'.

In 1982 Rudolf Nureyev returned to The Royal Ballet for the first time for five years, Peter Schaufuss danced with it, and also Antoinette Sibley. Guest artists continued to appear.

Young British dancers also continued to appear. In April 1981 a newcomer named Bryony Brind had danced Odette/Odile to a standing ovation, and at the end of that year she danced *Afternoon of the Faun,* a role Jennifer Penney had at this time established as her own. 'Bryony Brind bewitches us from the moment she picks her way on point into the mirrored room' one critic wrote and spoke of her 'long limbs rippling effortlessly'. She is described as tall, with a radically different physique from her contemporaries in The Royal Ballet and with a commanding presence which takes her naturally into the Imperial Russian grand manner. 'Her legs, tapering and unusually high in extension, are turned to much eloquent effect, sometimes fragile, sometimes . . . dangerously feathery and sinister, or darting, fine and sharp as needles.'[15] Other dancers much praised at this time were Fiona Chadwick, Deirdre Eyden, Pippa Wylde and Ravenna Tucker and, among the very young, Alessandra Ferri. Jonathan Cope was a notable newcomer.

Two main criticisms remained. The first was that, although so many talented young dancers appeared, they failed to develop into stars of the first order as their predecessors had done. When in 1987 Natalia Makarova produced a series for television on the female dancer, she still chose Antoinette Sibley as an example of the British *prima ballerina*. The second criticism, constantly made, was of the *corps de ballet*, which was said to be less disciplined, less technically sure and less elegant than in earlier days. Speaking of a performance of *La Bayadere* in 1982, Stephanie Jordan voiced a common complaint:

> Despite the excellent dancing of the female soloists, the *corps de ballet*, star of the opening of this piece, showed the lack of sufficient rehearsal and style that has characterised much of its recent work. The 32 women looked shakier than in past revivals in what should appear a majestic, hypnotic opening procession of Shades. The pattern of motion repeated over and over calls for the firmest stepping out and confident pressure of the back and leg into a fulsome *arabesque* arc. Such a test of *corps* mettle and other worldliness cannot withstand creaky, staid execution.[16]

The Sadler's Wells Royal Ballet was, on the other hand, disciplined and strong, and as much in request for foreign tours as the senior company. The repertoire now included some excellent productions of the classics, notably Peter Wright's production of *Giselle* about which Mary Clarke was able to say in 1984 that it was in the repertory of so many companies that guest stars could adjust easily when appearing at Sadler's Wells. And Sir Roy Strong in an article on stage design, speaking of economy productions, said that by far the most distinguished designs in this vein were those by Philip Prowse for the Sadler's Wells Royal Ballet *Sleeping Beauty*. The company had in addition much-liked productions of *Pineapple Poll* and of *La Fille mal gardée* as well as a distinguished *Petrushka*.

They also had David Bintley, probably the most interesting young talent in British ballet today. A product of the Royal Ballet School, he joined Sadler's Wells Royal Ballet in 1976 and soon proved a quite exceptional character dancer. Said by the critic of *The Times* to be the best British dancer he had ever seen in the role of Petrushka, and by Clement Crisp to be 'a character dancer of most rare and penetrating gifts' he was spoken of in the following terms by the critic of *Dance and Dancers:* 'It is an eerie sight during the curtain calls to see Bintley returning gradually to himself, a dancer in make-up and costume. Until the curtain falls, another creature has possessed the stage, a double image of puppet and suffering human soul. . . . Danced at this level *Petrushka* is a tragedy.'[17]

Bintley also gave notable performances of both the Widow Simone and Alain in *La Pille mal gardée* and as the blind reveller in *Prodigal Son*. However, he had always intended to be a choreographer, and after staging several works for the Royal Ballet Choreographic Group, began work for the Sadler's Wells Royal Ballet. He had considerable success with such ballets as the lyrical *Homage to Chopin*, *Night Moves* to Benjamin Britten's 'Frank Bridge Variations', and *The Swan of Tuonela* with music by Sibelius. His greatest success with the company was the ballet *Choros,* based on Greek dance themes. In 1983 he became company choreographer of Sadler's Wells Royal Ballet.

In 1983 Bintley created *Consort Lessons* for The Royal Ballet at Covent Garden. This is a ballet, without a plot, for twelve dancers, to Stravinsky's 'Concerto for Piano and Wind'. With Lesley Collier, Alessandra Ferri, Wayne Eagling and Stephen Jefferies in the leading roles, this was well received. *The Times* critic wrote:

> There is no uncertainty about Bintley's creation. He has stretched his dancers hard, especially in making them move much faster than they are accustomed to go, continually crossing a wide area with swift precise steps, and, although he too has cast his ballet from strength, mainly among the younger women with some more experienced men, you can see they find it an effort. If they catch up with him, not only this ballet but their other roles will benefit.

And speaking of Lesley Collier, he said:

> What a slow movement he gives her. The rest of the cast may have been made to hustle, but Collier has long sustained passages of balance and descent, changes of weight and direction, that sometimes look almost incredibly difficult. At least they would look difficult but for the radiant poise and smooth, crisp exactness with which Collier dances them. She meets the challenge of Bintley's choreography with shining assurance, pushes her admirable skills further than ever before, and as in other recent roles proves that she can still find qualities to match new demands.[18]

An important event of 1979 was the Far Eastern tour of the Royal Opera which visited Korea and Japan in the autumn of that year and performed *Tosca* with a cast which included José Carreras, and Monserrat Caballé; *Peter Grimes* with Jon Vickers and Geraint Evans; and *Die Zauberflöte* with Stuart Burrows, Thomas Allen, Leona Mitchell and Robert Lloyd. Colin Davis conducted all three. The Royal Opera had a phenomenal success in Tokyo—the normally passive audiences waving and shouting and hurling bunches of roses on to the stage. The tour, like so many of those of The Royal Ballet, did much to enhance the reputation of this country.

However, in the Annual Report of 1979/80, the Chairman had to explain that the financial situation was now such that, in spite of a generous donation, the new production of *Andrea Chénier* had had to be postponed. This, by a combination of extraordinarily fortunate circumstances, was replaced by a production of an *Otello*, in the old Wakhevich sets, of such memorable quality that it led David Cairns to observe that the Tories had done something for the arts at last.[19] Conducted by Carlos Kleiber, with Placido Domingo in the title role, Margaret Price as Desdemona and Silvano Carroli as Iago, this was an historic event. 'The house was ablaze', wrote Peter Heyworth, 'as it has not been since the heroic days of the centenary *Don Carlos* and the Callas/Zeffirelli *Tosca*, both of whose pale ghosts still stalk the boards.' Speaking of Domingo's 'Otello' he said those who heard this performance would be 'boring the young for years to come', while to describe Margaret Price as the ideal foil to this great Otello was in itself the highest praise.[20] 'Placido Domingo was born to be Otello', Tom Sutcliffe wrote. 'He is more thrilling to hear and to watch in this role than in any other.'[21] And David Cairns said: 'Margaret Price's Desdemona is simply the best I have ever heard.'[22] There was much praise for Silvano Carroli as Iago and above all for the unique genius of Carlos Kleiber who 'drew by far the finest playing to have emerged this season from Covent Garden's orchestral pit'.[23]

Shortage of funds caused the cancellation in the 1980/1 season of *Salome* and *The Rake's Progress*. However, there were new productions of *Les Contes d'Hoffmann*, with John Schlesinger making an impressive debut as an operatic producer; a *Macbeth* which brought Riccardo Muti back to the house in an outstanding performance, a *new Don Giovanni*, not in itself well received, but part of a Mozart Festival under Colin Davis which was a *tour de force*. Above all there had been the first performance in this country of the complete *Lulu*, 'a major achievement by our Music Director Colin Davis and the Producer, Götz Friedrich'. Max Loppert wrote:

> The splendours and rather more numerous miseries of the current Royal Opera season have been much in the air. For the moment, though, the house can hold its collective head high, can insist once again on being taken seriously as an artistic institution. For it has brought to London, in a strong . . . theatrically vivid, musically cogent staging, Berg's shattering masterpiece. . . .[24]

The year 1981 saw the cancellation of the Sadler's Wells Royal Ballet seasons in Glasgow, Leeds and Stratford, owing to a five-week dispute with the orchestra, and of *Eugene Onegin* through a wage dispute, the retirement of Josephine Veasey and the operatic farewell of Dame Janet Baker. The season began with a performance of a new *Samson et Dalila* in a production designed by Sidney Nolan. 'Forget Shaw', Max Loppert advised, and said there were good reasons for reviving this opera:

301

Not given at Covent Garden since 1928 and in London since 1968 . . . the new production has some flair, a handsomely distinguished appearance, vivid characterisations of the title roles, [by Jon Vickers and Shirley Verrett] and strong (if not always stylish) solo singing: it does much to persuade one of the manifold strengths of the piece.

It also has Colin Davis in the pit, and this is perhaps the prime-weapon in the Royal Opera advocacy of Saint-Saëns.[25]

Handel's *Semele* was given to mark the 250th anniversary of the first theatre at Covent Garden, with Valerie Masterson in the tide role, Marie McLaughlin as Iris, Gwynne Howell as Somnus and the American mezzo Kathleen Kuhlmann doubling as Ino and Juno – Sir Charles Mackerras conducting. The critics were mainly dissatisfied. Hande's opera has a libretto by Congreve and is described by Rodney Milnes as 'the greatest comic opera to an English text'. This critic, having said that if there was a producer who might have been expected to respond to 'the *double-entendre* suggestiveness, the hilarious classical obfuscations, the sheer wickedness of it all', it would be John Copley, went on: 'The first act passed with scarcely a laugh, the second sank in an ocean of designers' kitsch . . . and what jokes there were . . . were imposed on the text never drawn from it. . . . The decor was surely devised for some other, bad opera'.

At the end of his review, Rodney Milnes said: 'The only good news came from the pit, where Sir Charles Mackerras coaxed a properly Handelian sound from the orchestra and paced the work with expertise.'[26] However, his colleague, Max Loppert, wrote:

It was a strange and unsettling experience, to sit through a Mackerras performance persistently unconvinced, disagreeing over the choice of tempos for arias (which regularly sounded either too fast or too slow), failing to feel the unbroken momentum of each act, and becoming ever more troubled about the kind and quantity of decoration Sir Charles has added to the vocal lines.[27]

Although saying, as others did, that she was not at ease at first Mr Loppert spoke of 'the enchanting Valerie Masterson' and said 'it is already a beautiful performance of a great role'. Rodney Milnes, however, thought the first night vocally disappointing: 'Valerie Masterson was plainly ill at ease, as well she might be, having to sing Endless Pleasure miles up stage behind a tennis net' – and this affected her 'sense of pitch and normally crystalline tone'.

In 1983, in a double bill the Company gave its first production of Ravel's *L'Enfant et les sortileges* and its first at Covent Garden since 1919 of Stravinsky's *Nightingale*. These had designs by David Hockney in a production by John Dexter and choreography by Frederick Ashton.

The critics were more than normally divided. Bayan Northcott, having praised the conductor, David Atherton, and the singers, Phyllis Bryn-Julson, Philip Langridge and Ann Murray, remarked that he wished he could praise the productions and designs as highly. But by the end of the Stravinsky he thought the spectacle threatened

to become redolent less of exoticism than of thrift . . .

And the Ravel is surely altogether misconceived. . . . Hockney offers us the garish daubs of a child's colouring

303

book itself. The crudely costumed wall-paper shepherds and shepherdesses . . . are a particular betrayal of the score's nostalgic genre-piece, while Ravel's magically sinister evocation of the moonlit garden . . . could scarcely be less appropriately matched in slashes of crimson and sap green to set the retina zinging.[28]

Max Loppert on the other hand thought 'the decor the basic strength of the whole enterprise'.

With wonderful Tightness Hockney's language of painted screens, cloths, and pop-ups harmonises with both scores; for each, and in his own inimitably humorous and cultivated manner, he has divined a visual tone and texture, an organisation and reduction of colours that tell one something about the works that one wants and needs to know.[29]

Equally contradictory views were expressed about the Ashton dances, performed by Anthony Dowell and Natalia Makarova.

A major disappointment of this period was the failure of the intended association between Covent Garden and the Palace Theatre, Manchester, which had been renovated and the stage enlarged to the minimum specifications required by the Royal Opera Company. In May 1981 the Arts Council provided £200,000 additional funding to cover the extra costs of sending the company to Manchester. The Royal Opera gave twenty-one performances of four operas at the Palace Theatre and, although the box office results were disappointing (77 per cent of capacity), the season was generally regarded as successful. However, although a second visit was planned for September 1983, Covent Garden was told by the Arts Council that it could expect only a very limited increase of the basic grant, and that money to visit Manchester could not be guaranteed. In these circumstances, the second tour had to be cancelled.

In 1982/3 two new productions had also to be abandoned at Covent Garden, although through the generosity of the Hamburg Opera, Götz Friedrich's production of *Manon Lescaut* was given with Placido Domingo and Kiri te Kanawa leading the cast. The continuing necessity to cancel productions through inability to finance them was added to a degree of ill luck, probably no greater than normal but magnified by the circumstances. This drew from the critics a series of articles, ranging from savage disparagement of Covent Garden to cocksure and mildly patronizing praise. The following remarks by Max Loppert are quoted as representative of a good deal of press comment at the time: 'Once again, at the close of a year by no means without its good features, the sense came across of an organisation rudderless and demoralised, surviving from performance to performance without larger artistic goals or schemes in view.'

Having said that there had been instances of puzzling casting – 'How for instance, was it possible that Ursula Koszut should be invited to show us her (singularly unworthy) Mozart Countess when Heather Harper never has?'—he went on:

The two new productions framed by 1982 were both major disappointments—the devoutly dull Giulini *Falstaff*, and Handel's *Semele*, all but smothered in producer's and designers' kitsch (I wonder how much it cost). Passing speedily over the dim *Boccanegra* and *Sonnambula*, and respectful but very creaky *Khovanschina* (with the chorus at its lowest ebb in a year of generally poor standard), let me in fairness also record some happy revivals.

305

Mr Loppert then went on to praise *Hoffmann,* 'an enjoyable and worthwhile *Meistersinger'* just about the most involving *Pelléas* the house has yet produced', *The Rake's Progress* 'less flippant and fussy than when first exhibited three seasons ago', and the performance of various singers. Then he said: 'Colin Davis proved to some, if not all, his listeners – that his Wagnerian credentials are securely assembled; now might we perhaps be allowed a plurality of Wagner conductors in the future.'[30]

Discussing the criticism of the operatic side of Covent Garden's activities at a Board meeting early in 1983, the directors recorded a general feeling that the press had fastened on to a handful of isolated and well-publicized incidents, together with the shortage of new productions in the current season, while the range and quality of the major operatic repertory had been satisfactory. There appeared to be two reasons for this – the first that the public expected more of Covent Garden than high quality performances of the standard repertory, and it was widely felt that the recent programme had not generated as much excitement as was to be expected from the leading opera house; the second that the critics did not feel sufficiently regarded by Covent Garden, and the House should pay more attention to them.

In 1984 The Royal Opera appeared in Los Angeles, where they gave *Turandot* in a new production not yet seen in London with sets by Andrei Serban, 'a full blooded *Grimes* and a truly noble *Zauberflöte*[31] All these operas were tremendously well received, *Peter Grimes* possibly attracting the most interest:

Colin Davis, the conductor, dared stress the wrenching violence, the dark colors and brooding agonies that lay beneath the surface of the score and, in the process, made the moments of repose and nervous mystery all the more

306

affecting. Jon Vickers, as Grimes, made the outcast protagonist a monumental, heroic brute. His Grimes commanded elemental force. He wasn't just a dreamer . . . he was a fighter, a noble primitive, a formidable victim of common myopia.

Remarking that England used to be called 'the country without music', the critic of the *New York Times* went on:

But all that has changed in the past 50 years. British composers easily hold their own, internationally. British orchestras, conductors and singers proliferate on the world's stages. And now, if such proof were needed, we realise that English opera, too, need fear invidious comparison with no one.[32]

And the critic of the *Los Angeles Times* wrote:

The Royal Opera deserved the euphoria it created here. Our British visitors set standards. . . . This was grandiose opera produced by a major company. Los Angeles hadn't seen anything like it for a long, long time. . . . Most important, perhaps, this company commands the services of a great conductor, a great chorus and a great orchestra. That claim cannot be made for many companies here or abroad.[33]

17

Administration 1979–1984
The Priestley Report

The Royal Opera House, like other institutions unable to increase productivity, could not combat the combination of depression and high inflation of the early eighties. As Sir Claus Moser wrote in the 1979/80 Annual Report:

> These are rough times for everyone, and the arts cannot escape some pressure. . . . But there is no hiding our anxiety. We are grossly under-financed in relation to comparable houses abroad and this year the increase in our grant has been substantially less than the rate of inflation. The results are seen in artistic cancellations (two operas this season), in increases in seat prices which we deeply regret, and almost certainly in unbalanced books.

He went on to say that high standards could not be achieved

cheaply, although this was not principally due, as was so often said, to costly productions. 'The fact is that production costs are well under 10 per cent of our total expenditure.' Sir Claus said that the administration would nevertheless continue to do their best on the resources available and he thanked the Minister for the Arts and the Arts Council for their support, without which 'we could not have remained in being'.

During the Heath, Wilson and Callaghan governments of the seventies, a period during which Kenneth Robinson succeeded Lord Gibson as Chairman of the Arts Council, there was a spirit of unquestioned support for the arts, and this persisted when Norman St John Stevas and, following him, Paul Channon were at the Ministry of Arts in Mrs Thatcher's Goverment.

In the financial year 1980/1 the Chairman reported that, at the expense of two operatic cancellations, the Opera House had kept close to budget and by careful management had been able to carry £704,000 forward into the current year. 'However, on current projections we do not expect to carry any of this sum forward into next year, and our anxiety for 1982–83 and the years immediately beyond is greater than I have ever known it.'

In the same report Sir Claus recorded that 'by the acid test of ticket sales our enterprise must be judged extremely successful', and that at 94 per cent of capacity, opera attendances were the highest for some years, while ballet audiences were 88 per cent of capacity.

Since we are sometimes falsely represented as performing only to an elite minority, it may be worth noting that in addition to 269 performances at Covent Garden itself by our three companies (125 by The Royal Opera, 135 by The Royal Ballet and 9 by Sadler's Wells Royal Ballet), we gave a further 257 in this country and abroad; and were able to continue the promenade performances, attended by a great many young people, the children's matinees and performances in the Big Top.

Television and radio performances also allowed millions of people to see opera and ballet from Covent Garden and in the year under review there had been five television and radio relays, while an agreement had been signed with Covent Garden Video Productions Limited in association with the BBC which would make broadcasts more profitable for the Opera House.

The last quarter of the financial year 1980/1 – the spring of 1981 – saw an alarming falling off in attendances at theatres all over London, many being dark as a result of the depression, others only half full, while orchestral concerts were attracting audiences of 60 per cent or less. The Opera House suffered for a short time, chiefly as the result of a rise in prices, but by 1982 opera was back at 89 per cent of capacity and ballet at 87 per cent. However, the deficit for that year, after the Arts Council grant of £9,550,000, amounted to £1,050,000, 'reduced to £220,000 by bringing forward Arts Council guarantees of £380,000 and a supplementary grant of £450,000.'

As a result the Minister for the Arts, Mr Paul Channon, decided to undertake a government scrutiny into the financial affairs of the Royal Opera House and of the Royal Shakespeare Company, both of which had declared themselves unable to eliminate substantial financial deficits. The scrutiny was undertaken by the Government's Management and Efficiency group (the Rayner Unit), under the direction of Mr Clive Priestley, its head.

Mr Priesdey's team consisted of a former Treasury economic

adviser, a member of Cooper & Lybrand Associates, a member of Deloitte, Haskins and Sells and six assignment staff from the Management and Personnel Office. The scrutiny was to cover all aspects of the Royal Opera House's policy and administration, and members of the team sat in at rehearsals and studios to observe the work of stage staff, and saw the companies' performances of opera and ballet at Covent Garden and on tour. They also visited the New York Metropolitan Opera, Deutsche Oper, Berlin, La Scala, Milan, Staatsoper, Vienna and the Bolshoi and Kirov Ballet Companies.

> The *overall approach of the scrutiny* has been to question on the ground why things are done as they are; why they are done at all; and whether they could be done more effectively at less cost. This approach was undertaken against the background of the three fundamental questions: Why did the Royal Opera House go into deficit after funding in 1982/83? Why will it go into deficit in 1983/84? What can be done to prevent this happening again?[1]

Mr Priestley reported in September 1983. The first paragraph of the overall conclusion of his examination of the financial affairs of the Royal Opera House explains that the 1982/3 deficit 'is projected to accumulate to £1.16 million by the end of 1983/4 and approaching £3 million by end 1984/5, with the *annual* deficit after funding in 1984/5 being £1.8 million'.[2]

He then explains that the deficit is not temporary or new, but the consequence of expenditure rising faster than the general level of price and wage inflation (particularly in the two ballet companies and in the overtime working throughout the Royal Opera House); a drop in the level of the attendance at Covent

311

Garden; and an annual Arts Council grant which 'although broadly keeping pace with movements in the Retail Price Index over the past four years has not kept pace with the more appropriate Average Earnings Index, to reflect the labour intensive nature of ROH's activities'.[3] There is a footnote to this paragraph which states that the Arts Council had assessed the full needs of the Royal Opera House for 1983/4 at £12.9 million. Paragraph 3 of the conclusions stated:

> There is nothing which the Royal Opera House can do this year significandy to reduce the forecast end-year deficit of £1.16 million; and even over the next two years, whilst the financial situation can and must be stabilised, only limited economies can be achieved to reduce the funding requirement unless the House is required to lower substantially its artistic sights, to try and withdraw from commitments necessarily entered into in planning ahead and to change its nature. *I recommend* that the Government should provide additional funds to write-off the forecast accumulated deficit at 31 March 1984 of £1.16 million; and in 1984/85 should raise the base level of grant to the budgeted funding requirement of £12.35 million (an increase of £1.8 million on present projections) although the precise level of funding in 1984/85 will need to be decided in the light of a detailed assessment of the budget for that year.[4]

The Priesdey Report also recommended that the Royal Opera House grant should be based on what it called 'targeted funding', which would set a minimum standard for Covent Garden to be translated into various operational needs (e.g. an orchestra of a certain size) with the grant based largely on such targets. Against this background Priestley also recommended that the Royal Opera House should make savings of £600,000 per annum in two years.[5]

This was all rather bad luck for the Government who had clearly expected the Report to suggest that, with ordinary business efficiency, savings of a much larger order could be made. However, Sir Claus Moser's annual report of the following year explained that what had actually happened as a result of the recommendations was that the grant for 1984/5 had been implemented to the level of 18 per cent, which, 'though short of the Arts Council's estimate of our needs (22.50 per cent), was enormously welcome'; that between the Treasury and the Arts Council the accumulated deficit had been eliminated; but that there were no signs of the recommendation that the grant for the coming two years should be increased, at least in line with a weighted increase of the Retail Price Index and Average Earnings Index appropriate to the expenditure being implemented; or of the grant being based on 'targeted funding'. 'We are, therefore, left in an uncertain position. Neither do we have the security of a grant reflecting the rise in earnings, as recommended by Priestley, nor the rational basis for funding which "targeted funding" would provide.'

There was little more the Royal Opera House could do to help itself. It must be apparent that the effort to acquire private funding had been determined, imaginative and enormously successful. A list of the corporate members and sponsors can be found in all the programmes at the Opera House, and leaves no doubt of the extent of sponsorship. Nevertheless, the business world was also hit by the depression, while the success of the Development Appeal made it harder to raise money for productions and other activities. In any case, funds from private sources represented only a very small percentage of the annual income (5 per cent according to the 1982/3 Annual Report), although without it the number of new productions would have been even more reduced. Seat prices could be put up, but only at the risk of diminishing audiences, and in the certainty of a gradual narrowing of the audience's social range, to the detriment of the purposes and reputation of the administration. One of the results of the grant being gradually reduced in real terms was that it encouraged the belief that subsidy contributed only to the pleasures of the rich.

For the purposes of his scrutiny, the Minister for the Arts had appointed two specialist advisers to Mr Priestley – Mr Peter Diamand, a former director of the Edinburgh Festival and now with the Orchéstre de Paris, and Monsieur Hugues Gall, formerly with the French National Opera in Paris and now Director of the Geneva Opera. Some of the comments made in the Report by Mr Priesdey himself and his two advisers, particularly Monsieur Gall, are an important contribution to the history of the Opera House:

> By our own observation and the reports we have received it is clear that Sir John Tooley has a high world standing and reputation in the fields of opera, ballet and opera house administration; that much of the international reputation of Covent Garden as a house free of intrigues of the kind which afflict many other houses and, more important, as welcoming, friendly and supportive to visiting performers and others is due to him and to the style he has established; and that, in turn, the reported willingness of performers to come to Covent Garden at fees somewhat lower than they might command elsewhere is also due to him; and that the

imaginative exercises in 'out-reach' represented by the opera Proms and the ballet Tent seasons are his initiative. Even though my colleagues and I end this scrutiny with reservations about some aspects of the management at Covent Garden, as well as with commendation for others, we have no doubt that in Sir John Tooley the Royal Opera House is fortunate to have a servant of exceptional knowledge, experience and quality or that he has made an immense personal contribution to the preservation and development of the House. And it is too often overlooked in human affairs, that much of the best work of such senior administrators as Sir John Tooley is done unobserved and therefore wants the credit it merits.[6]

Mr Priestley said that Sir Colin Davis's artistic responsibilities did not come within the scope of his enquiries, but he added:

As a layman I am far from convinced that all the criticisms levelled at those responsible for the artistic direction of the ROH, including Sir Colin Davis, are objective and just. All too seldom is enough credit given to those who, like Sir Colin, bear the actual responsibility for the affairs of such an institution as an international opera house. And I would expect his musicianship, name and contribution to Covent Garden to be recalled with honour when much else is forgotten.[7]

During the course of his scrutiny, Mr Priestley invited newspaper and other critics to let him have any comments on the Royal Opera House, 'which they would wish me to have in mind in making my report'. He showed a summary of these criticisms to Mr Peter Diamand and Monsieur Hugues Gall. Their comments on this are also recorded and have particular interest in the case of Monsieur Gall (although Mr Diamand, too, has experience of opera in other countries).

A point made here, as constantly elsewhere, was that it was unnecessary to spend high fees on visiting artists. To this Monsieur Gall replied: 'Not one of the great Western opera houses can guarantee the required musical quality by limiting itself to the employment of national singers only.'[8] After saying that records, television, films and video had set the level of quality demanded by the public very high and the resulting competition had made for the disappearance of such permanent ensembles of national singers as were known before the war, he went on to say that it was not possible for a house like La Scala at Milan to cast suitably a large number of works in the Italian repertory by restricting itself only to Italian singers.

> This phenomenon repeats itself everywhere. . . . In the course of the last six years, to take a precise example the part of Marguerite in Gounod's *Faust* has been played at the Paris Opera by Mirella Freni or by Valerie Masterson. Similarly the part of Faust has required the presence of Nicolai Gedda (Swedish) and Kenneth Riegel (USA).[9]

And he went on to give other examples of the sort. On the same or a related subject he said:

> There is to my knowledge no important British singer, or one who may so become, who has not regularly had the opportunity to perform on the leading British stage. It is right to think that the ROH should contribute to perfecting

young British talents, but it seems to me that it has fulfilled this task to general admiration for many years. One often speaks enviously in mainland Europe of a phenomenon of 'anglo-saxon singing'. But the ROH should not be considered as the only place where it is fashioned. Its mission, in my view, is not to be a 'trial theatre' for promising talents. It stands at the junction of the consecration and the extension of a training which must remain essentially the appanage of provincial operas or even of the ENO. In the pyramid of British lyrical life, the ROH must be the summit and not the base.[10]

Mr Diamand agreed with what Monsieur Gall had said, making the point that British singers of note receive invitations from other international houses and often devote more time to guest appearances abroad than to making themselves available to the Royal Opera House.

Many of the criticisms were directed to the idea that the Royal Opera House was too much associated with 'the Establishment' (the new term for 'the snobs'), and comparisons were made between it and ENO and WNO (Welsh National Opera). To this Monsieur Gall replied that if the managers of WNO or ENO were in charge of the Royal Opera House it was unlikely that they could take a line of artistic or financial policy palpably different from that of Sir Claus Moser and Sir John Tooley: 'Can one seriously imagine the leading stage of Great Britain finding itself faced with the following dilemma: either removing whole tracts of the repertoire because it is unable to cast the works concerned suitably, or offering operatic masterpieces at a level of musical performance worthy of a provincial stage?'[11]

In reply to the criticism that the Royal Opera House had no

317

'house style', Monsieur Gall replied: 'The only house style which should inspire a house of international rank must be to present throughout the season the widest range of the heritage complemented by some contemporary works, and that at the highest level of performance.'[12]

Mr Diamand said that only the Royal Opera House was equipped to give as wide a spectrum of the repertoire as possible under the best possible artistic conditions:

[It] does not detract from one's great admiration and respect for the results achieved by the ENO and the regional companies under the circumstances in which they operate. It may well happen that one or other of their best productions outshines a less happy one given by the ROH, but they are not in 'competition' with the ROH as long as it continues to be an international opera house. There is no room, money, talent for more than one in this country, as in practically every other one. It is to be welcomed that the regional companies, on the whole, enjoy the critics' and the audiences' goodwill, but it should not be overlooked either that – rightly and tacitly – a different yardstick is being applied for the judgement of their efforts as compared to those of the ROH.[13]

In reply to the criticism that the Music Director did not conduct enough and had not a sufficiently developed policy for bringing on British singers, Mr Diamand said that it was much to the credit of Covent Garden's management that conductors like Abbado, Haitink, Kleiber, Mehta, Muti were being attracted to the Royal Opera House, and that few international opera houses could boast similar results.

A third consultant, Mr Michael Haines, who had no experience of the running of an opera house, but who was an ardent opera lover, agreed that the standard of singing and orchestral playing at the Royal Opera House was commendably high, but felt that there had been a lack of flair over the last few years: 'Only *Lulu* and *Samson et Dalila* were, in my view, productions of real excellence. At the other end of the scale was *Alceste* where the production fell far short of musical excellence.'[14] He also complained of a reluctance to employ certain native artists, and cited Dame Janet Baker (who sang regularly at Covent Garden only towards the end of her career), Pauline Tinsley and Reginald Goodall.

In the Annual Report of 1984/5 Sir Claus Moser confirmed that the Priestley recommendations had been implemented only for the first year. On the other hand he said that box office receipts were once more buoyant and private funding, 'thanks to the Royal Opera House Trust', ahead of budget (£1,773,000 against the budgeted £1,360,000). 'Cash control was tight, and we were able to carry forward an unused guarantee of £882,000.'

Alas, Sir Claus said, it was a different story for the 1985/6 season. The Arts Council grant had been increased by only 1.9 per cent – a cut in real terms with reference to the Retail Price Index, and well below the Average Earnings Index. In the following year he reported a cut of 2 per cent in real terms and said: 'It was a sad blow that, having begun by implementing the recommendations of the Priestley Report in the first year, the Government abandoned it for the critical next two years. We, on the other hand, have played our part by continuing to implement all the principal recommendations of the Report.'

Happily, private funding was up by 7 per cent, even on the

319

high level of the previous year. 'We had to adjust our plans and budgets by £0.7 million', Sir Claus said, 'with a real loss artistically.' But he added:

> As a result of tight housekeeping, we have ended up with a surplus. . . . This, however, has to be seen in relation to the essential contingency reserve we must build into next year's budget. As a result . . . above all of the substantial fall in the real value of the grant, the carry forward into 1986/87 has had to be radically reduced. The implications of this for our future activities are now being considered. They are likely to be serious. I should stress that, if we had enjoyed 'level funding' (in real terms) for the last two years we would have a balanced budget for next year.

In 1982 Sir William Rees-Mogg succeeded Sir Kenneth Robinson as Chairman of the Arts Council, and in 1983 Lord Gowrie became Minister for the Arts in succession to Paul Channon. The fortunes of the Royal Opera House have to be seen against what came to be regarded as a real change in the constitution and spirit of the Arts Council. In the days of Lord Goodman, Lord Gibson and Sir Kenneth Robinson the Arts Council had seemed to stand between the Treasury and the arts, but the Chairman was seen as leading the arts from in front. Both Lord Gowrie and Sir William were known to be exceptionally cultivated intellectually, but they were both also known to be in sympathy with the financial policies of Mrs Thatcher's Government, at that time labelled 'monetarist'. More than this Lord Gowrie doubled the functions of Minister for the Arts and Treasury spokesman in the House of Lords. Sir Denis Forman (a member of the Covent Garden Board), in an open letter to Lord

Gowrie, published in the *Listener* in 1985, asked: 'Is it right . . . for the functions of a spending Minister and those of a Treasury Minister to be united in one person?' (The spokesman in the Lords is in fact not a Treasury Minister but he must necessarily agree with the policies of the Treasury.) Sir Denis Forman went on to say that many forms of umpiring between the claims of the spenders and the non-spenders had been devised, but the two sides had been heard 'if not always in Cabinet, certainly in some Forum, where after the appropriate measure of open debate a deal was struck'.

> But in the case of the arts today, the only available court of adjudication – and, indeed, of appeal – lies within the mind of one person, namely yourself. . . . You have said that . . . you agree profoundly with your government's (economic) basic approach *and* (my italics) with their manifesto commitment to the arts. This is a Delphic utterance because it would seem to be saying that you believe in two policies which may conflict. We can now clearly deduce from your actions, however, that you believe primarily in the economic doctrine and will only support the arts in so far as they comply with the economic imperative.[15]

In reply to this letter, Lord Gowrie said that he went through the 'same process of haggling as every other spending Minister'. He quoted the figures for the funding of the Arts saying that such a low uprating could be described as 'bad' but that the public services, especially the health service, held large claims on public affection, and many people would consider it 'bad' for quite different reasons. 'Try selling greater public funding for opera to those who want greater provision of kidney machines.'[16] In a further letter Sir Denis Forman stated that quoting statistics did not present the 'whole, true picture', and wondered why, when the Arts are a 'profitable business', the Government did not invest in them more heartily.

In 1984 The Arts Council issued a strategy document called 'The Glory of the Garden', with the sub-title 'The Development of the Arts in England'. In the preface Lord Keynes is quoted as saying, at the time of the formation of the Arts Council, that it was its business 'to make London a great artistic metropolis, a place to visit and to wonder at'. But, primarily he said:

> We of the Arts Council are greatly concerned to decentralise and disperse the dramatic and musical and artistic life of this country, to build up provincial centres and to promote corporate life in these matters in every town and country. . . . We look forward to the time when the theatre and concert hall and the gallery will be a living element in everyone's upbringing.[17]

This was a preliminary to the announcement that the Arts Council proposed to 'come to grips' with Keynes's first priority and 'to decentralise and disperse the dramatic and musical and artistic life of this country'. The financial steps were admitted to be the most difficult.

> The Arts Council recognises the financial constraints inside which the Government is working. We have therefore decided to make a start, even if it has to be a relatively small one, out of our own existing level of funding. [In other words funds must be diverted from London to the regions.]

322

That does mean painful choices, including transfers inside existing provision. Yet it has one great advantage: it demonstrates the determination of the Arts Council to carry out this strategy even though it involves decisions of great difficulty and hardship for respected clients.[18]

The trouble with this strategy was that the lack of extra funding made it unpopular with almost everyone. Sixty-two companies had their grants withdrawn altogether (among them the Old Vic) and the degree of under-funding of the major companies was increased. It was difficult to decide which regional companies to support, and, inevitably, the regions were disappointed with what they received.

'What cake is left for the rest of the country?' asked Michael Bogdanov, in an article in the *Guardian*. 'Nothing but arguing and bickering over the few crumbs that might fall on empty plates.'[19] And, in the *Observer*, Lord Goodman said that the idea that the Arts Council could develop and employ a new strategy was a misleading one. 'It suggests that there is a latitude available to it which is not bound by rigid restraints. The truth of the matter, alas, is very different.'[20] And in fact, in pursuance of the policy of cuts across the board – 'equal misery for everyone', the Arts Council grant was in real terms reduced in subsequent years. It was against this general background that the second generation of those responsible for opera and ballet at Covent Garden played out their last years.

18

1984–1986
A Wider Public

The triumphs of the Drogheda/Webster regime, which succeeded in establishing Covent Garden as a international opera house, were difficult to follow, and Sir Claus Moser and Sir John Tooley might well have been content simply to maintain the standards they took over. In fact their achievements have been imaginative and wide-ranging, although often undervalued.

The repertory of opera at Covent Garden is now planned according to three categories – the first consisting of forty or so standard works which are never out of the repertory for more than three years; the second of works of marginal popularity, to be performed occasionally, for example: *I Lombardi, Werther, La clemenza di Tito*; the third of modern operas, including commissioned works. As a result the repertory of the last fifteen years has probably been the widest of any opera house in the world.

In the same way the roster of conductors far exceeds in quality that of any other house. When Sir Claus Moser took over as Chairman he believed that as a matter of deliberate policy as much importance should be given to conductors as to singers. With the generous co-operation of Sir Colin Davis, who was often willing to conduct revivals so that guest conductors could be enticed into the house with the new productions, he succeeded in this policy. In recent years guest conductors have included Kleiber, Giulini, Solti, Böhm, Mehta, Muti, Abbado, Mackerras, Pritchard, Downes and many others. Both singers and conductors enjoy coming to Covent Garden, although for obvious reasons the fees paid are often lower than elsewhere. They find the atmosphere sympathetic – professional and disciplined, but pleasandy informal.

Attempts to raise private funds have been very successful. In 1986 nearly £3 million was raised from a combination of sponsorship, corporate members, premium stalls and boxes.* Separately, Mrs Jean Sainsbury (not related to the Sainsbury family who have supported the arts so much) gave a donation of £i million as an endowment fund, the income to be used towards sponsorship of new productions and, in alternate years, to help with the redecoration of the house.

Everything possible has been done to make opera and ballet accessible to the less well-off. By 1986 the price of the best stalls was often as much as £40, but more than 40 per cent of the seats were on sale at prices under £12. The schools matinees and the

---

* This is a scheme whereby some corporations and businesses, in return for guaranteed seats throughout the year, pay considerably more than the price to the public.

proms have flourished and in January 1986 the first Hamlyn week took place. During this week sponsorship by the Paul Hamlyn Trust enabled tickets to be sold for five performances by The Royal Ballet—four evening and one matinee—for from £1 to £3, the purpose being to encourage people to attend who had never previously visited the Royal Opera House. Tickets were distributed through charitable and voluntary organizations and the TUC. In the first year the audience came mainly from London, but it was announced that in July 1987 there would be seven performances by The Royal Ballet, designed to attract a new audience from outside London. During the first Hamlyn week the GLC granted permission for a row of seats in the stalls circle to be taken out to make spaces for twenty wheelchairs. This will be done in future at certain performances, including all schools matinees.

The Friends of Covent Garden, chaired by Sir John Sainsbury since Sir Leon Bagrit's resignation in 1969 and in 1982 by Angus Stirling, have gone from strength to strength. By 1986 there were approximately 17,000 members—14,800 full members, 2,000 junior associates and 200 American Friends. (Junior associates pay £7 against a full member's £21.) The privileges, in addition to priority booking, attendance at some rehearsals and the excellent *About the House* magazine, include lectures and concerts, Lunch and Listen (at which musical celebrities are interviewed in the Crush Bar) and tours of the theatre. The Friends have supported exhibitions, schools matinees, made contributions to bursaries, to the Royal Ballet School, to the Royal Ballet Choreographic Group, to the archives, and generally to opera and ballet education. In the 1986/7 season they gave £350,000 to cover sponsorship of two orchestral concerts, new productions of *Jenufa* and *Norma*, the televising of *Turandot*,

326

sponsorship of the new David Bindey ballet *Allegn Diversi,* and a substantial contribution to five other new Sadler's Wells ballets. HRH Prince Charles became President in 1978 and in 1986, when he and the Princess of Wales attended the Christmas party, the Princess danced on stage with Wayne Sleep.

The most effective method of widespread exploitation of opera and ballet is through television and radio. Television performances of opera and ballet were at an unsatisfactorily low level in the early eighties; television because neither the Royal Opera House nor the BBC could afford the heavy costs of transmission, and radio because of the failure of the BBC and Equity to reach agreement on relay fees. In 1984/5 new productions of *Der Rosenkavalier* and *Andrea Chénier,* as well as a performance of *Don Carlos,* were recorded by BBC Television and Covent Garden Video Productions. However, the dispute between the BBC and Equity remained unsettled and for the fourth year prevented transmission of opera with chorus – a disgraceful situation which for all this time has prevented the widest exploitation of the public investment in opera.[†]

Probably the fastest expanding area of activity at the Royal Opera House has been the Education Department. In 1983 and 1984 education officers for ballet and opera were appointed, and since then they have organized an extensive programme of workshops in schools and at the Opera House. With the aid of artists and staff of the two Companies, they have demonstrated— often in connection with some performance the children were to see —most of the things which go into a theatrical performance. The children have also been encouraged to dance and sing and

---

[†] Now at last settled.

to improvise on what they have been shown. The John Lea School at Wellingborough and the Prince William School at Oundle actually mounted a production of *Carmen,* in which the two leading roles were taken by Royal Opera singers but all other roles sung by local people, and the chorus parts by the children. The orchestra consisted of a mixture of professional and school musicians and the costume department and design team from Covent Garden gave advice.

An ambitious programme of education has been designed to reach adults as well as young people—not merely those already committed to or interested in opera or ballet, but also the unaware or uninterested, in particular teachers, community workers and all those concerned with youth organizations. By the end of 1983/4, contact had been made with 20,000 people and it had become clear that there was a vast potential for future work of this kind. Then in 1986 an organization called 'Invitation to the Ballet' was formed to visit hospices and hospitals thoughout the country and, with company dancers, to present classical ballet, demonstrating aspects of training, rehearsal and performance.

The most concrete achievement of the Moser/Tooley regime at Covent Garden was the Phase 1 extension to the theatre (see pp. 282–5). In 1986 plans were revealed for Phase 2. The key objectives of this plan are to modernize the stage, to enable The Royal Ballet to move from Barons Court to a permanent home at Covent Garden; and to provide greater public accessibility to the theatre. The Opera House authorities have had to accept that no Government money would be made available and that part of the available site would have to generate finance towards the cost of the requirements of the theatre. The scheme is therefore a mixture of new buildings for the Opera House, refurbishment of existing Opera House premises, and new offices, shops and public parking.

However, in the years since the fruit and vegetable market moved to Nine Elms, the Covent Garden area and particularly the piazza has become unusually successful as a lively meeting place and it is understood that 'it is crucial that the new buildings should take account of the history, character and use of this important area of London'.

The planning of Phase 2, from the first consideration to the actual production of plans by the architect, Jeremy Dixon, took six years. When the plans were shown at an exhibition at Covent Garden in 1986 they were acclaimed for their architectural merit and thought by many people to be a potential asset to the capital city. Particularly attractive is the design for an arcade to form a continuous frontage to the piazza, which provides a shopping frontage at ground level, a new entrance to the theatre and, at roof level, a promenade which connects directly with the new amphitheatre foyer. Studios and offices for The Royal Ballet are created at the top of the building by linking new studios and company offices with the existing studios of Phase I.

The figures submitted to the Westminster City Council in an application for planning permission were in round figures: for the opera house £56 million; for commercial development £75 million, of which £33 million would be retained as profit, leaving £23 million to be found. At the time of writing it is known that the Covent Garden Community Association – an experienced and powerful body who helped to defeat the property dealers when the fruit and vegetable market moved – oppose the plan. They accept the case for the theatre developments, but object to the scale of commercial development necessary to finance them. They also object to the destruction of the existing Victorian and eighteenth-century façades.[‡]

In 1984/5 all three Royal Companies mounted successful foreign tours, supported by the British Council. Sadler's Wells Royal Ballet toured New Zealand, South Korea and India, its performances of *Giselle* in India being the first in that country of a full-length classical ballet with live orchestra. The Royal Ballet went to Hungary, the German Democratic Republic, Spain and Portugal. The Royal Opera paid a first and triumphantly successful visit to Greece, performing in the open air at the Herodes Atticus theatre, as part of the Athens Festival.

Two operas, *Macbeth* and *King Priam* were performed alternately on four consecutive nights. The first, conducted by Edward Downes and produced by Elijah Moshinsky, 'bristled with energy, pulsed with musical energy, culminated in an unforgettable choral splendour', and the second, conducted by Elgar Howarth, was said to be 'probably the strongest and most authentic performance the work has ever received'. The success of the Athens tour added much to The Royal Opera's international reputation.

In London in 1984 David Bintley followed a one-act ballet called *Metamorphosis*, at Sadler's Wells with *Young Apollo* at Covent Garden. Clad in white costumes, Mark Silver, Bryony Brind and a group of eighteen women danced against three backdrops by Victor Pasmore. 'Here is an exciting and unusual new ballet, moving and satisfying in spite of a somewhat underdanced premiere. It may be that David Bintley's choreography has

---

[‡] See p. 338.

outrun the Royal Ballet's abilities. Will they, can they, catch him up?'[1] The music for *Young Apollo* was by Britten, supplemented by Gordon Cross. Other new ballets by young choreographers first performed in 1984/5 were *Number Three* by Michael Corder and *Half the House* by Jennifer Jackson.

One of the most exciting events of the 1985/6 season was the appearance of the French ballerina, Elisabeth Platel, dancing Aurora in *Sleeping Beauty*. Clement Crisp wrote:

> In a performance of lambent authority she demonstrated that she is without peer in the West in this role. Here is an interpretation which fulfils the rigorous outward canons of classic dancing – harmony of form, clarity of statement, beautifully rounded technique – and, no less important, those inward qualities of the true classic artist.[2]

The Royal Ballet's new productions for 1985/6 included a new staging of *Giselle*, by Peter Wright, and a new one-act ballet, *The Sons of Horus*, by Bindey. Also performed at Covent Garden by the Sadler's Wells Royal Ballet was Bintley's three-act ballet *The Snow Queen* (first performed in Birmingham). In this the choreographer was generally regarded as not 'at his inventive best'. 'There are gems in *The Snow Queen*', Julie Kavanagh wrote, 'but the ballet itself is a disappointment.'[3]

At the end of the 1985/6 season, Norman Morrice resigned his post as Director of The Royal Ballet. Sir Colin Davis also retired in 1986, and, as it happens, his last years give good examples of all three categories of the operas regularly performed. The first two were revivals of the second category of works – *Samson* and *Ariadne auf Naxos* – neither of them entirely well received by the critics. *Samson* was praised for 'some beautiful and skilfully deployed tableaux and the grandeur of Timothy O'Brien's massive sets', but the conductor, Julius Rudel, of the New York City Opera, was the subject of much critical dissatisfaction, as was the singing of Jon Vickers, which, remembered as 'movingly heroic in 1958', was now thought 'mannered and monotonous'.

The opening sentences of the reviews of *Ariadne* by Max Loppert and John Higgins would have brought joy to the heart of Ernest Bean, the creator of 'Point Counterpoint', the programme notes at the Festival Hall which regularly compared the views of the critics. 'In planning its frightful, unmusical, anti-verbal new production of *Ariadne*, the Royal Opera House was evidently unable to schedule a single set of performers for the complete run',[4] wrote Loppert. But John Higgins, having begun by saying that the last shot at *Ariadne* a decade before carried few fond memories, went on:

> Ample amends have been made with the production just opened, which arrives in London via Paris' Opera Comique. Everywhere it substitutes strength for weaknesses : in the assurance of touch from Jeffrey Tate in the pit, in the solid achievement of a cast led by Jessye Norman in the tide role and in the sheer theatricality of Jean-Louis Martinoty's staging.[5]

The first staging of Rossini's *La donna del logo* since 1851 was also given in June of that year, and was chiefly notable for the singing of Marilyn Home, of whom Peter Heyworth said that to hear her was to be reminded of the gulf that separates a great from a good singer.[6]

The Stockhausen *Donnerstag aus Licht* (Thursday from

Light) – said to be the first electronic masterpiece, and welcomed by all as a necessary production in an international opera house, was more appreciatively received by audiences than might have been expected at a first hearing. The critics were divided, Bayan Northcott saying that 'What the Covent Garden production reminds one at inordinate length is that he [Stockhausen] has never amounted to much of a composer';[7] while Peter Heyworth began his review as follows:

> A great artist establishes his own norm. Look once at a Francis Bacon picture and your eye is seized by the horror it depicts. Look again and you begin to perceive what lies beneath. So it is with Stockhausen's opera *Donnerstag aus Licht*.
>
> At first its ludicrous aspects seize your attention. You are liable to be irritated by the work's coy humour, oppressed by its ponderousness, repelled by a heady brew of metaphysical notions and mystical ideals told from east to west. Yet the fact remains that its music dwarfs almost everything as yet achieved in the field of opera by the generation of composers that emerged in Europe in the wake of World War II. Even as I write, the boredom and irritation I experienced at Covent Garden on Monday recede from my memory. What remains is the work's resplendent beauty.[8]

The production by Michael Bogdanov and the designs by Maria Bjornsson were generally praised and Covent Garden thought to have made amends for having limply allowed the privilege of giving the opera's premiere to slip through its hands.[9]

The Zemlinsky double bill, *A Florentine Tragedy* and *The Birthday of the Infanta,* were borrowed from Hamburg in a production by Adolf Drese with designs by Margit Bardy.

The Flying Dutchman of 1986 was a production which few people liked. Try as I will', David Cairns wrote, 'I can make no sense of the new, updated *Flying Dutchman* at Covent Garden or find in it anything but emptiness – no trace of an illuminating idea to make up for the desolating ugliness of the designs.'[10] And Edward Greenfield in the *Guardian* asked: What, one wonders, has Wagner done to deserve such gratuitously ugly new productions in three days?'[11] (The English National Opera at the Coliseum had a new production of *Parsifal* equally disliked.)

Booing, nowadays, as Tom Sutcliffe remarked in the *Guardian,* is reserved for producers and designers, and on the first night of *The Flying Dutchman* Mike Ashman and David Fielding were unmercifully booed and jeered by a surprisingly large number of the audience.

All the sadder then that Sir Colin Davis, on the first night of *Fidelio,* his last production as Music Director, got well booed (said by some to be the loudest booing heard at Covent Garden since the production of *Don Giovanni* in 1973). This again was inspired by the strength of emotional dislike of the production – by Andrei Serban – about which there was however more difference of opinion than there had been about *The Flying Dutchman.* Max Loppert found it 'so roundly unworthy of the piece that Wednesday's performance came as near collapsing in ignominy as the sublime work ever could',[12] and this was the view of many of the critics, as well as large parts of the audience.

Sir Colin, like all concerned at Covent Garden, was in his final years receiving a rough time from the press. Due partly to ill luck – for example, the cancellation of a *Tosca* with Pavarotti, in circumstances which were not understood – and the failure of one or two borrowed productions in an attempt to deal with serious under-funding, there had been some disappointing performances. The press, always ready to rally to the cry of 'Snobs!' are quick to gang up against what are nowadays termed centres of excellence. (This is said to be the same in other countries.) At Covent Garden in the eighties there was often critical contempt not only of obviously unsatisfactory performances, but also of performances which people with taste, experience and sensitivity thought to be of an inadequate standard for an international opera house.

There was also much hostility of a general kind: Why not let the culture-lovers pay?' was the heading of an article which began What you can't afford you can't have', and which represented a strong – if minority – view.[13] Because this is a constantly recurring theme it cannot be said too often that the purpose of the Arts Council grant is to bring art to people whom it otherwise would not reach. If there were no subsidy the rich would certainly pay for opera – in Milan, Vienna and New York, and possibly in short summer seasons at Covent Garden which nobody else could afford.

At the height of the criticism Sir Georg Solti attempted a rescue in the columns of *The Times*. In Paris, he said, he had been told by a senior government official that Covent Garden was 'one of the few stable operatic institutions in the world'. 'In 1946 there was no opera here', Solti went on, 'Before the war Covent Garden seasons were short; you could probably hear more opera in Catalonia than in London. But last year over a million people heard opera in London and other cities in Britain. So much for the charges of elitism.'[14]

Sir Colin Davis was by now too well established for booing either at the beginning or end to affect his reputation. Hugh

Canning in the *Guardian* described his personal contribution to opera at Covent Garden:

> As the world's leading Berliozian he'd been given *The Trojans* by his predecessor, Solti: he revived it twice and conducted a series of *Benvenuto Cellinis* at Covent Garden and La Scala in 1976. His *Peter Grimes* and *Rake's Progress*, both collaborations with Elijah Moshinsky, confirmed his pre-eminence as a Britten and Stravinsky interpreter.
>
> Then there have been the Mozart operas, always conducted with love and zest, the Tippett premieres, Berg's *Lulu* – one of the highlights of his regime – and even the *Ring* grew into a considerable joint achievement with Friedrich over the seasons. Before Chereau, it was the most significant anywhere in the world.[15]

Bernard Levin also paid a special tribute to Sir Colin, saying:

> This man has done our musical life great service, and he still has not ceased growing; to the imperceptive, his lack of flamboyance may disguise the fact that he is now one of the foremost of the world's conductors. At Covent Garden, in his 15 years as musical director, he has had his failures and made his mistakes but . . . I for one have never doubted that he had the mettle of greatness in him, and no one can doubt it now.[16]

Epilogue

This history properly ends with the season of 1985/6 which coincided approximately with the end of an era. Yet life goes on and the last, and perhaps the most important, job of the old regime is to appoint the new. In the time I have taken to bring the record of the period up to date, the names and personalities of those responsible for the future have been revealed to us.

Of the new generation, Dame Merle Park was appointed Director of the Royal Ballet Schools in 1983, and has already made her mark. New teachers of dancing, some of them Russian, have been introduced, and at the same time the level of academic tuition has been raised. Since the ballet school is the foundation on which the standards of a company are built, much depends on Dame Merle and at the present moment one can say that the signs are hopeful.

As Director of The Royal Ballet, Anthony Dowell succeeded Norman Morrice. Dowell, one of the greatest of the *danseurs nobles* England has produced and world-famous for his partnership with Antoinette Sibley, has in the last years extended his experience in America. His first production as director – a new version of *Swan Lake* – was seen in the autumn of 1986, and, although some of the critics disliked the designs and thought the production too fussy, there was a sense of authority on the stage and excitement in the audiences at the first performances which augured well for the future.

Bernard Haitink, successor to Colin Davis as Music Director, is well known in this country. For the last ten years he has been Musical Director at Glynde-bourne, where he formed a famous partnership with Sir Peter Hall. He rose to fame as Director of the Concertgebouw and is acknowledgedly one of the finest conductors in the world.

Haitink will be assisted by Jeffrey Tate as Principal Conductor, a new position created for him. Mr Tate was a member of the music staff at Covent Garden from 1971 to 1977 and conducted *La clemenza di Tito* there in 1982, *Ariadne auf Naxos* in 1985, and *Manon* in 1987. He is also principal conductor of the English Chamber Orchestra.

At the end of the season, 1986/7, Sir Claus Moser resigned the Chairmanship, held with distinction and devotion for thirteen years. His achievements have been recorded in the course of this account, but one can say here that probably no one in the history of the Royal Opera House will do more to raise funds or show greater ingenuity in the effort to bring opera and ballet to an increasingly wide public. He will be remembered for his rigorous musical standards, and for his friendliness and devotion to everybody at Covent Garden – it is said that he knew all, including the cleaners, by name. Two of the innovations of his last years were an experiment in the use of surtides in the theatre and the first use of the big screen in the piazza, which allowed a crowd of several thousand people to see and hear a performance of *La Bohème* with Placido Domingo. He will be succeeded by Sir

John Sainsbury, who has been on the Board of Covent Garden for many years, is married to the ballerina Anya Linden, and known to a much wider public than that for opera and ballet as the Chairman of Sainsbury's.

Sir John Tooley will remain the General Administrator for a year or so more, to the great benefit of this new team. He will be followed by Mr Jeremy Isaacs, well-known to the public as the Chief Administrator of Channel 4.

On 30 June 1987 the Westminster City Council gave planning permission for the building of Phase 2 of the Royal Opera House development, on the condition that the balance of £23 million to be raised from private funds was found.

So apparently all should be well. Yet in practice, the future of the Royal Opera House seemed less assured than at any time since 1946. In November 1986 the grant from the Government to the Arts Council for the 1987/8 season was announced as £138 million. However, this was against a request for £164 million, and was an increase of only 3.4 per cent on the previous year – less than the rate of inflation. This caused the Arts Council to hold the national companies, apart from the English National Opera (whose development was thought of a particularly high order) on standstill – that is to the figure of the previous year. In the case of the Royal Opera House, the Arts Council did not in the end announce a standstill grant because it wished to negotiate a longer-term arrangement to make it possible to provide a balanced budget over a three-year period. However, the settlement finally agreed was that the Royal Opera House would receive an increase of 1 per cent in 1987/8, with 2 per cent for each of the following two years.

The effect of this on the already under-funded Opera House appeared to be disastrous. The recommendations of the

339

Priestley Report were designed to avoid the necessity to budget regularly for a deficit, after making all reasonable allowance for box office receipts, the efforts of the Trust, the Friends and private funding. In relation to those recommendations the grant for 1987 represented a cumulative shortfall of £1.25 million and, with the agreed maximum for the following two years, this might well be doubled.

The Board considered every possible means of meeting the situation, and their deliberations obviously cannot be quoted at any length here. Yet because of ill-informed criticisms that are often made, some points seem worth explanation. In the first place the Chairman stated that the Royal Opera Houses's financial problems – a deficit of £2 million on a turnover of about £28 million – were in relative terms little different from comparable problems of other Arts organizations, but the Arts Council would not be able to meet its needs. Because of the overhead costs of the orchestra, production departments, stage and administration, the direct saving which could be made by abolishing one of the companies was limited.

Two other methods of improving the prospect were considered. The first was by an absolute reduction in opera performances with some dark nights; and the second by longer runs of fewer performances. Neither would improve the outcome: because of the heavy incidence of fixed costs, the marginal net revenue of each performance was positive; longer runs of fewer productions would mean that the cost of cancelling productions at this stage would exceed the net gain in revenue from longer runs of other productions.[1]

The overall difficulty was that there was an inconsistency between the repeatedly stated policy of the Board, which was to run three companies fully and at the highest artistic standards, and the decline in real terms of the Arts Council grant. As a result, the situation of the Opera House was like that of an under-capitalized business which operated with only limited scope for improving its profitability.[2]

At a press conference held at Covent Garden on 3 June 1987, Sir Claus Moser said that the position of the Royal Opera House in terms of the projected deficit for next year was due 'Very simply to the cumulative effect of three years of Arts Council funding well below the inflation rate'. He added: 'Now, we are in the throes of considering various new ways of improving the revenue situation and in due course there will be announcements about seat prices, about new sponsorship schemes.[5] Announcing the operas for the coming year, the Chairman said that whether they achieved the programme which he was about to put forward (for four new productions and three others borrowed or done in association with other houses) depended 'on what turns out from the discussions with the Arts Council and Government after the election and what the Arts Council finally decide about the ROH grant and the arts in general'.

When at the end of the season, Sir Claus Moser retired, the new generation therefore took over rather in the spirit of a task force relieving a beleaguered garrison – sustained only by faith in the ultimate value of their purpose. Then on 5 November 1987 the Minister for Arts, Richard Luce, took the Arts world completely by surprise with a statement which seemed to bring an end to what one journalist called 'his policy of pinch and squeeze on funding'.[4] He announced a new departure in funding the Arts, involving a 17 per cent increase in the Government's Arts budget over the next three years. The biggest increase of

10 per cent was to be used in the first year and was designed to 'create a positive atmosphere in which we can move forward'. The Arts Council grant would be increased by 8.4 per cent to £150 million in the current year and will reach £160 million by 1990/1, a rise of 15.6 per cent over the three years. The Minister also announced that in future all financial arrangements would be on a three-year rather than an annual basis.

Some of the Arts Council new money is marked for special purpose but there is a substantial surplus. The Minister's announcement has been very generally welcomed and seems to suggest a change of mood which augurs well for the future of British art – and more particularly for opera and ballet at Covent Garden.

Appendix A

The Royal Ballet Companies' Tours Abroad

	The Royal Ballet	*SWRB*
1932	Copenhagen	
1936	Paris	
1938	Dublin	
1940	Holland	
1945	Belgium, France, Germany	
1946	Vienna	
1947	Belgium, Czechoslovakia, Poland, Sweden, Norway	
1948	Holland, Paris, Germany	Dublin
1949	Italy, USA, Canada	Dublin
1950	USA	
1951	Canada	Canada, USA
1952	Portugal, Germany	USA
1953	USA, Canada	Holland, Belgium, Germany, Bulawayo
1954	USA, Holland, France, Italy	South Africa
1955	USA, Canada	Dublin
1956		Spain
1957	Dublin, USA, Canada	Spain, Germany, Switzerland, Holland
1958	USA, Canada, Belgium	Dublin, Australia
1959		Australia, New Zealand

	The Royal Ballet	*SWRB*
1960	USA	South Africa
1961	Canada, USA, Leningrad, Moscow	Japan, Hong Kong, Manila, Baalbeck, Syna, Monte Carlo, Greece
1962		Dublin, Switzerland, Germany, Italy, Denmark, Norway, Sweden
1963	USA, Canada	France
1964	USA, Canada, Italy	Germany, Switzerland, Belgium, Holland, Italy, Baalbeck
1966	Monte Carlo, Athens, Florence, Luxemburg, Prague, Brno, Bratislava, Munich, Belgrade, Sofia, Bucharest, Warsaw	Finland, Denmark, Belgium, Holland, Germany
1967	USA, Canada	
1968	USA	Germany, Switzerland, Portugal, Italy, France, Holland, Spain
1969	USA, Vienna	Egypt
1970	USA	Germany, Austria, Belgium, France, Switzerland
1972	New York	Portugal, France, Switzerland
1973	South America, Belgium	Israel
1974	USA	Holland
1975	South Korea, Japan	Greece
1976	USA	Switzerland, Italy, France
1977		West Germany, Luxemburg, Holland, Belgium, Teheran, Greece
1978	Korea, USA, Greece	
1979	USA, Canada, Mexico City	
1980		South Korea, Philippines, Singapore, Malaysia, Thailand, Hong Kong
1981	USA, Canada	Yugoslavia, Monte Carlo
1982	Italy	New Zealand, Australia, Singapore, Thailand, Italy
1983	USA, Japan, South Korea, China, Hong Kong	Canada
1985	Hungary, East Germany, Spain, Portugal	New Zealand, South Korea, India
1986	Canada	USA, Mexico, Venezuela, Brazil, Israel
1987	Holland, South Korea, Japan	Czechoslovakia, Poland, East Germany, Bulgaria

Appendix B

The Royal Opera Tours Abroad

Date	City	Operas	Conductors
1948	Brussels	Peter Grimes	Rankl, Goodall
	Paris	Peter Grimes	Rankl, Goodall
1952	Paris	Billy Budd	Britten
1953	Bulawayo	Aida	Barbirolli, Goodall, Young,
		La Bohème	Gellhorn
		Gloriana	
		Figaro	
1954	Wiesbaden	Peter Grimes	Goodall
1961	Schwetzingen	A Midsummer	Davies
	Festival	Night's Dream	
1964	Lisbon	– ditto –	Bryan Balkwill
1970	Berlin	Don Carlos	Solti, Downes
	Munich	Falstaff	Downes
		Victory	
1976	La Scala,	Benvenuto Cellini	Davis
	Milan	Peter Grimes	Davis, Atherton
		La clemenza di Tito	Pritchard
1979	South Korea	Tosca	Davis
		Peter Grimes	
		Magic Flute	
	Japan	Tosca	Davis
		Peter Grimes	
		Magic Flute	

345

Date	City	Operas	Conductors
1984	Los Angeles	Turandot Peter Grimes Magic Flute	Davis
1985	Athens	Macbeth King Priam	Downes Howarth
1986	South Korea	Carmen Samson et Dalila Turandot	Barker & guest conductors
	Japan	Carmen, Samson & Dalila Cosí fan tutte Turandot	Barker & guest conductors

Appendix C

Board Members

	COVENT GARDEN OPERA TRUST	ROYAL OPERA HOUSE, COVENT GARDEN LTD.
	Trustee	*Director*
ANDERSON, Sir Colin		1961–1972
ANNAN, Lord		1966–1978
ARMSTRONG, Sir Thomas		1958–1969
BAGRIT, Sir Leon		1962–1969
BENSON, Christopher		1984 to date
BERLIN, Sir Isaiah		1955–1965
		1974 to date
BLISS, Sir Arthur		1954–1957
BONHAM-CARTER, Lord		1958–1982
BOOSEY, Leslie	1946–1950	1950–1954
CLARK, Hon. Colette		1974 to date
CLARK, Lord	1946–1950	1950–1953
COKE, Gerald		1958–1964
COLDSTREAM, Sir William		1957–1962
COURTAULD, Samuel	1946–1947	

Appendix D

Arts Council Subsidies to the Royal Opera House

	£		£		£
1945/46	25,000	1959/60	473,000	1973/74	2,195,000
1946/47	55,000	1960/61	500,737	1974/75	2,650,000
1947/48	98,000	1961/62	505,991/10/-	1975/76	3,410,000
1948/49	145,000	1962/63	690,041/7/-	1976/77	4,300,000
1949/50	170,000	1963/64	815,000	1977/78	4,850,000
1950/51	145,000	1964/65	1,055,000	1978/79	5,475,000
1951/52	150,000	1965/66	1,026,500	1979/80	7,000,000
1952/53	265,000	1966/67	1,225,000	1980/81	7,805,000
1953/54	240,000	1967/68	1,280,000	1981/82	9,020,000
1954/55	250,000	1968/69	1,280,000	1982/83	10,379,682
1955/56	250,000	1969/70	1,400,000	1983/84	11,584,776
1956/57	270,000	1970/71	1,420,000	1984/85	12,350,000
1957/58	302,000	1971/72	1,640,000	1985/86	12,593,000
1958/59	362,000	1972/73	1,750,000	1986/87	13,096,000

Appendix E

Inflation

A note from the distinguished economist who kindly supplied this table reads:

The numbers (e.g. 34.2 for 1850) mean that you should multiply any money figure, such as a fee, by them to convert to 1985 prices. I think I need hardly tell you that calculations of this kind are extremely ropey. An index for 1850 would, you may be sure, be full of candles, horses, footmen & growlers. The 1985 index has ball-point pens & long-playing records. This means that the figures cannot be given the unconditional imprimature of a great research institute.

1800	21.2	1938	21.4	1965	6.4
1850	34.2	1946	12.7	1970	5.1
1900	38.5	1950	10.5	1975	2.8
1914	33.6	1955	8.5	1980	1.4
1920	13.5	1960	7.5	1985	1.0

351

Notes

Some of the early press criticisms consulted in the ROH archives are un-credited. Where it has proved impossible to identify the newspaper and/or date of publication, the quotation is credited to the ROH archives.

Introduction

1 Quoted in *History of the London Stage,* H. B. Baker & Sons, 1904, p 163

2 Baker, *op cit,* p 165

3 Quoted in Baker, *op cit,* p 166

4 *Dramatic Criticism,* Leigh Hunt, OUP, 1950, p 214

5 Baker, *op cit,* p 180

6 *Musical Recollections of the Last Half Century,* Rev T. C Cox, Tinley 1872, quoted in *Opera at Covent Garden,* Harold Rosenthal, Gollancz, 1967, p 27

7 Rosenthal, *op cit,* pp 36-7

8 *Covent Garden,* Desmond Shawe-Taylor, Marc Parrish, New York, 1948, p 32

9 *Thirty Years Musical Recollections,* Henry C. Chorley, Knopf, 1926, p 325

10 *Two Centuries of Opera at Covent Garden*, Harold Rosenthal, Putnam, 1958, pp III—12

11 *Ibid* p 114

12 *Thirty Years of Musical Life in London*, Hermann Klein, New York, 1903, P44

13 Chorley, *op cit*, p 375

14 Hermann Klein, quoted in *Opera at Covent Garden*, Rosenthal, p 51

Chapter One

1 *Strand* magazine, ROH archives, undated

2 *About the House*, Spring 1987

3 *The Golden Age of Opera*, Hermann Klein, T. Fisher Unwin, 1920, p 269

4 *Covent Garden*, Desmond Shawe-Taylor, p 53

5 *Music in London*, Bernard Shaw, Constable, 1932, vol 1, p 250

6 *Strand* magazine, ROH archives

7 *Percy Pitt of Covent Garden and the BBC*, J. Daniel Chamier, Arnold, 1938, p 92

8 *Ibid*, p 53

9 *About the House*, Xmas 1971, p 38

10 *About the House*, Xmas 1982, p 35

11 *About the House*, Spring 1985, p 33

12 *About the House*, March 1966, p 36

13 *Daily Telegraph*, November 1913

14 *About the House*, Spring 1982, p 54

15 *About the House*, Xmas 1983, p 31

16 Chamier, *op cit*, pp 137-8

17 *Ibid*, pp 138—9

18 *Ibid*, pp 151-2

19 *Ibid,* p 153

Chapter Two

1 *A Mingled Chime,* Sir Thomas Beecham, Hutchinson Ltd, 1944, p 87
2 *Ibid,* p 88
3 *Ibid,* p 88
4 *Evening News,* 7.1.11
5 *The Times,* 2.3.10
6 The *Chronicle,* 7.1.11
7 ROH archives, 7.1.11
8 *Globe,* 12.11.10
9 Beecham, *op cit,* p 106
10 Beecham, *op cit,* p 108
11 *Thomas Beecham: An Independent Biography,* Charles Reid, Gollancz, 1961, p 138
12 *Sir Thomas Beecham,* Neville Cardus, Collins, 1961, p 9
13 Beecham, *op cit,* p 153
14 *New Statesman,* 29.3.19
15 *London Mercury,* January 1920
16 *Glasgow Herald,* 17.12.25
17 *Sir Thomas Beecham,* Alan Jefferson, Macdonald & Jane's, 1979, p 144
18 *Ibid,* p 145
19 *The Times,* 12.2.24
20 *The Times,* 19.2.24
21 *Punch,* 9.5.28
22 *Observer,* 22.2.20
23 *Opera at Covent Garden,* Harold Rosenthal, p 109
24 *Covent Garden,* Desmond Shawe-Taylor, pp 60-2

25 Quoted in *Two Centuries*, Rosenthal, p 462

26 *Ibid*, p 438

27 *The Times*, 11.10.33

28 *Daily Express*, 25.4.29

29 *Evening Express*, 16.10.35

30 Shawe-Taylor, *op cit*, p 66

Chapter Three

1 *Beecham Remembered*, Humphrey Procter-Gregg, Duckworth, 1976, p v

2 *The Baton and the Jackboot*, Berta Geissmer, Hamish Hamilton, 1944, p 267

3 *Sir Thomas Beecham*, Alan Jefferson, p 162

4 ROH archives, 20.11.31

5 ROH archives, 11.10.31

6 White Paper, Cmnd 3884

7 Quoted in *Opera at Covent Garden*, Harold Rosenthal, p 115

8 *Ibid*, p 118

9 *Covent Garden*, Desmond Shawe-Taylor, p 64

10 Ibid, p 65

11 *Ibid*, pp 65-6

12 *Two Centuries*, Rosenthal, p 426

13 *Sunday Times*, 24.5.36

14 *Wings of Song*, Lotte Lehmann, Kegan Paul, 1938, p 171

15 *National Press*, 1.5.34

16 *The Royal Ballet: The First Fifty Years*, Alexander Bland, Doubleday and Co., New York, 1981, p 15

17 *Ibid*, p 17

18 *Lydia Lopokova*, Milo Keynes (Editor), Weidenfeld & Nicolson, 1983, p 109

19 Bland, *op cit*, p 25

20 *Glyndeboume: A Celebration,* John Higgins (Editor), Cape, 1984, pp 103-4

21 *Ibid,* pp 101-2

22 *Glyndeboume,* Spike Hughes, David & Charles, 1981, p 90

23 *Ibid,* p 88

24 *Ibid,* p 128

Chapter Four

1 *John Maynard Keynes,* R. F. Harrod, Macmillan, 1951, p 521

2 *Ibid,* p 521

3 *The Quiet Showman,* Montague Haltrecht, Collins, 1975, p 52

4 *Duet for Two Voices,* Hugh Carey, CUP, 1979, p 184

5 *The Other Half,* Kenneth Clark, Murray, 1979, p 131

6 *On and Off the Record: A Memoir of Walter Legge,* Elisabeth Schwarzkopf, Faber & Faber, 1982, p 161

7 *Ibid,* p 161

8 *Thomas Beecham,* Charles Reid, p 236

9 Schwarzkopf, *op cit*, pp 60-1

10 *Ibid,* p 93

11 *Glyndeboume,* Spike Hughes, p 153

12 *Observer,* 29.1.50

13 Boosey to Webster, ROH archives, 3.12.57

14 Clark, *op cit*, p 131

15 Arts Council archives, 1946

16 Arts Council archives, 1946

17 Carey, *op cit*, pp 139-40

18 *Ibid,* p 183

19 Arts Council archives, 30.7.45

20 Halbrecht, *op cit*, p 68

Chapter Five

1 *Leader,* 23.2.46
2 *Glyndebourne: A Celebration,* p 91
3 Quoted in *The Royal Ballet,* Alexander Bland, p 41
4 *Ibid*
5 ROH archives, 1946
6 ROH archives, 1946
7 ROH archives, 1946
8 Quoted in *The Quiet Showman,* Montague Halbrecht, p 72
9 ROH archives, 1946
10 ROH archives, 1946
11 *Time and Tide,* 2.3.46
12 ROH archives, 1946
13 ROH archives, 1946
14 *The British Council: The First Fifty Years,* Frances Donaldson, Cape, 1984, p 150
15 Bland, *op cit,* p 94
16 *Christian Science Monitor,* 1949
17 *New York Journal,* ROH archives, 1949
18 *New York World Telegraph,* ROH archives, 1949
19 *Chicago Tribune,* 14.11.49
20 *New York Times,* ROH archives, 1949
21 *Invitation to the Ballet,* Ninette de Valois, The Bodley Head, 1937, pp 98-9

Chapter Six

1 *The Quiet Showman,* Haltrecht, p 93
2 *The Tongs and the Bones: The Memoirs of Lord Harewood,*

Weidenfeld & Nicolson, 1981, pp 150-1

3 Haltrecht, *op cit*, p 35

4 *New Stateman and Nation*, 19.1.46

5 ROH archives, 26.12.44

6 ROH archives, 7.3.46

7 ROH archives, 12.3.46

8 ROH archives, 16.3.46

9 ROH archives, 22.3.45

10 ROH archives, 22.3.45

11 ROH archives, 412.44

12 Haltrecht, *op cit*, p 15

13 *The Other Half,* Kenneth Clark, p 132

14 Frank Howes, Obit. Rankl, ROH archives, 1968

15 ROH archives, 1968

16 *John Anderson,* John Wheeler-Bennett, Macmillan, 1962, p 362

17 *Ibid,* p 365

18 ROH archives, 26.7.46

19 ROH archives, 1.8.46

20 Haltrecht, *op cit*, p 38

21 *Two Centuries,* Harold Rosenthal, p 566

22 Haltrecht, *op cit*, p 96

23 Boosey to Webster, ROH archives, 16.12.46

24 *Time and Tide*, 25.11.47

25 *Time and Tide*, 8.2.47

26 *New Statesman and Nation,* 10.2.47

27 *New Statesman and Nation,* 3.5.47

28 *Time and Tide,* 3.5.46

29 *Sunday Times,* 27.4.47

30 *New Statesman and Nation,* 3.5.47

Chapter Seven

1 *New Statesman and Nation*, 7.8.48

2 *New Statesman and Nation*, 7.6.47

3 *Musical Times*, ROH archives, 1947

4 *New Statesman and Nation*, 7.8.48

5 *Sunday Times*, 17.10.48

6 *Manchester City News*, 15.8.48

7 Memorandum by John Christie, undated (early 1947), ROH archives

8 Public Record Office, T227/84,29.6.48

9 Public Record Office, T227/84,28.7.48

10 Arts Council archives, 14.8.48

11 ROH archives, opera sub-committee minutes, April 1949

12 *Two Centuries of Opera at Covent Garden,* Harold Rosenthal, p 582

13 *The Times*, 5.1.49

14 *The Quiet Showman*, Haltrecht, p 126

15 *New Statesman and Nation*, 6.4.48

16 *Sunday Times*, 13.11.49

17 *Sunday Times*, 20.11.49

18 *Observer*, 27.11.49

19 *Thelsis*, 23.11.49

20 *Time and Tide*, 26.11.49

21 *Sunday Times*, 27.11.49

Chapter Eight

1 Philip Hope-Wallace, ROH archives, 15.4.50

2 *New Statesman and Nation*, 22.7.50

3 Webster to Rankl, ROH archives, 2.3.50

4 Rankl to Webster, ROH archives, 2.3.50

5 Webster to Rankl, ROH archives, 3.3.50

6 *The Quiet Showman*, Haltrecht, p 141

7 ROH archives Board minutes, 26.1.50

8 Webster to Rankl, ROH archives, 14.11.50

9 *New Statesman and Nation*, 16.12.50

10 *Observer*, 24.12.50

11 *Spectator*, 22.12.50

12 *Sunday Times*, 1.7.51

13 *The Times*, 15.12.51

14 *Gramophone*, July 1950

15 ROH archives Board minutes, 26.10.51

16 Rankl to Webster, ROH archives, 1,11.50

17 Frank Howes, Obit. Rankl, ROH archives, 1968

18 *The Royal Ballet*, Alexander Bland, p 100

19 Arts Council archives, file EL4/55, paper 330

20 *Opera at Covent Garden*, Harold Rosenthal, p 155

21 *Spectator*, 1.2.52

22 *Sunday Times*, 5.5.50

23 *The Times*, 16.5.50

24 *New Statesman and Nation*, 2.12.51

25 *Financial Times*, 16.5.50

26 *Time and Tide*, 24.6.50

27 *Daily Telegraph*, 10.11.52

28 *New Statesman and Nation*, 9.2.54

29 Rosenthal, *op cit*, p 156

Chapter Nine

1 *The Tongs and the Bones: The Memoirs of Lord Harewood*, p 106

2 ROH archives, 24.5.68

3 *Double Harness*, Lord Drogheda, Weidenfeld & Nicolson, 1978, p 229

4 Harewood, *op cit*, p 152

5 *English Singer*, Margaret Steward, Duckworth, 1970, p 214

6 Drogheda, *op cit*, p 237

7 Harewood, *op cit*, p 153

8 *Financial Times*, 11.5.54

9 *Manchester Guardian*, 12.5.54

10 *New Statesman and Nation*, 28.5.54

11 *Sunday Times*, 3.6.56

12 Harewood, *op cit*, pp 156-7

13 Drogheda, *op cit*, p 238

14 Harewood, *op cit*, p 168

15 *The Royal Ballet*, Alexander Bland, p 220

16 *Ibid*, p 251

17 *Ibid*, p 117

18 Quoted in *Opera at Covent Garden*, Harold Rosenthal, p 160

19 Harewood, *op cit*, p 159

20 *Daily Telegraph*, 9.6.56

21 *Daily Telegraph*, 13.6.56

22 *The Times*, 23.6.56

23 *The Times*, 27.6.56

24 Drogheda, *op cit*, p 247

25 *Ibid*, pp 246-7

26 to *Statesman and Nation*, 7.7.56

27 *Manchester Guardian*, 5.6.57

28 Daily *Telegraph*, 7.6.57

29 *Observer*, 9.6.57

30 *Financial Times*, 7.6.57

31 *Observer*, n.5.58

32 *New Statesman and Nation*, 17.5.58

33 *Financial Times*, 23.4.59

Chapter Ten

1 *Double Harness*, Lord Drogheda, p 232
2 *Ibid*, p 230
3 Members of the Board in conversation
4 Drogheda, *op cit*, p 131
5 ROH archives, opera sub-committee minutes, 27.11.56
6 ROH archives, 15.2.57
7 Drogheda, *op cit*, pp 259-61
8 *Two Centuries*, Harold Rosenthal, p 660
9 *The Tongs and the Bones*, p 162
10 ROH archives Board minutes, Feb. 1959
11 ROH archives Board minutes, 27.10.59
12 Drogheda, *op cit*, p 234
13 *Manchester Guardian*, 22.10.49
14 ROH archives, 26.7.61
15 Harewood, *op cit*, p 172
16 Webster to Drogheda, ROH archives, undated
17 Drogheda to Webster, ROH archives, undated
18 Drogheda to Donaldson, 20.3.53
19 Drogheda, *op cit*, p 268
20 ROH archives
21 ROH archives Board meeting, 16.1.62

Chapter Eleven

1 *Daily Telegraph*, 21.6.59
2 *New Statesman and Nation*, 5.6.59
3 *Observer*, 6.12.59

4 *Double Harness,* Lord Drogheda, p 243

5 Drogheda, *op cit,* p 280

6 *About the House,* Summer 1971

7 Drogheda, *op cit,* p 281

8 *About the House,* November 1962

9 *About the House,* Summer 1971

10 *Observer,* 17.9.71

11 *About the House,* Summer 1971

12 *Financial Times,* 3.2.61

13 *The Times,* 3.2.61

14 *About the House,* November 1972

15 *Observer,* 11.2.62

16 *The Times,* 10.2.62

17 *Financial Times,* 31.5.63

18 Drogheda, *op cit,* p 285

19 *The Times Educational Supplement,* 5.2.65

20 *The Times,* 30.961

21 *Guardian,* 30.9.61

22 *Observer,* 7.10.61

23 *Sunday Times,* 15.963

24 *About the House,* Summer 1971

25 *The Times,* 22.1.64

26 *Financial Times,* 22.1.64

27 *Guardian,* 29.12.86

28 *Guardian,* 8.7.68

29 *The Times,* 13.4.64

30 *The Times,* 29.6.65

31 *Financial Times,* 29.6.65

32 *The Times,* 6.7.66

33 *Guardian,* 6.7.66

34 *Sunday Telegraph,* 21.2.71

35 *Sunday Times*, 21.2.71

Chapter Twelve

1 *Frederick Ashton and His Ballets*, David Vaughan, Adam and Charles Black, 1977, p 302

2 *Ibid*, p 314

3 *Guardian*, 30.1.60

4 Quoted in ROH Annual Report, 1961/2

5 *Ibid*

6 *The Royal Ballet*, Alexander Bland, p 132

7 *John O'London's Weekly*, 8.3.62

8 *Spectator*, 2.3.62

9 *Observer*, 25.2.62

10 *Financial Times*, 2.1.61

11 *Guardian*, 4.5.62

12 Bland, *op cit*, p 139

13 *Ibid*

14 Vaughan, *op cit*, p 336

15 *Spectator*, 12.4.64

16 Vaughan, *op cit*, p 343

17 *Daily Mail*, 12.2.65

18 *Financial Times*, 23.3.65

19 *Financial Times*, 1.3.65

20 *Sunday Times*, 28.2.65

21 The *Times*, 2. 11.68

22 *Sunday Telegraph*, 27.10.68

23 *Kenneth MacMillan*, Edward Thorpe, Hamish Hamilton, 1985, p 94

24 *Double Harness*, Lord Drogheda, pp 316-17

25 *Ibid*, p 317

Chapter Thirteen

1 *Double Harness,* Lord Drogheda, p 326
2 *Ibid,* pp 329-30
3 *Ibid,* p 335
4 *Ibid,* p. &2
5 I&¿, p 333-4
6 ROH archives, 16.5.73
7 *Observer,* 15.10.67
8 Drogheda, *op cit,* pp 348-9

Chapter Fourteen

1 *Double Harness,* Drogheda, p 317
2 *The Times,* 23.7.71
3 *Financial Times,* 23.7.71
4 The *Times,* 8.3.74
5 *Kenneth MacMillan,* Edward Thorpe, p 119
6 *Financial Times,* 27.3.72
7 New York *Times,* 45 77
8 *Guardian,* 4.11.76
9 *Observer,* 5.12.71
10 The *Times,* 2.12.71
11 *Daily Mail,* 8.5.74
12 *Sunday Times,* 5.12.71
13 The Times, 23.4.74

Chapter Fifteen

1 *Double Harness,* Drogheda, p 344
2 *Yorkshire Post,* 18.p.76

3 *Guardian,* 18.9.76

4 tywsr, 12.9.78

5 *Financial Times,* 2.10.78

6 *The Times,* 7.12.76

7 *Observer,* 8.1.78

8 *Financial Times,* 29.1.77

9 *Sunday Times,* 30.1.77

10 *Observer,* 10.7.77

11 *Sunday Times,* 10.7.77

12 The Times, 10.3.78

13 *Jewish Chronicle,* 17.3.78

14 *Financial Times,* 11.3.78

15 *Sunday Times,* 25.6.78

16 *Financial Times,* 15.11.78

17 *Guardian,* 20.6.79

18 *Spectator,* 21.4.79

19 *Observer,* 15.7.79

20 *Guardian,* 13.2.76

21 *Herald Tribune,* 14.2.76

Chapter Sixteen

1 *Guardian,* 9.3.79

2 *Guardian,* 15.3.79

3 *The Times,* 16.2.78

4 *Financial Times,* 16.2.78

5 *Financial Times,* 17.10.77

6 *Times,* 29.10.77

7 *Financial Times,* 17.3.80

8 *International Daily News,* 13.8.80

9 *New York Post,* 22.6.81

10 *New York Post,* 25.6.81

11 *New York Post,* 30.6.81

12 *Ibid*

13 *New York Times,* 1.7.81

14 *New Yorker,* 27.8.81

15 ROH archives, 1981

16 *New Statesman and Nation,* 12.3.82

17 *Dance and Dancers,* Dec. 1984

18 *The Times,* 9.12.83

19 *Sunday Times,* 10.2.80

20 *Observer,* 10.2.80

21 *Vogue,* 15.3.80

22 *Sunday Times,* 10.2.80

23 *Observer,* 10.2.80

24 *Financial Times,* 18.2.81

25 *Financial Times,* 30.9.81

26 *Spectator,* 4.12.82

27 *Financial Times,* 27.11.82

28 *Sunday Telegraph,* 25.9.83

29 *Financial Times,* 20.9.83

30 *Financial Times,* 13.1.83

31 *New York Times,* 22.7.84

32 *Ibid*

33 *Los Angeles Times,* 1984

Chapter Seventeen

1 Financial Scrutiny of the Royal Opera House Covent Garden Ltd and the Shakespeare Co. Cabinet Office Management and Personnel Office. Prefatory note, p 3

2 Report to the Earl of Gowrie by Clive Priestley, CB p 3

3 *Ibid*

4 *Ibid*

5 *Ibid*, p 4

6 Financial Scrutiny, vol 1, p

7 *Ibid*

8 *Ibid*, p 297

9 *Ibid*, p 298

10 *Ibid*, pp 298-9

11 *Ibid*, p 301

12 *Ibid*

13 *Ibid*, p 303

14 *Ibid*, p 305

15 *Listener*, 4.4.85

16 *Listener*, 18.4.85

17 'The Glory of the Garden', p iii

18 *Ibid*

19 *Guardian*, 9.4.82

20 *Observer*, 25.3.84

Chapter Eighteen

1 *The Times*, 19.11.84

2 *Financial Times*, 3.12.85

3 *New Statesman and Nation*, 17.5.86

4 *Financial Times*, 19.6.85

5 *The Times*, 19.6.85

6 *Observer*, 30.6.85

7 *Sunday Telegraph*, 24.9.85

8 *Observer*, 24.9.85

9 *Ibid*

10 *Sunday Times*, 23.3.86

11 *Guardian*, 18.3.86

12 *Financial Times*, 4.7.86

13 Daily *Telegraph*, 2.4.84

14 *The Times*, 18.3.86

15 Guardian, 9.7.86

16 The Times, 16.7.86

Epilogue

1 ROH Board minutes, 23.12.86

2 ROH Board minutes, 27.7.86

3 ROH Board minutes, 23.12.86

4 *Guardian*, 6.11.87

A NOTE ON THE AUTHOR

Lady Donaldson of Kingsbridge (1907–1994), a British writer and biographer, was the daughter of Freddie Lonsdale, a playwright. In 1935 she married John George Stuart Donaldson, Baron Donaldson of Kingsbridge (known as Jack), a left-wing intellectual, social worker, and dilettante Gloucestershire farmer. As the daughter of the playwright Frederick Lonsdale, she grew up in the frivolous world of 1920s café society, yet she became a committed socialist. As the wife of Lord Donaldson, who was on the board of both London Opera houses and was subsequently Minister for the Arts, Frances Donaldson was at the cultural centre of British life.

Her body of work included topics such as farming, and biographies of writers Evelyn Waugh and P. G. Wodehouse, as well as of her father, Freddie. Her biography of King Edward VIII won the Wolfson Literary Award and was the basis for a six-part television series, "Edward and Mrs. Simpson," starring James Fox and Cynthia Harris.

12520874R00229

Printed in Great Britain
by Amazon.co.uk, Ltd.,
Marston Gate.